TOTALLY
VEGETARIAN

TONI FIORE

TOTALLY
VEGETARIAN

Easy, Fast, Comforting

Cooking for Every Kind

of Vegetarian

Da Capo

LIFE
LONG

A MEMBER OF THE PERSEUS BOOKS GROUP

Copyright © 2008 by All Art Media, Delicious TV
Photographs copyright © 2008 by Betsy Carson

Designed by Pauline Neuwirth, Neuwirth & Associates, Inc.

Set in 10.5 point Whitman by the Perseus Books Group

Library of Congress Cataloging-in-Publication Data

Fiore, Toni.
  Totally vegetarian : easy, fast, comforting food for every kind of vegetarian / Toni Fiore. — 1st Da Capo Press ed.
      p. cm.
   Includes index.
   ISBN 978-0-7382-1183-1 (alk. paper)
   1. Vegetarian cookery. I. Title.
   TX837.F476 2008
   641.5'636—dc22

                                                            2008007706

First Da Capo Press edition 2008

Published by Da Capo Press
A Member of the Perseus Books Group
www.dacapopress.com

Da Capo Press books are available at special discounts for bulk purchases in the United States by corporations, institutions, and other organizations. For more information, please contact the Special Markets Department at the Perseus Books Group, 2300 Chestnut Street, Suite 200, Philadelphia, PA 19103, or call (800) 810-4145, extension 5000, or e-mail special.markets@perseusbooks.com.

1 2 3 4 5 6 7 8 9

To my family and friends.
With love and gratitude.

Contents

TOTALLY
VEGETARIAN

Introduction

AS THE HOST of a vegetarian cooking show on national television, I'm frequently asked why I decided to become a vegetarian. How old was I when I made the change? How do I subsist on seeds and grass? What are my protein sources? Where did I learn to cook?

I believe people's confused curiosity to be genuine. After all, I wasn't born a vegetarian and looking back, I realize I had the same questions when trying to imagine my meals without meat. This is because vegetarianism has largely been shrouded in mystery and misconceptions. A big part of the reason I enjoy what I do is that I can relate to my audience members, many of who aren't vegetarians but are interested in learning how to cook healthy meals. With my show, and now with this book, I demystify the vegetarian world by offering practical advice, sensible solutions, and simple recipes and techniques to make new ways of eating and cooking easy and accessible.

As far as my formal training goes, I've never attended culinary school and I didn't want to. Because I enjoy preparing a meal and love to eat, I was content to find my own way to a finished dish by trial and error. Mistakes are how you find your way to success. They teach you how to develop your own style, how to indulge your particular tastes, and help you gain confidence in the kitchen. For me, cooking is a passionate pursuit. Anyone who has the desire and a little imagination can become an excellent cook.

As to why I made the switch from meat eater to vegetarian, myriad thoughts and experiences had a cumulative effect on me. I've always had a natural affinity with and sensitivity to animals. When I was growing up in Europe, I struggled to discern the difference between pet animals and food animals. In many parts of the world, unlike much of America, the origins of meat are out in the open. There were no neat little cellophane packages of meat or chicken at the grocery store that seemingly have no connection to a life. European markets and butchers still display whole and partial animal carcasses, their heads, fur, and feet intact so consumers can determine just how fresh the meat is. There's no opportunity to deny the reality that animals are raised and killed to feed humans. Although I continued to eat meat, my conscience was getting the better of me and it became harder and harder to keep doing so.

I moved to Maine in my late twenties, drawn by its beauty and a quality of life I found similar to the one I enjoyed in Europe. I joined and eventually became president of the Maine Animal Coalition, a statewide animal advocacy organization. Farm animal campaigns were my focus and I became an overnight vegetarian. I have never missed eating meat. In fact, I was relieved to let it go.

At that point, I still loved cooking, was good at it, and prepared three meals a day, but it had become routine rather than inspired. I explored more and more vegetables, grains, and legumes—far more than I'd known existed—and a life-changing shift took place. The lack of practical information available about vegetarians and the misunderstandings about meatless meals (supposedly complicated to prepare and fairly boring to eat) became a challenge rather than an obstacle to me. My interest in cooking was reawakened and reinvented. Not only was I going to be a vegetarian, but I was also determined to create meatless meals that were easy, healthy, humane, and so delicious they would satisfy even the most ardent carnivore.

I sorted through my repertoire of meatless meals—pastas, casseroles, soups, and pizzas, to name a few—which became my foundation. Next came the meals that contained meat as a flavoring agent. These were pretty simple to modify: swap chicken or beef broth with vegetable broth, leave the ham hock out of the lentils and drop in a little liquid smoke flavoring; these were easy, small ingredient omissions and substitutions. Overall, the basic recipe remained unchanged.

Then came the real work: meat-centered recipes. It was clear, considering the finished dish I was aiming for, that potatoes weren't going to replace pork and artichoke couldn't stand in for chicken. True, I could skip an ingredient altogether, but by doing so an important component was missing, a certain flavor, texture, even a particular "look." These are all crucially important elements, especially when you're reinventing a recipe. That was when I learned about soy products.

Growing up in Germany and Italy, I'd had no exposure to tofu, tempeh, or other soy foods so I had a lot to learn. In the early eighties, when I made the transition to being a vegetarian, shopping for meat alternatives and soy products wasn't easy. Only a handful of stores stocked these items and even then, product lines were limited. Creativity became my essential ingredient. With that in mind, I decided to just start cooking and figure out how to work these unfamiliar foods into my everyday recipes as I went.

Although my decision to become a vegetarian was made for ethical reasons, I was also aware of the negative health impact that came with a saturated fat–laden diet: heart disease, diabetes, arthritis, and obesity to name a few health issues. I didn't wish to resort to substituting eggs and cheese for meat, because I'd simply be trading one high-fat, high-cholesterol food for another. Instead, I tracked down a couple of cookbooks in hopes of finding alternatives. The only ones I found either relied heavily on animal by-products or went in the opposite direction and eliminated everything, offering a narrow scope of recipes. I had no choice. I had to create recipes of my own.

Over time, with practice and commitment, I became proficient at building textures and flavors in foods. For instance, Mediterranean recipes naturally utilize different methods of cooking vegetables based on region or season. So, my experience with roasting, grilling, or baking vegetables to achieve a variety of textures taught me how to transform vegetables into stand-ins for meats, fats, and even cream. White beans become "butter" to spread on bread. Baked eggplant becomes "chewy meat" for stews. Potatoes add creaminess when pureed and added to soups. I learned that there are infinite imaginative ways to prepare and combine vegetables. Sometimes what I originally intended to create went completely wrong, but something else unexpectedly delightful was the result. I experimented constantly with my recipes. I took copious notes, shared ideas with fellow foodies and throughout my travels, both local and abroad, was always on the lookout for new culinary inspirations. I tested everything on myself, my family, and my friends, many of whom were carnivores, and all of whom came back for seconds. And thirds. Before I knew it, I had a book's worth of recipes.

At a Maine Animal Coalition reunion, I ran into my old friends Kate Kaminski and Betsy Carson who owned a production company. We noted that there was a distinct lack of programming highlighting vegetarian cooking and healthy eating in general. On a whim and a few glasses of wine, we decided to produce one episode of a cooking show for public access, focusing on vegetarian holiday dining. With my recipes in hand, we produced a thirty-minute program in my kitchen and sent it off to our local station. The response was overwhelmingly positive and there were numerous requests for additional episodes. *Delicious TV Totally Vegetarian* was born.

Over the years, I've received hundreds of viewer comments and questions from all over the world. They helped reshape my style of cooking, my philosophy, and my presentation and continue to do so. When we decided to put together this cookbook, my first thoughts were that the recipes within these pages may appear too easy, nonprofessional, or completely homespun. But the reality is, that's just what they are. In fact, that's the very thing about *Delicious TV* that people relate to. It's evident from the feedback the show receives that accessible home cooking is something every mother, father, and child

If You Like . . . Then Try . . .

IF, LIKE I once did, you can't imagine some of your favorite foods without the meat, you'll be surprised at how many vegetarian dishes are just as delicious and satisfying (even more so, I'd say) than traditional meat-based fare. To help ease your switch to eating less meat, I've included "If You Like . . . Then Try . . ." (pages 258–259), an at-a-glance guide that highlights dozens of my recipes that are especially good choices, if you're looking to replace a favorite meat-based dish.

craves. It's how many of us grew up, or perhaps wished we had. Everyday family life has become extremely complicated. My goal is to help make everyday healthy cooking as tasty, fun, and effortless as it can be. With this in mind, following are four basic guidelines that help make this easier.

THE MOST IMPORTANT step in preparing any meal is to purchase the best ingredients possible. The best ingredients will give you the best results. I learned this while growing up in Italy where there's an emphasis on local produce. So much so that it's not uncommon to see Italians foraging along the sides of roads, fields, and forests for wild greens. These amazing vegetables are superior in nutrition because they haven't been exposed to the various, often chemical or genetic, manipulations of mass cultivation.

Ingredients purchased at farmers' markets and farm stands or harvested from your garden taste better and last longer than those purchased from supermarkets. After all, they haven't spent the better part of their lives in trucks moving across the Americas. Nothing lasts forever, so plan to eat what you buy as close to the purchase date as possible. Ask questions. Farmers know what they grow. They are chock-full of good advice, recommendations, and even recipes. Ask about what's best now, what's coming up in the next few weeks or months, how to properly store your produce, and so on. More often than not, it's the farmers themselves who are doing the answering. There's a wealth of knowledge to be gleaned from those who live off the land.

It's Easy Being Green

IN ADDITION to being mindful of the foods we eat, it's also good to be mindful of the land that produced these foods. In light of this, I like to reuse "disposable" items whenever possible. If I use paper towels to blot water, I'll hang them up to dry. Tucking them over a cupboard door—the majority toward the outside, just a smidgen to hold them in place on the inside— works nicely, as does draping them on a dishtowel rack. They're dry in about an hour. Plastic zipper-lock bags get washed after each use with soapy water, then hung to dry hanging off wooden spoons, inverted glasses on the dish rack—anything that will allow them to drain. And the cardboard roll in the middle of paper towel makes a nifty place to store grocery store produce bags. I cut the roll in thirds, stuff it with bags—bottoms first so the air gets out— drop it into my purse and reuse them at the store.

IN OUR SUPERMARKETS everything is available at all times of the year, so it can be tricky to get your head around not eating, say, guacamole in Maine in

January or roasted acorn squash in Florida in May. But seasonal eating encourages a connection to the community, the land, and the seasons that enrich our meals and our lifestyles and encourages greater care of our planet. It also expands your palate and sense of adventure as your food becomes inspired by what's fresh, fragrant, and available.

In Europe, this knowledge is so ingrained that people can be startled if you don't know what's in season. I remember once inquiring about artichokes in a trattoria during the summer. I was "politely" informed that this wasn't the best season for them. If I didn't mind waiting a few months, the waiter was sure they could rustle me up some. Mind you, artichokes in some form are available pretty much year-round. But Italians aren't interested in "some form." Quality ingredients are extremely important in their dishes, whether in home kitchens or restaurants. It's not unusual to discover several items on a menu aren't available because the chef couldn't find satisfactory produce at the market that morning. An awakening to the use of high-quality, local, and seasonal ingredients is becoming more evident in home and professional kitchens across America.

A respect for the seasons lends itself well to vegetarian cooking. In a sense, you're forced by nature into varying your diet and this in turn ensures that you're eating well-rounded and well-balanced meals. Vegetarian cooking isn't about what you don't or can't eat, but about the amazing choices, interesting preparations, and downright delicious dishes that you *can* eat. Eating seasonally breaks what I think of as a vegetable rut. You may be unknowingly preparing lackluster dishes because the vegetables you're using aren't at their peak. Also, seasonal shopping teaches you to recognize fruits and vegetables in their prime, so you're more inclined to showcase them as an entrée rather than simply as a side dish. For example, when beets are in season, especially here in Maine, they're not only wildly flavorful, but reasonably priced, providing the perfect opportunity to experiment with a variety of recipes. Maximizing what and how vegetables can be used is the hallmark of vegetarian cooking.

BUY ORGANIC

MUCH HAS ALREADY been written on the importance of organic food and it's not my intention to have this book serve as a primer on these larger, more complex issues, so suffice to say: whenever possible buy organic. It's better for your health, it's better for the health of the farmers and the planet, and it's simply more flavorful.

Having said that, for the majority of people to purchase organic goods they need to be both affordable and accessible. Increasing consumer interest has motivated mainstream supermarkets to stock more organic produce, and co-ops and small markets are sprouting up faster than roadside weeds. This certainly addresses accessibility. But what about affordability? It's true, due to their hands-on, chemical-free cultivation methods, organic foods are more expensive to produce than conventionally farmed or imported produce. This can present a challenge for budget-minded shoppers. It's important to also understand the leap in real value these foods take. Not only are they fresher and taste better, they're significantly higher in vitamins and minerals; free of pesticides, chemicals, and other toxins that are believed to be at the root of many of our modern diseases. And they are grown in a manner that respects the environment. All of which makes them the best choice for your money. Here are a few tips to help keep organic foods within your budget:

- Shop at farmers' markets. When food is purchased at the peak of its growing season, it's always the best value.
- Buy in bulk or on sale and divide your purchase with friends and family.
- Join a food co-op. Co-ops are essentially member-owned buying clubs where food is purchased in bulk and the savings is divided among its members. Co-op shopping can save you as much as 40 percent off the retail price of food. If you don't have a co-op in your area, contact the Cooperative Grocers Information Network (www.cgin.coop) for guidelines on starting your own.
- Join a CSA (Community Supported Agriculture) program or partnership. Many local farms offer shares or produce subscriptions where members or subscribers receive weekly or monthly baskets of produce directly from the farmer. Some CSA farmers require up-front payment for the season and others accept weekly or monthly payments. A typical CSA season runs from late spring through late fall. For more information about how to participate in a CSA, inquire at your local farmers' market or check out Sustainable Agriculture Research and Education on the web (www.sare.org). Browse around or head straight for the Consumers tab.
- Freeze, freeze, freeze. Proper freezing preserves nutrients and ensures you'll get more mileage from the vegetables and grains you purchased at a great price. Inquire at the market for the best methods and vegetables for freezing.
- Don't overbuy unless you plan on canning, freezing, or drying extra produce. Buy just what you'll need for a few days. Throwing out food amounts to throwing money in the trash.
- Use your buyer power. The more frequently you purchase quality organic foods at mainstream markets, the more you'll see it available on supermarket shelves. By purchasing compromised chemical-laden foods grown in countries we can't even pronounce

(let alone find on a map), by workers who are paid two cents an hour, we're in essence subsidizing the industry. Buy cheap and pay tenfold with your health and resources.

MY MOTHER IS an excellent cook. Not one to venture into uncharted territory, she's nevertheless game to adjusting a recipe according to season, availability, and culinary whim. When I was growing up, she relied on traditional German dishes, most passed down from her mother. But if there weren't any fresh vegetables in the pantry, she knew how to transform her would-be stew into a hearty goulash by letting her instincts guide her. I learned from her that cooking, with the exception of baking, isn't about putting together a preformulated set of ingredients or about following predetermined rules. Rather, it's about getting in touch with your own intuition, your own tastes, and utilizing those to create delicious and healthy meals.

This rooted me in a satisfying relationship with food I still enjoy today: equal measures playful and empowering. It doesn't mean that any consideration to seasoning or cooking times, for example, should go the way of the dodo bird. It *does* mean that with a flexible attitude toward food—especially what we eat daily—and sound basic techniques, we can eat well at every meal. In other words, cooking doesn't have to be complicated, intimidating, or particularly rigid to be really good.

Sometimes flexibility is born of necessity. Just the other day I set out to make some pasta with fennel, a classic Sicilian dish, but there was no good fresh fennel to be found. There was, however, nestled in a basket at my local farmers' market, some small, just-picked zucchini with their edible flowers still intact, so dinner was grilled marinated zucchini with lightly fried blossoms.

My hope is that you use this book to create and develop your own foundation for making delicious vegetarian food, and that you do so in your own way. My recipes, except for the baked goods, should be considered guidelines. To become a good cook (and *everyone* can become a good cook), listen to your intuition. Think about the various transformations that happen to foods when you boil, fry, bake, or grill them. What are the ingredients like in their raw state? How do they react with acids or sugars? How does a particular vegetable or other item look, smell, and sound? Are you pleased with the final results of a particular dish? Is there any way you can make it taste better next time? You're not looking for scientific answers. You're learning to pay attention to how *you* feel about the food. If the recipe calls for grilled asparagus, but you prefer it boiled, adjust the recipe to suit your taste. It's a learning process. It's what makes a good meal exceptional. I rarely make the same thing the exact same way twice and I've been enjoying cooking for thirty-three years now. I encourage you to embark upon the same adventure.

Vegetarian or Vegan?

DESPITE ALL the designations assigned to vegetarians who eat chicken, fish, or game, true vegetarians do not consume any meat of any animal. They do, however, consume products that come from animals such as eggs, butter, milk, cheese, and honey. Even these foods can and often do have negative consequences for the animals who are the sources of these products. Egg-laying hens, for example, have their beaks sliced off when they are a few hours old so they don't attack and cause damage to one another when they're caged by the tens of thousands in airless warehouses. They're also force-fed antibiotics in an attempt to ward off illness caused by these unsanitary and inhumane living conditions. Dairy cows have their calves taken away within hours after birth so that humans may harvest the milk for themselves. Many cows are subsequently injected with growth hormones to both lengthen lactation and increase the quantity of milk produced. While the female calves may be raised, in varying conditions, into future dairy cows, the male calves are typically taken to veal farms, where as infants they're short-chained in crates, deprived of proper nutrition, sanitary living space, and basic humane treatment for the duration of their short lives. The end result is prized anemic veal, or erroneously labeled milk-fed veal. Veal calves were the national poster children of farm animal reform efforts in the mid- to late-eighties. The issue to ban veal crates was my first campaign and was ongoing for many years.

Growing up in Europe, I was regularly exposed to the realities of slaughter, however the conditions of the farm animals I've just described, and many other inhumane practices, have now been outlawed in most of Europe for decades. Over the past twenty years in America, there's been a growing awareness with respect to eggs, dairy, and intensive factory style farming practices, resulting in more humane, organic, chemical- and hormone-free options slowly becoming available, but the overall industry has done little to change.

In light of this, vegetarians who choose to eliminate all animal products from their diets and their lifestyles are known as vegans. Veganism may sound like a radical concept, but it really isn't as challenging as you might think. Most of the recipes in this book easily become vegan because they're inherently flexible and not heavily dependent on the addition of animal ingredients.

Stocking the Kitchen

YOU DON'T NEED all sorts of timesaving gizmos, nor every size pan or dish known to mankind to be proficient in the kitchen. In fact, by the time you figure out how to use those gadgets, or wade through your overstuffed cupboards to get the appropriate pan, you could have finished the job five times over and be relaxing with a nice cup of tea. A selection of the right items, however, does make short work of certain tasks.

Viewers often write in and ask me about this pan or that particular knife and why I use it. I decided to go through my cupboards and drawers and come up with a list of what I consider to be my basic kitchen necessities along with their virtues and applications. Because I have a cooking show, I have a wider variety of pots, pans, and casseroles than most, so I'm in no way suggesting you need every one of these. Assess your own personal needs, storage space, how and what you cook most often, and select those pieces that best support your cooking style.

WHEN IT COMES to creating space, it's not the size of the kitchen that counts, but rather how well it's organized. Spacious counters are of little use if they're crowded with mail, keys, non-cooking books, knickknacks, things you're about to get to, plants, or anything else you don't quite know where to put.

MAKING SPACE

Find a new home for all your counter's nonessentials. Once this is complete, your kitchen should feel calmer. More relaxed. I can't emphasize this enough. Clutter can create subconscious barriers to enjoying yourself in the kitchen, so create an inviting atmosphere for yourself and for your guests.

Next, check your light bulbs. I know dim light makes us look more youthful, but you need to be able to see what you're cooking. I have dimmer switches on my lights. When I'm cooking, I crank them up. When I'm entertaining, I turn them down.

Now that you're relaxed and can see properly, go ahead and fling open a cupboard or slide open a drawer. If you can't remember what something does—out it goes. Just like there's a man out there for every woman (or every man), there's someone out there who will provide your castoff with a good home.

A few tips for the purge:

■ **SENSIBLE PLACEMENT.** Try to keep your prep and cooking tools—wooden spoons, knives, etc.—within easy reach.

■ **CREATE EASY ACCESS.** Items you use infrequently can go in the back of the cupboard, things you grab on an almost daily basis go in front. Common sense.

DON'T SCRIMP ON knives. They can be quite expensive, I know, but if you take good care of them (wash by hand, dry well, and keep blades protected), they can conceivably outlast you. I recommend starting with four knives (vegetarian cooking eliminates the need for a few styles right off the bat, like a boning or carving knife):

■ **FIVE-INCH HOLLOW-EDGE SANTOKU CHEF'S KNIFE.** This is the knife you see most chefs using on television because it has evenly spaced indentations, or hollows, along the entire cutting edge of the blade to help prevent food from sticking to the knife. This knife also reduces friction, which means there's less drag on the knife and smoother, faster chopping. I own a seven-inch and a five-inch, but use the five-inch most often, because it's lighter and more maneuverable for everyday tasks.

■ **PARING KNIFE.** A good paring knife is essential for peeling and trimming, and slicing small items like garlic. I prefer a three-inch blade to a two-inch one because that extra bit of length makes delicate slicing easier.

■ **SERRATED TOMATO KNIFE.** Not only does this knife cut through tomatoes without creating a mess, it's also makes slicing soft and citrus fruits easier.

■ **SERRATED BREAD KNIFE.** This knife makes easy work of slicing even the heartiest, crustiest bread loaf into thin slices without crushing it. Also cuts a tomato, squirt-free, in a pinch.

Because knives are an investment, I encourage you to ask questions when shopping. Personally, I find the celebrity chef lines to be overpriced, overrated, and under-crafted. I'd suggest visiting a kitchen specialty store where you can handle the knives before purchasing. Each knife is weighted differently and has a unique handle style, so one size doesn't fit all. If it doesn't feel right in your hand, it's not your knife.

Also, each manufacturer has a graduated level of quality: three, four, and five stars. Oftentimes, there's little difference between a four- and five-star knife, especially if you're not a professional chef. Once you make your decision, shop around; these days pricing is fairly competitive.

Buy individual knives, not sets. While sets may seem like a good deal, they usually come with a couple of completely useless knives.

And, finally, keep your knives sharp. A dull knife is an accident waiting to happen. Rather than gliding through food, dull knives need to be forced, often landing right in your thumb. I use what's called a *steel* to keep mine honed. It looks like a fireplace poker only much shorter and without the prongs. It's handy, stores easily, and works well for daily touch-ups. Serrated knives require special care. I suggest you ask at the time of purchase about how to properly maintain your knives. Options may include annual sharpening services at the store or with the manufacturer.

NOW THAT YOU have your sharp knives at the ready and your kitchen is decluttered, well lighted, fairly organized, and several pounds lighter, it's time to have a glass of wine and focus on what appliances you need. A food processor, blender, immersion blender, and mixer top my list.

KITCHEN APPLIANCES

- **FOOD PROCESSOR:** Select one with a six- to eight-cup capacity. They're ideal for chopping, shredding, and processing foods that have a drier texture, such as dips, cheeses, greens, vegetable burgers, nuts, and fillings. I prep most things by hand, but a food processor can transform a half-hour chopping job into thirty seconds. I find mine indispensable when making Beet Burgers (page 190), Tofu Cannoli (page 250), pesto, and pastry dough. Warning: it's not hard to get carried away with the ease a food processor provides at the expense of texture. Maintaining texture is vital in vegetarian cooking, and those blades spin at a powerful enough rate to turn even the chunkiest ingredients into mush. Fortunately, processors come with a pulse button, which is your insurance against overprocessing. And don't forget about your knives. Some chopping, dicing, and mincing is better done by hand.
- **BLENDER:** There are people out there who believe that owning both a food processor and a blender is akin to putting both whipped cream and ice cream on their slice of pie, but they're wrong. A blender is useful for liquefying soups and smoothies— anything liquid. A food processor loves drier mixtures, but doesn't work well for liquids. See, it's a perfect match.
- **IMMERSION BLENDER:** This is like a magic wand with a blade on the end. The downside to a stand blender is that you have to wait for very hot foods to cool before liquefying them. An

immersion blender goes right into the pot, bowl, or cup no matter the temperature or size. It's an inexpensive blending option.

- **MIXERS:** Mixers come in hand and stand models. If I had to pick between them, I'd go for the hand mixer, but that might be because I'm not the world's biggest (or most successful) baker. Nevertheless, hand mixers have improved over the years and a good one will get you through pretty much everything short of bread or pizza dough.

THESE DAYS, SHOPPING for cookware is almost as much fun as shopping for shoes. The choices are as glamorous as they are endless. As with shoes, I'd recommend, if possible, investing in a few quality pieces that will last you a lifetime. This is not to say you can't make tasty and nutritious food in less expensive pans. You can. Two of my favorite pans were made back when disco balls were the rage. Nevertheless a few carefully selected essentials can make the difference between, say, Pumpkin-Bulgur Chili (page 124) that tastes like pumpkin and bulgur and Pumpkin-Bulgur Chili that tastes like tin. The better brands heat well, heat evenly, and don't impart any flavor other than the ones you want. Plus, trust me, you'll burn through the cheapies. Start small and shop smart. For instance, consider purchasing discontinued colors on the sale table.

I have a full set of cast-iron skillets, which I've had for more than thirty years. I get older, but they don't: they're as black and smooth as the day we met. I love cooking with cast iron because it distributes the heat evenly, and consistently retains that heat. This means you can cook at lower temperatures, and cooking at lower temperatures means your food will stay moist and flavorful. Plus, it adds dietary iron to food, which we all need. I'm from the generation where we actually seasoned our cast iron (oiling and baking them, then waiting a few months for them to get that lovely black, mostly nonstick patina), but nowadays you'd be hard pressed to find cast iron that hasn't been preseasoned by the manufacturer. There are a variety of cast-iron pans on the market in all sorts of price ranges. To my mind, the Lodge brand still makes the best. While not outrageous, they can be on the pricier side, but cheap look-alikes eventually will crack, warp, and pit. And, frankly, they don't conduct heat as well. One of the many pluses of cast iron is it moves easily from the stove to the oven and back again. Another is the delicious crispy, browned, seared crust on foods that only cast iron can deliver. This is important for vegetarian cooking, because it increases the texture and flavor of food

If straight cast iron doesn't resonant with you, there's enamel-coated cast iron. These have all the heat-conducting qualities of straight cast iron, only they're prettier. For enameled cookware pots, I love the Le Creuset brand. The pots come in various colors with cream interiors that, over time, turn a lovely burnished brown patina, which should never be bleached or scrubbed away. Not only is it a layer of history, as with the straight cast iron, it keeps them nonstick. Avoid scratching them by using wood, melamine, plastic, or resin utensils—never metal. Be sure to remove plastic utensils while cooking as when they come in contact with the bottom of a hot pot they can melt. Also, enamel is fragile, so chipping is a possibility. Find charm in the imperfections and you'll have these forever. Naturally, there are less expensive versions of enameled pots available, many of which are quite good. Explore what best suits your needs. The lack of a certain size or brand of a pot should never impede your desire to cook. It took me many, many years to collect my set.

Some people find both plain and enameled cast iron too bulky, price-prohibitive, or simply not their thing. Not to worry. I firmly believe you can cook anything in anything, what matters most is that you're comfortable with the anything you're using. Nonstick coated aluminum is a popular choice these days. Aluminum cookware is lightweight and inexpensive and heats up quickly. Because they're lightweight, these pots and pans can also dent easily, and the nonstick anodized coating is susceptible to scratching, so once again, be sure not to use metal utensils. Stainless steel is another option. It's shiny, durable, and resists denting or warping. Available in a huge variety of styles and prices, quality can vary. Viking, Calphalon, All-Clad, and even Le Creuset make top-notch stainless pots and pans. The downside to stainless steel is it's not an efficient conductor of heat (to solve this problem the higher-end lines have an aluminum or copper core in the base of the pan that may run up the sides) and it can take a bit of extra effort to keep clean. But it is more durable, and less likely than aluminum to transfer unpleasant flavors or colors to your food.

Here's a list of the cookware and bakeware that I recommend. Each piece is available in cast iron, enameled cast iron, stainless steel, and aluminum.

POTS

- **ONE-QUART SAUCEPAN WITH LID.** The perfect size for a small quantity of sauce. Before I had one of these, I used my 2-quart pot. While not as thrilling (yes, there is a thrill to finding the exact piece of cookware for your recipe), it worked very well. If you're on a budget or have limited space, the 2-quart is the size to start with.
- **TWO-QUART SAUCEPAN WITH LID.** This is one of my most-used pots. It's great for sauces, steaming vegetables, or a simple stew for one or two.
- **THREE-QUART SAUCEPAN WITH LID.** Another of my most-used pots. This size is ideal for pasta, soup, sauces, stews, and deep-frying.
- **FIVE- OR SIX-QUART DUTCH OVEN.** This has more surface space, which makes it easier when cooking for a large number of people. Soups, stocks, stews, pasta, braising—all work well in one of these.

- **FIVE-QUART BUFFET CASSEROLE WITH LID FROM LE CREUSET.** I adore this pan. I use it as my everything: wok, skillet, sauté pan, risotto pan, baking dish, and a gorgeous serving dish. It's the pan that most viewers want to know more about.

PANS

- **EIGHT-INCH CAST-IRON SKILLET:** The perfect size for scrambling one egg (or an egg-substitute), toasting nuts, and sautéing anything that you don't need a lot of. And when you're cooking in a larger pan, it's just the right weight to press a panini sandwich or delicately, but firmly, flatten a portobello mushroom.
- **TEN-INCH CAST-IRON FRYER:** Roomy and deep, use this for sautéing all sorts of those yummy things that need a fair dose of oil. I use mine for stews, beans, fried potatoes; the taller sides keep things from spilling out. Added bonus: it comes with a lid.
- **TEN-INCH CAST-IRON GRILL PAN:** I refer to this (well, "these," as I own two of them) as my "saving grace pan." I live in Maine, so my outdoor grill is burrowed away for a good part of the year, but this pan brings a bit of summer to even the gloomiest days. A fraction of the cost of a fancy stovetop grill, lightweight, and stackable, use it for vegetables, bread, pizza, fruit—really anything you're craving. Preheat your grill pan on the stovetop for at least 15 minutes, then brush it with a little vegetable oil. Your food will sizzle when it hits the pan.
- **TEN-INCH CAST-IRON GRIDDLE PAN:** This is a lot like the grill pan, except it's flat with no rim and no lines. Heat up sandwiches, cook tortillas, or make pancakes. This is the pan I prefer when I employ my eight-inch skillet as a press.
- **TEN-INCH CAST-IRON SKILLET:** This pan has sloped or slanted sides, which makes it a great lightweight all-purpose skillet. I use it when making Tarte Tatin (page 253), Vegan Corn Bread (page 131), and Pan-Fried Pizza (page 144).
- **TWELVE-INCH CAST-IRON SKILLET:** This is the largest pan I own. Weighty and broad, it is the pan to turn to when there are a lot of ingredients or I need a spacious surface area. I use it for any kind of noodles or if I'm making more than four burgers. I also put it to work when roasting potatoes or vegetables in the oven. Warning: It's a two-fister, so have a couple of potholders nearby.
- **TEN-INCH SLOPE-SIDED NONSTICK SKILLET.** It's always helpful to have at least one of these around, ten inches or larger. It's perfect for a light sauté or for foods that tend to stick, like eggs, crepes, and tofu.

Plus, it allows you to use little to no fat. I occasionally call for one in my recipes. Here I recommend a mid-range pan. I find it works very well for just as long as its pricier counterparts and it's much less painful to replace. Farberware makes good, affordable nonstick skillets and some of the Italian pans available in outlet stores are also nice. Be sure to use only a plastic or rubber spatula or a wooden spoon on the tender surface.

Caring for Cast Iron

IRON IS porous so it requires a little bit of special care. If I've just been roasting nuts, heating a tortilla, or toasting a sandwich, I don't submerge the skillet in water, but wipe it out with a damp sponge (it's fine to soak the enameled cast iron). If scrubbing is necessary, use hot soapy water and a brush. Rinse well and dry very, very well (iron rusts). Never use an abrasive cleanser because no matter how much you rinse, you'll still leave a bit behind. Once the pan is clean, daub a piece of paper towel with a little vegetable oil and wipe it around the surface of the pan. In essence, you're re-seasoning it, which will maintain its timeless nonstick finish. A little bit of care goes a long way. I know of cast-iron pans that have been handed down through three generations.

OVEN EQUIPMENT

- **PIZZA STONE.** For homemade pizza with a crisp crust, a pizza stone is a must. They're lighter and less expensive than ever and easy to use. Just preheat your stone at 500°F for at least 45 minutes, and it does the rest. Rather than using a pizza peel to place my pizza on the stone, I use a somewhat unconventional method that guarantees crispy pizza every time. To remove the pizza, I use a round, lightweight cheapie cookie sheet which not only slides easily under the pizza, but I can slice on and serve off it as well. When the stone has cooled, scrape off any cheese, drippings, or oil. No need to clean it with soap and water. And it's safe to leave the stone in the oven even when you're baking. Over time, it will turn black and become seasoned. This is good. If the look of it bothers you and you have a self-cleaning oven, run it through the clean cycle, dust off the ashes, and it will be good as new. Note: It's best to place the pizza stone on the lower level of the oven when cooking cakes, cookies, and other more delicate foods. Bread, focaccia, or savory foods, like a pan of potatoes, baked directly on a stone taste out of this world.

■ **CASSEROLE AND CERAMIC BAKING DISHES.** I have a variety of each in a variety of shapes and sizes. I use them for cooking lasagna, roasting vegetables, baking tempeh and tofu, and creating desserts. These sorts of dishes are perfect for oven-to-table service and allow for easy cleanup. You can find beautiful European casseroles here for a fraction of what they cost in Europe. Be sure that they are labeled "oven safe," and not intended solely for serving. And don't use them on your stovetop. These dishes are strictly for oven and broiler use.

■ **CAKE PANS AND COOKIE SHEETS.** A kitchen without cake pans and cookie sheets is a kitchen without homemade cakes and cookies. And that's not much fun. Most pans and sheets are made from tin, aluminum, or metal. Look for ones made from baker's steel (black or silver), tin, glass, terra-cotta, or ceramic. Heavy materials are best for cookie sheets—rimmed (jelly-roll pan) or flat—because they won't buckle or warp in the oven. A good basic assortment should include:

- 9- or 10-inch pie pan: glass or tin
- 13 × 9 × 2-inch baking dish: glass, ceramic or tin
- 8-inch square pan: glass, ceramic, or tin
- Two 8 × 4-inch loaf pans: glass or tin
- 9-inch tart pan with removable bottom
- 9- or 19-inch springform pan: glass bottom is a nice feature
- Two to four cookie sheets or jelly-roll pans: heavy metal
- Cupcake or muffin tin
- Wire cooling rack
- Parchment paper or reusable silicone liners like Silpats for lining pans

OTHER KITCHEN EQUIPMENT

■ **BENRINER.** This great little tool, also known as an *Asian mandoline,* performs all the same tricks as the French version—cuts vegetables into perfectly even thin slices—for a fraction of the cost. It's lightweight, easy to use, and easy to clean. Didi Emmons, a Boston-based chef, introduced me to it and cabbage slaws have never been the same.

■ **COLANDER/STRAINER.** Select a reasonable size based upon how many folks you normally cook for and what it is you most often cook. A mesh strainer is a good choice because it allows you to strain or rinse small foods like rice without half of it rushing down the drain. A colander with holes is good for fruit, in particular berries, so that bits of debris can wash away. You may find you need one of each.

■ **CUTTING BOARD.** Forget about the modern plastic or glass option, and go for the old-fashioned wooden cutting board. It's naturally bacteria-resistant, comfortable to work on, doesn't dull your knives, and looks beautiful resting on your countertop. And cleanup is easy: wipe, wash, and dry.

■ **MEASURING CUPS AND SPOONS.** The first thing to know is that a one-cup liquid measure is not the same as one-cup dry measure. I do a lot of my measuring by sight, and encourage you to develop this knack as well, but for those recipes where accuracy means the difference between a Bundt cake and a pancake, it's crucial to use the right measure. Pyrex makes classic, tried-and-true graduated measuring cups for liquids. They can be microwaved and are excellent for pouring sauces. For dry measures—flour, sugar, etc.—I recommend metal cups. Metal is also preferable for measuring spoons. Look for ones that are narrow and fit easily into the slots atop spice and herb containers.

■ **MICROPLANE GRATER.** This is the best tool around for a quick grating of cheese or zesting of citrus. It comes in a variety of sizes for a variety of jobs. Pick the one that most matches your needs. What I especially love about these graters is that they're narrow and fit easily in a drawer.

■ **MIXING BOWLS.** These come in all shapes, sizes, and price ranges. I tend to grab my stainless steel bowls most often; they're inexpensive, stackable, easy to find, and oversized, which is nice for mixing everything from a vegetable burger to a salad. Plus, you never have to worry about breaking them. If you're a bread baker, pick up a large ceramic bowl; bread dough loves ceramic.

■ **MORTAR AND PESTLE.** This may not be essential, but I'm such a fan I have two: a large one made from stone and a small porcelain one. Giving dry spices a grind prior to cooking releases their natural essential oils and wakes up their flavors like nothing else. Mortars do an exceptionally good job with spices, garlic, nuts, salt, and herbs—even the occasional aspirin.

■ **OLIVE OIL CRUET WITH A SPOUT.** Pick up a nice, big economical can of extra virgin olive oil, pour some into your cruet and tuck it somewhere handy for a quick drizzle on a salad, pizza, or pasta. Ceramic is your best choice for a cruet because olive oil should be protected from the light, which diminishes both quality and shelf life.

■ **PLASTIC STORAGE CONTAINERS.** These are absolutely indispensable: handy, practical, and easy to use. They make my cooking life much easier. But, like the proverbial partnerless sock, I always seem to end up with more tops than bottoms. And I can't seem to stack them so they fit either inside of each other or inside the

Going with the Grain

PROPER CARE of your wooden utensils and cutting boards is essential and, fortunately, easy. Apply a few drops of food-grade mineral oil to a cloth or paper towel, rub into clean wood, and buff off any excess with a dry towel. Repeat this treatment every two to three months to prevent drying, splitting, and fading.

cupboard. Nevertheless, it's helpful to have them in a variety of sizes ranging from 1 cup to 2 quarts.

- **PEPPER MILL.** If you want pepper that tastes like pepper, a pepper mill is essential. Pepper out of tin tastes flat and bitter. Don't bother with one of those fancy foot-long numbers, a simple comfortable size works best. Chances are, there'll be a matching salt mill nearby, but you can skip it if you have mortar and pestle for grinding coarse salt.

- **ROLLING PIN.** Essential for making pastry and pasta dough, choose a rolling pin that feels comfortable in your hands and rolls easily. For a while there, marble was all the rage. I know, I bought one. To my mind, marble doesn't work any better than your basic wooden version and is quite heavy.

- **RUBBER SPATULAS.** These flexible spatulas are handy for getting every last bit of soup, sauce, or batter out of a mixing bowl, food processor, pot, or casserole dish. A must for nonstick finishes.

- **SALAD SPINNER.** I'm not sure why, considering all the other nonsense I bought, I resisted getting one of these for years. Instead, I flung mesh bags around my frightened kitchen in the hopes of separating water from greens, wrapped them in a small forest of paper towels, and even tried leaving them out to air dry. I always ended up with soggy, slimy greens that my dressing wouldn't adhere to. A salad spinner is inexpensive and efficient. You can wash your greens all at once, spin dry, then store what you don't need in a plastic container or a reusable zipper-lock bag. That way when you're ready to go, your greens are too. It's also ideal for herbs, preventing those disturbing bits of grit from ending up in your pesto.

- **SCRUB BRUSH.** I keep a small stiff scrub brush near my sink so I can give my vegetables a good wash. I also keep a two-sided sponge scrubber nearby for potatoes and smoother vegetables. Although you'll be tempted to use either one for dishes or to clean the sink, don't.

- **SPIDER.** This resembles a metal nest and is great for removing fried food from oil and pasta from boiling water. The handle is long and the basket angled, making it a more practical option than a slotted spoon. Spiders are inexpensive, versatile, and easy to find. Most come with bamboo handles, so keep them out of the dishwasher.

- **SPOONS AND LADLES.** I recommend having a few of each. As far as ladles go, invest in a larger size—meaning a larger bowl—for soups and stews, and a smaller size for sauces. A few larger serving spoons—make one a slotted spoon—are nice to have around. I have bunches of wooden spoons. My most treasured ones are made of olive wood. I picked them up at a trade fair in Florence, Italy, fifteen years ago and they're with me still. Wooden spoons are sanitary, don't scratch your pots, inexpensive, long lasting (if you keep them out of the dishwasher), and widely available. I suggest starting with the traditional spoon shape, angled (to get into those corners), and a spatula type.

- **STEAMING BASKET.** This is a must if you like to steam vegetables. Look for one that will fit into the pot and be wary of the ones that come with an unnecessarily tall center stem. They make a lid impossible to fit. Asian markets usually stock them. They're stainless steel and quite inexpensive.

- **THERMOMETER.** Frying at the proper temperature, 375°F, will keep your food from absorbing excess oil and produce a crispy exterior without burning—so a thermometer is a must. I find that an inexpensive candy/fry thermometer works well. Choose one with easy-to-read numbers that clips to the side of your pan. The clip keeps the thermometer in place, and lifts the probe off the bottom and away from the sides of the pan ensuring an accurate temperature reading.

- **TIMER.** I'm notorious for becoming so wrapped up in doing something else that I forget I have food on the stove or in the oven. In this multitasking world of ours, a timer is essential for peace of mind. I use one with a clip so I can carry it with me everywhere I go. Personally, I believe the adage "out of sight, out of mind" was coined by a chef.

- **VEGETABLE PEELER.** Find one that fits nicely in your hand: some of those with oversized handles can be cumbersome and interfere with developing a "peeling rhythm," which means you'll just be hacking away. Peelers now come with serrated carbon steel blades, which I like. I suggest buying one with a swivel head. They make swift work out of peeling potatoes, carrots, and fruit. With this said, I should note that whenever possible I buy organic produce and as a result of this I'm less inclined to peel fruits and vegetables for the sake of preserving nutrients. I still peel non-organic produce.

- **WHISK.** One medium or large whisk will do the trick. Pick a nice sturdy one; flexible whisks do a mediocre job. A whisk is great for stirring sauces, polenta, or flour mixtures. It also comes in handy when you're sifting dry ingredients together while baking. I have a small salad whisk with an angled, coiled base that draws a lot of attention from viewers. This fantastic little tool fits into a small bowl and emulsifies oil and vinegar like nothing else because it lies flat so you don't have to tip the bowl. It's one of my favorite prep tools. And it's inexpensive.

THE EMPTY SINK SYNDROME

NOW THAT YOUR kitchen is clean and stocked, you're ready to begin. I first have one bit of advice that will come in handy: before preparing your meal, empty your sink. Better yet, empty it and fill it with hot soapy water. Have paper towels and a clean sponge close at hand too. Cleaning up along the way helps keep you on task. When I'm filming my show, I really do clean up as I go and the same is true in my off-camera life. With step one out of the way, I'm able to see step two with much more clarity. Make it a habit to plunk used mixing bowls and utensils in the sink to soak. This makes the final cleanup easier and clears the way to creating more usable space. When something is simmering or boiling use that time to wash dishes. If you're caught up and have a few minutes to kill, stay near the stove and knock out thirty or forty squats.

Stocking the Pantry

COOKING IS ABOUT getting in touch with your intuition. Rather than opening your cupboards and seeing a bunch of unrelated cans and boxes, think how it would feel to see a wide choice of meals. This happens quite naturally as you become acquainted with the textures, smells, tastes, under-tones, and reliability of your staples. The more you cook, the more you'll know that you don't need to have every ingredient under the sun to satiate a personal craving or make dinner for four in a hurry.

As time goes on, you'll realize that with a few tweaks and pinches you can transform Thursday's roasted eggplant sauce with the simple addition of a few chopped Kalamata olives and some capers into Friday's bruschetta top-ping, or add capers or olives to some white beans, pasta, and stock for a nourishing minestrone. You'll begin to know—without even a conscious thought—how to turn what you have on hand into what you want.

No matter your favorite foods or cooking skills, here are a few basics it's good to have around:

BAKING POWDER AND BAKING SODA

Both are necessary leavening agents for baking. I usually have baking powder forever, because I hardly use it. But it's best if used within six months of opening, so mark the can or box with a date. If you want to test your baking powder to see if it's fresh and active, put a little in some hot water. If it "sizzles," it's good. In a pinch you can make your own baking powder by combining ½ teaspoon cream of tartar and ¼ teaspoon baking soda. This makes the equivalent of 1 teaspoon baking powder. Use this immediately or add ¼ teaspoon cornstarch to absorb moisture and pre-vent a premature chemical reaction.

BEANS

Having a selection of beans on hand is an easy way to ensure dozens of meal options with little fuss. Low in fat, high in protein, folate, B vitamins, and complex carbohydrates, beans—all of which are varieties of legumes—are a vital part of a balanced and nutritious diet. They're also high in fiber, which is important because it slows down the rate that sugar enters the bloodstream, provides a steady source of energy, and supports proper digestion. A pleasure to cook, beans add texture and interest to just about any dish including soups, stews, sauces, and salads.

Beans are available dried or canned. I recommend organic beans, especially when purchasing canned. Organic beans are firmer, have less (or no) added salt and sugar, and, well, just taste better. Some Italian- and Latin-based recipes call for the addition of canned bean liquid to increase body and thickness. If this isn't the case, simply drain and rinse. Heartier beans, such as kidney beans, can be added at the beginning of a recipe. Most other canned beans retain their texture better if mixed in toward the end.

Dried beans, except lentils, require presoaking before cooking, so you'll have to plan ahead. It's well worth it, though, as home-cooked beans are always more delicious and more economical. Once cooked, they can be stored in the fridge for up to five days, or may be frozen in plastic containers. Whenever possible, shop for dried beans where you know there's a rapid turnover. Look for beans that are shiny, unbroken, and plump. These are signs of freshness. Stored in an airtight container in a cool dry place, beans should keep for up to a year. A 15-ounce can of beans is the equivalent of ¾ cup of dried.

While there are myriad beans available, a good starter collection includes:

- **BLACK BEANS.** A staple of Latin and Caribbean cuisines, these earthy, rich beans are a sumptuous balance to assertive, spicy flavors such as garlic, onion, hot or sweet peppers, and cilantro. They're frequently used in soups, dips, salads, and Mexican recipes.
- **CANNELLINI BEANS.** Smallish, white kidney-shaped beans with a soft creamy texture, cannellini beans are excellent when simply dressed with olive oil and lemon, in hummus, soups, and salads, or blended with hot water and whipped into a creamy dairy-free emulsion for vegans. They're popular in Italian and Mediterranean cooking and far easier to digest than navy beans.
- **CHICKPEAS.** To me, chickpeas are the king of beans. Resembling shelled hazelnuts, packed with protein, and easy

Quick-Soak Method for Dried Beans

OVERNIGHT SOAKING has been the tried-and-true method for preparing dried beans for cooking. Now, new studies show that the quick-soak method is not only more convenient and efficient, but is more effective in reducing the flatulent effects that beans often cause.

All beans can be quick-soaked with the exception of soybeans and fava beans, which require a minimum of 12 hours in water. Other legumes such as lentils, peas, black-eyed peas, and split peas require no soaking and can be used right out of the bag. Be sure to sort through all dried beans for little pebbles or stones lurking beneath the surface.

To quick soak, place the beans in a pot and cover with 3 inches of unsalted water. Bring the uncovered pot to a rolling boil and boil for 2 minutes. Remove from the heat and cover. Allow the beans to steep in the cooking liquid for 1 hour. Drain the beans, return to the pot, and cover again with fresh water. After 5 minutes of rest, drain and rinse again. The beans are now softened, free of troublesome elements and ready to be cooked in water, soup, or a stew.

to digest, they are prominent in many cuisines—from Spanish to Greek to North African to Indian. They are also roasted and ground into flour (marketed as *besan, garbanzo flour,* or *gram flour*), which I use in one of my favorite recipes, Chickpea Crepes (page 132). The whole beans add texture to soups, fritters, salads, and appetizers.

- **LENTILS.** Lentils are low in fat, rich in protein, and high in fiber, iron, and folate and other B vitamins. They are used often in vegetarian cooking as a protein source and blend well with textured foods like nuts and grains. Lentils readily absorb the flavors of fellow ingredients and look dramatic on the plate. They come in many varieties and colors: red, yellow, brown, and green, to name a few—and, my favorite, Puy. Red and yellow split lentils tend to break down during cooking, into almost a puree, making them ideal for thickening soups and stews. Brown and green lentils retain better texture but take a bit more time to cook. Puy lentils, sometimes called *French lentils* because they're grown in Le Puy in the Auvergne region in central France, have a superior texture and a beautiful blue-green color. They retain their bead-like firmness during cooking, making them ideal for preparations where the integrity of a whole lentil is desired. Lentil Stew (page 123) is a tasty and easy recipe that highlights their fine qualities. Unlike other beans, lentils require no soaking before cooking.
- **PINTO BEANS.** Few beans have the flexibility of texture and flavor as pinto beans. Closely related to kidney beans, they are versatile and nutritious. Served whole or mashed—as in

refried beans—they make hearty appetizers, soups, and salads. In the Deep South, they're even used in pies and other desserts.

- ■ **SPLIT PEAS.** Dried split peas are usually green or yellow, although you may stumble across other varieties. Sweet and tender, they don't retain their texture or shape during cooking, making them perfect for soups and pureed dishes. Peas share many of the same nutritional benefits as lentils.

BOUILLON, VEGETARIAN

Bouillon is one of the mainstays of Italian cooking, especially in restaurants. Vegetarian versions are available in powder, pastes, and cubes. It's an inexpensive, easy, and immediate way to add tremendous depth of flavor. Unfortunately, with most bouillon you're also adding massive amounts of salt and sometimes MSG. But if you shop wisely (health food stores have a selection of low-sodium, MSG-free vegetarian bouillons) and use judiciously, you'll be thrilled with the results. I much prefer powdered because it dissolves quickly, you can control the measure used, and it is available in bulk, ensuring freshness. Pastes are also good but are extremely concentrated and therefore require a bit of practice. Cubes are my last choice, but in a pinch they work well. Whatever your preference, store in a cool dry place.

BREAD CRUMBS

Dried bread crumbs are always handy for adding to vegetable meatballs, breading a burger, or toasting with spices to top pasta. I suggest buying "regular" bread crumbs over "seasoned." That way if you'd like a bit more flavor, you can add your own granulated garlic, salt, Parmesan, oregano, or whatever seasoning you might be craving. I love frying with Japanese-style panko crumbs that look like coconut flakes. They're inexpensive, available everywhere, and have a unique flavor and crisp texture. I like them for recipes like Mock Maryland Crab Cakes (page 196) and also for a quick breading on vegetables or tofu. In a pinch, if you find yourself crumb-less, you can crush croutons.

CAPERS

Capers are immature buds harvested from a small bush native to Mediterranean and Middle Eastern regions, then sun dried. Those preserved in salt are much more flavorful than those preserved in vinegar brine. Give them—salted or in brine—a good rinse and they're ready to go. Even though they're small, capers pack a punch so use sparingly. Great with tomatoes, on pizza, or on their own, capers make a nice vegetarian stand-in for anchovies.

CHILI SAUCE

During the past few years, I have come to adore chili paste. So much so that I now consider three to be my basics. These sauces are widely available in supermarkets and specialty food stores. Sambal oelek, a southern Asian condiment, is a bright red fiery sauce made from pure crushed red chiles. It has a smooth consistency and adds a spicy kick to sauces, soups, and dressings. Spicy harissa hails from North Africa and is made with smoked, ground red chiles, salt, and olive oil. You may find brands that contain other spices. I use harissa in curries, Moroccan stews, chickpea dishes, and Italian cooking—anywhere that neither a vinegar nor a sugar influence is desired. Sriracha is a Thai hot sauce made with chiles, vinegar, a dash of sugar, and garlic. I use it as a dressing for burgers, mixed into salad dressings, or anywhere a smooth texture is called for. Once opened, store all of them in the fridge.

COCONUT MILK

Not cream of coconut, but real coconut milk. Cream of coconut is extremely sweet and used for making piña coladas. Coconut milk comes in a variety of styles; I prefer first-pressed, unsweetened regular. Coconut milk and oil have received a bad rap over the years, being misrepresented as one of the only vegetable foods that could somehow transform into artery-clogging cholesterol. In reality coconut milk and coconut oil contain saturated fats that are easily metabolized and not only give your body instant energy, but also contain potent antiviral and anticarcinogenic properties. Use as a replacement, measure for measure, for dairy milk in stews, baking, and curries. Once opened, pour into a jar or container and store in the fridge for up to a week.

FLOUR

I keep unbleached white all-purpose flour, whole wheat or white whole wheat flour, and chickpea or garbanzo bean flour in my pantry. Stored in an airtight container, flour should stay fresh for up to eight months. Large quantities may be stored in the fridge where it will keep for up to a year. I use all-purpose flour for bread and pizza dough; however, if you're a dedicated baker you may want to purchase bread flour that has additional gluten.

GARLIC

People often think that Italians use a lot of garlic in everything. Many cooks use garlic often but not in great quantities. Good cooking is about balance. Using too much of a good thing, and garlic qualifies as a good thing, can overwhelm the subtlety of all your other ingredients. Fresh garlic comes in a wide range of flavors, depending on the varieties and its age, moving from pungent and astringent to sweet and delicate. Use only fresh garlic from whole heads. There's something so decidedly artificial tasting about jarred garlic that I would omit the garlic from my recipe before using it. Fresh garlic is inexpensive, easy to use, and can be stored for long periods in a dry, dark place. Should your garlic begin sprouting green shoots, pop them out with the tip of your paring knife as they tend to impart a bitter flavor. If you can hit the farmers' markets in the summer, you'll find "new" garlic, which is so gentle tasting you can eat it raw. Garlic can be roasted or boiled to enhance its sweet mellow qualities. To bring out a more intense flavor, crush, smash, or process raw garlic. But don't bother investing in any of those garlic peeling or mincing gadgets. Your paring knife is the best tool.

GINGER

Spicy, peppery, and downright warming—there is no substitute for fresh ginger, especially not powdered ginger. I use ginger often in my dressings and marinades. Buy a piece of fresh ginger that is firm and thin skinned. If my ginger is very fresh, I don't peel it before I mince it, though many people insist you should. If I have to grate ginger, then I peel it first for a finer texture. Avoid wilted, dry, wrinkled ginger, as this is a sign of age and can result in a bitter flavor and fibrous texture. Store ginger in a paper bag in the fridge.

GRAINS

Whole grains are inexpensive, readily available, and packed with complex carbohydrates, protein, fiber, vitamins, and minerals. Cooked simply in water, grains have a hearty, nutty taste. To enhance their flavor, briefly toast in a dry pan or sauté in olive oil before boiling, substituting stock for water, or adding herbs and spices to the cooking water. Store in a cool dry place and use as quickly as possible since moisture can cause grains to become rancid. Here are the ones I suggest you keep in your pantry.

- **BUCKWHEAT.** Actually not wheat at all, buckwheat—also known as *kasha*—is related to rhubarb. The gluten-free grain is available untoasted or toasted. Toasted buckwheat has a richer nut-like flavor, but nutritionally they are the same: rich in iron, protein, some B-complex vitamins, and essential amino acids. Buckwheat is delicious prepared as a side dish, blended with other grains, or as a binder for vegetable burgers.
- **BULGUR.** This light, nutty grain comes from cooking wheatberries, then crushing the dried grain. Bulgur is available in supermarkets in coarse, medium, or fine grain. I prefer and use

medium textured bulgur most frequently in my recipes. Because bulgur is already cooked, it simply requires a soak in warm water for about 20 minutes, a plus on a busy day. It's the main ingredient in Lentil Tabbouleh (page 234) and Pumpkin-Bulgur Chili (page 124). Bulgur is a quick and easy way to add nutrition and texture to a variety of vegetarian dishes.

- **CORNMEAL.** Used primarily for baking corn bread and muffins, cornmeal is also the key ingredient in polenta, which is both the name of the dish and the Italian name for cornmeal. I usually use steel-cut organic cornmeal when baking and a finer grade of imported Italian cornmeal when cooking polenta. I happily admit to using quick-cooking polenta. The difference is 45 minutes of constant stirring versus 5 minutes and, honestly, I can't tell them apart once they are cooked.

- **MILLET.** Yes, this is the same millet that turns up in most birdseeds. The tiny, yet firm grains have a mild flavor that lends itself well to rice dishes, stews, and vegetable burgers. A staple in many parts of the world, millet is high in iron, zinc, and B vitamins. Because it's gluten-free, it's suitable for people with wheat sensitivities.

- **OATS.** One of the most familiar grains in North America, oats come in many forms including whole oats, groats, and oat bran, and is widely used in breads, cereals, and baked goods. High in fiber, vitamin E, iron, calcium, and B vitamins, I recommend eating oats frequently. Vegetarians often add whole oats to burgers, breads, and cookies to boost nutrition and add fiber and texture. To change the texture of whole oats from large coarse flakes to medium or fine, often more appropriate for baking, simply give them a quick whiz in the food processor. Quick-cooking rolled oats have diminished nutritional value since they're processed and precooked.

- **QUINOA (PRONOUNCED KEEN-WAH).** Commonly referred to as a super grain, quinoa is actually more closely related to dark leafy greens like spinach, kale, and chard. Quinoa contains all eight amino acids, is a complete protein, and a superb source of calcium, potassium, B vitamins, and iron. It's been cultivated in the Andes for hundreds of years and is now widely available here. It has a mild, pleasant yet slightly bitter flavor. The bitterness is due to its outer covering called *saponin*, which may be reduced by rinsing well before cooking. Quinoa has a firm, crunchy texture perfect for adding umph to stews and vegetable burgers, or mixed in with rice. And, like millet, it's gluten-free.

- **RICE.** There is a wide variety of rices available, much wider than most of us realize. Unlike America, where rice is relegated to the side dish sector, in many other parts of the world it's a main dish and for good reason. It's a valuable source of fiber and complex carbohydrates and whole grain rice is a good source of vitamin B. Additionally, rice is easily digested, inexpensive, and versatile. It's delicious plain and also pairs beautifully with vegetables, nuts, and fruits in both sweet and savory dishes.

  I favor the absorption method when cooking rice. Rather than boil and rinse (like pasta), sending all the valuable nutrients down the drain, take advantage of rice's ability to absorb liquid. Place one part rice into two parts boiling water, then simmer until all the liquid is absorbed. I keep several types of rice in my pantry:

  - **ARBORIO AND CARNAROLI RICE.** These rice varieties are grown in northern Italy and are essential for risottos. Beware of cheap imitations. The good stuff comes at a premium; don't settle for anything less. Check the box and make sure it's labeled "Grown in Italy." Arborio and Carnaroli have a short, flat grain and are extremely starchy. They shouldn't be rinsed or boiled. Rather, first sauté in oil, then incrementally add heated stock while constantly stirring to release the creamy starch, resulting in a dish that is as delicious as it is spectacular.

  - **BASMATI RICE.** Long, slender, fragrant, with a mellow nutty flavor, basmati is one of my favorites. Typically grown in India and the Middle East, basmati is a now a popular domestic crop. The grains are light and fluffy and separate easily. They're tasty paired with spicy foods. It's fantastic in Basmati Rice Pudding (page 252), because it lacks the sticky starchiness ordinary rice imparts.

  - **JASMINE RICE.** A mild floral fragrance gives jasmine rice its suggestive name. It's a long-grain rice with a delightful, delicate flavor. The silky grains pair well with flavors that are more assertive.

  - **LONG-GRAIN BROWN OR WHITE RICE.** The most popular rice, long-grain cooks quickly, but is difficult to overcook. The light and fluffy rice is perfect for side dishes, pilafs, and soups. Fairly neutral in flavor, it's best paired with nutrient-rich vegetables or savory, well-seasoned foods.

Long-Grain Rices

LONG-GRAIN white rice, also called *converted rice*, has its hull, germ, and bran removed during milling, is steamed under pressure and, oftentimes, is whitened with chalk (so rinsing is recommended). This process strips the rice of vital nutrients, which must then be added back in. This, in turn, hardens the grain. But hardened grain allows for consistent cooking—it's nearly impossible to overcook it—and fluffy, non-sticky rice. Long-grain brown rice has its outer husk removed during the milling process, leaving the bran intact. It takes a bit more time to cook than white rice and retains a lovely chewy texture.

- **SPELT.** Similar to the Italian grain known as *farro*, this is another ancient grain with solid nutritional value. High in vitamins and minerals, with a pleasant, chewy, and easily digestible texture, spelt can be used in place of rice in risottos, added to soups, and stews, and served as a side dish. While spelt does contain gluten, it's tolerated in moderate amounts by some gluten-sensitive people and is often used as a substitute for wheat flour in breads and pastas.
- **WHEAT GERM.** Wheat germ, especially the toasted variety, has a pleasant, nutty flavor that's lovely sprinkled on cereal or added to baked goods, such a cookies and muffins. Really, it's good in any dish where you'd like to add some crunch. Derived from the heart of the wheatberry, it's a rich source of protein, B vitamins, vitamin E, and iron.

HERBS

In most of my recipes when I call for the addition of herbs, I'm referring to fresh herbs. Dried herbs don't deliver the same vibrant colors and deep aromatic flavors as fresh ones. Having said that, dried herbs certainly do have their place in the everyday kitchen. The ones that best retain their flavor are oregano, thyme, and bay leaves. Excluding bay leaves, be sure to give any dried herb a quick rub in your palms before using to release essential oils and aromas. I find that the flavors of oregano and thyme intensify when dried, so use with moderation. Blended together with fine salt, black pepper, red pepper, or lavender, dried herbs can make a perky Mediterranean mix or a soothing herbes de Provence. These herbal seasonings can add a flavor kick to dips, roasted vegetables, dressings, or marinades.

On the other hand, fresh herbs are more fragrant and delicately flavored. Generally fresh are best when warmed, not cooked: therefore add them to a dish shortly before serving.

I'm pretty successful growing herbs outdoors. Indoors, however, can be a bit trickier. I envy people who are successful with indoor herbs, as homegrown ones provide flavor, quality, and accessibility. Rosemary, sage, thyme, chives, and oregano happily move inside with the rest of the family when the cold weather hits. Others, like basil, tarragon, cilantro, and parsley tend to be more finicky. From there, it only gets worse. Luckily, for those of us with flesh-tone thumbs, fresh herbs aren't expensive, come in manageable bunches, and are easily stored in the fridge; some can even be frozen.

No matter how you come by them, fresh herbs should always be washed and dried well. A salad spinner makes this step quick and efficient. Many people advise that you should not wash herbs until you're ready to use them, however, I like the convenience of ready-to-go foods so I'll wash a bundle at a time. After spinning, wrap in a paper towel and let sit for 5 or 10 minutes. This is key. If your herbs aren't thoroughly dried, they'll become slimy and useless. If your herbs are clean so is the paper towel, so be sure to let it dry and reuse when you're done. Store herbs in an airtight container or resealable plastic bag for up to ten days. For longer storage, simply follow the same steps for cleaning, drying, and bagging, then pop the herbs into the freezer. Their color will darken, but their flavor will remain intact.

My basic refrigerator pantry of herbs includes:

- **BASIL.** Bright green and incredibly fragrant, basil comes in many varieties. While basil loves the sun—I remember colorful pots of it hanging from terraces all over Italy—it doesn't react well to high heat from cooking. Italians drop chopped basil into recipes just before serving, often allowing the residual heat of the pasta or potatoes to wilt it. When used fresh in salads or on sandwiches, basil adds a peppery spike. A fragile herb, it tends to wilt easily. If you find yourself with a little more than you need, whiz the leftover leaves in your processor with a drizzle of olive oil, then store in a covered container in the fridge or freeze—an ice cube tray specifically for this purpose works well (transfer the cubes to a plastic bag once frozen). Basil stored this way will darken, however, the flavor will add a boost to everything from soups to toast. This whiz-and-freeze method also works well for large amounts of parsley, mint, and cilantro.

- **CHIVES.** Easy to grow indoors or out, chives add a mild onion flavor and pop of color to just about anything. They remind me of Chia Pets: you keep snipping and they keep sprouting.
- **CILANTRO.** Also known as *Chinese parsley,* cilantro is the world's most popular herb. It's often used in Southwestern, Indian, Asian, and Latin dishes. People either love cilantro or hate it. Rarely do you find a fence-sitter when it comes to this bright, lemony herb. I use it a lot. The stems are sweet and can be chopped and used to complement the delicate leaves, especially in deep, robustly flavored dishes.
- **DILL.** Light and feathery, fresh dill imparts a mild anise flavor. Use it in creamy dressings, egg dishes, and sauces, or sprinkle over vegetables such a cucumber and zucchini. Add dill just prior to serving as a tasty edible garnish.
- **MINT.** Fresh mint, when used judiciously, adds a crisp clean flavor to soups, salads, potatoes, dips, and grain dishes. Lemon juice—not vinegar—brings out the best in fresh mint.
- **OREGANO.** Very intense and pungent, oregano is one of the most recognizable of all herbs. Fresh oregano is delicious, but this is one herb I use most often dried. But do so with caution: some people find dried oregano to be so potent that their lips become numb. Dried oregano made from your own fresh is also less sharp than packaged dried. To dry your own, simply cut the stalks from the plant and hang them upside down in a warm, dry, well-ventilated area. Once dried, slide the leaves off the brittle branch and store them in an airtight container or a zippered plastic bag.
- **PARSLEY.** I'm partial to the flat-leaf Italian parsley since it has tons more flavor and is less bitter than the curly variety. Although parsley is high in vitamin C and vitamin A, many people only use it as a garnish and rarely consume it. Make an effort to toss a little extra into soups, salads, and vegetables. Parsley stems become sweet when finely chopped and cooked, so use the whole herb. Parsley is notorious for residing in small spaces, so be sure to check your teeth after eating.
- **ROSEMARY.** Rosemary is a staple in European cooking. Robust, intense, and piney, it is pungently aromatic. The trick is not to overuse, overcook, or over-garnish with it. A little goes a long way and complements everything from sweet squashes to savory potatoes. It's easy to grow indoors and out.
- **SAGE.** Like cilantro, folks either love or hate sage. I happen to love it, especially when cooked in a simple butter sauce,

quickly fried in a little olive oil, or tossed whole into vegetables when roasting. Sage has a musty, though not unpleasantly so, taste that adds a woodsy-ness to sweeter vegetables such as squash. When dried, the flavor is much more aggressive; therefore the trick is to use a light hand. Sage plants are a beautiful addition to any garden and are easy to grow.

- **TARRAGON.** Tarragon has a hint of anise flavor and pairs especially well with mushrooms, eggs, dressings, rice, and grains. It holds up well to longer cooking times and when used in dressings, the flavor will intensify over time. A good thing to keep in mind if you're tempted to add more to boost the flavor in a dish—usually it's best to let tarragon sit and the flavor mature.

- **THYME.** Thyme, another easy-to-grow herb, is earthy and warm and adds a nice touch to tomato sauces, beans, hearty stews, and marinades. Thyme is frequently used in Mediterranean cooking and works well with high-heat cooking methods such as roasting and grilling. Be sure to pull the leaves off the tough stems before using.

HONEY OR BROWN RICE SYRUP

Honey is lovely in dressings, marinades, and teas, or as a simple spread on a nice hunk of hearty bread. Look for organic honey produced locally in your area or other countries such as Greece, Spain, or France. When I visit Italy, I'll pick up some acacia or chestnut honey, both my favorites. Brown rice syrup is a good vegan alternative to honey that can be used in baking and cooking or wherever sugar is called for. Brands vary so read the label for substitution amounts.

Honey: Medicine of the Gods

THE GREEKS, Romans, and Egyptians believed honey was the medicine of the heavens. And it seems they were on to something. Considered by many today to be a super food, honey is rich in essential amino acids, B-complex vitamins, as well as C, D, and E vitamins. It also contains enzymes, and antibacterial and antimicrobial compounds. Over the centuries, people have used it as everything—from a facial cleanser to a cure for hay fever. To enjoy its full benefits, buy raw, unfiltered honey.

LEMONS AND LIMES

Nothing surpasses the bright, tart, citrus flavors of fresh-squeezed lemon or lime juice. When my recipes call for lemon or lime juice, squeeze fresh fruit. Bottled versions have a cloying artificial flavor that, quite frankly, can ruin a dish. Thin-skinned lemons tend to be juicer that their thick-skinned counterparts. Limes are always thin skinned and have few to no seeds. Leaving your citrus out at room temperature, then giving them a quick roll on the counter with a little pressure will also net you more juice.

LIQUID SMOKE

This hickory-flavored concentrate adds a pungent smoky undertone to soups, marinades, and dressings, which is especially helpful if you don't have access to a charcoal grill or smoker. Use sparingly; a few drops go a long way.

MIRIN

While I steer clear of cooking wine and their awful artificial flavors, I'm fond of this Japanese sweetened rice wine. It pairs beautifully with soy sauce, toasted sesame oil, and assertive flavors such as garlic and ginger. I use it to balance and mellow salty dishes, Asian or otherwise.

MUSTARD

Mustard adds zip to many dishes. I use Dijon, a spicy brown mustard that is salty and slightly sharp, for marinades and general cooking. When a less aggressive flavor is called for, I use a canned powdered dry mustard.

NUTS AND SEEDS

Nuts and seeds are extremely healthy, in part because they're full of protein. Toasted or roasted, they add texture and variety to any dish. Because of their high oil content, nuts and seeds can become rancid quickly. Store them in sealed containers, away from light and moisture. If you're not planning on using them within a week or two, store them in sealed bags in the freezer. I purchase mine raw and roast them myself. A good variety to keep on hand includes: almonds, cashews, chestnuts, peanuts, pine nuts, pumpkin seeds, sesame seeds, sunflower seeds, and walnuts.

OILS

In this fat-free age, oils have been given a bum rap, but our bodies need the fat found in oils to run smoothly. Good-quality fat, that is. With this in mind, choose unrefined, partially unrefined, or expeller-presser oils. The less heat used in processing, the more nutritious and flavorful the product. Refined oils are stripped of their natural nutritional properties, treated with additives, and then clarified. Unrefined oils are a bit more expensive, but this is one area you don't want to cut costs, otherwise, down the road, you'll end up spending more in doctors' bills than you saved on groceries. Plus, there's nothing like the flavor a good-quality oil can impart. But keep in mind, oils contain saturated fats so use them with a light hand.

There is a trend these days toward oils flavored with everything from curry to lavender. Some are luscious; others taste like a science project gone awry. By all means, have fun experimenting; variety and change are two of the cornerstones of cooking. At roughly two-dollars-an-ounce, however, many of these fancy oils are beyond the reach of everyday cooking.

- **OLIVE OIL.** Is there anything more pleasurable than a heavy drizzle of olive oil on a slice of crusty bread, some grilled vegetables, or over a salad? Olive oil comes in more than fifty flavor designations. I most enjoy peppery, fruity, and grassy, with fruity being my favorite. It's usually greener, richer in color, and more fragrant than its counterparts. Some oils are produced from a combination of two or more olives. These can also be delicious. What's most important is that you enjoy and appreciate the flavor of the one you've selected.

  No matter the type you decide upon, look for a first cold-pressed extra virgin olive oil. These oils have not been altered by heat, have a low acid level, and taste just like olives. The taste and quality of olive oil will vary widely depending upon where the olives are grown and when they're pressed. The most common olive oil–producing countries are Italy, Spain, Greece, and France, but there are also many quality ones made domestically. Very high-quality oils, known as *estate oils*, are dense and superb. True condiment oils, they're not suited to cooking. For light sautéing, cooking, and dressings, I use a less expensive Sicilian extra virgin oil pressed from a single olive variety.

- **VEGETABLE OIL.** Lighter than olive oil, vegetable oils are frequently used for frying, in dressings, and for general cooking needs. Canola, corn, grapeseed, coconut, peanut, and safflower are most suitable for everyday uses. I prefer canola for frying. It has a deep golden color, heats well, and has a balanced flavor—not too assertive, yet not too bland or lifeless. Plus, it's very economical.

- **SESAME OIL.** The lighter sesame oil has a subtle nutty flavor and is good for frying and general cooking. The darker Asian variety is toasted and has an intense nutty flavor and aroma. As a condiment, a few drops or a drizzle usually do the trick. I'm referring to the toasted oil when I call for it in my recipes.

- **CHILI OIL.** This is oil that's been infused with hot chiles. It adds a peppy spike to finished dishes and dressings.

How to Store Oils

🌿 OXYGEN, HEAT, and sunlight are the enemies of oil. They will turn your oil rancid quicker than butter melts in the Missouri sun. Whenever possible, buy oils packaged in dark glass bottles. Always cap them and store them in a cool, dark place. It can be economical to purchase oil in quantity, in which case pour small portions into your lovely cruet and store the rest. Ceramic cruets work best against the elements, but sometimes sentiment wins over. For instance, I use a beautiful tall glass bottle from Italy for my olive oil, clear as a new day. It's so comfortable to hold and so meaningful to me that I allow myself this indulgence. I use it daily, refill it often, and enjoy it completely.

OLIVES

Niçoise and Kalamata olives are useful to have on hand to add to salads, pizza, and pasta dishes. Best of all, a few olives can flip leftovers into something altogether different. With their salty pungent flavor and meaty texture, they pair beautifully with more subtle foods like fresh tomatoes, cheese, and pasta salad. Purchase them with pits or without, whichever suits you. Olives will keep for a good long time, however, their texture eventually breaks down and the saltiness becomes concentrated. For the best taste, buy what you'll use within a week or so.

PASTA

Pasta is versatile, affordable, healthy, tasty, easy to cook, and remarkably comforting. High in complex carbohydrates, it fuels the body while also providing a good source of protein. Plus, it's low in fat. Whole wheat varieties offer greater concentration of vitamins, minerals, and fiber. Having grown up in Italy, I can confirm that the rumors are true: pasta is eaten at least once a day, sometimes more. This is in no small measure because pasta works well with most ingredients you're likely to have on hand, such as beans, vegetables, herbs, tofu, cheese, and soups. Pasta also stores very well—dried pasta at least—so if you find any on sale, stock up. Fresh pasta is best eaten the same day, though you can keep it in the fridge for a few extra days. Frozen pasta should remain frozen until ready to use, then cooked while frozen. Designer brands, hand cut with a lovely textured surface that helps the sauce adhere, come at a hefty premium. I tend not to buy these, but they do make a nice hostess gift or a treat from time to time as their textures and shapes are unique.

For the record, there are more than 350 shapes and styles of pasta, some so regional they are unknown outside of a particular town. For this book, I've narrowed the scope to those that are easy to find and are my personal favorites. It's important to choose good-quality brands. I buy imported Italian pasta; however, there are some good domestic brands available. The important thing is to look for pasta that's made with 100 percent durum wheat to ensure the best results. Here are my favorites:

- **FARFALLINI, ORECCHIETTE, QUADRUCCI, AND DITALINI.** These four pasta shapes are quite small and typically used in soups and stews. Their small size adds just the right amount of pasta texture while not overwhelming the dish.

- **FARFALLE.** Also known as *bow ties*, farfalle is one of my favorite pasta shapes for pesto. In Liguria, where pesto is king, a pasta called *trofiette* is generally served with pesto. Its short, gently rolled (not twisted) shape suits pesto perfectly, just grabbing enough of the rich emulsion without filling up all the spaces. While trofiette can be tricky to find in America, this provides the perfect opportunity to improvise. I like the way farfalle catches a small amount of pesto right at the center twist. This is just one example of the craft of matching the right pasta with the appropriate sauce. Also try serving farfalle with Dried Tomato Pesto (page 73) or Cilantro-Mint Pesto (page 74). Experiment with various pastas and sauces until you find the combination that pleases you.

- **OTHER PASTA SHAPES.** White or whole wheat ziti, penne, rigatoni (short or long), shells, fusilli, the list goes on. I keep a variety of these shaped pastas on hand. Sturdy, robust, and compatible with any sauce, they're especially good with hearty toppings. They are perfect for Ziti with Summer Tomato Sauce and Arugula (page179), the topping from Tomato and Basil Bruschetta (page 56), and Penne with Onions and Vegetarian Bacon (page 175).

- **NO-BOIL LASAGNA.** I enjoyed cooking with these handy pasta sheets in Italy and am thrilled they're now available here. With these precooked and dehydrated noodles, all that's required is a good sauce or filling. They turn out perfectly every time. Try them with Vegetable Lasagna (page 187) and you'll be as big a fan as I am.

- **SPAGHETTI.** White or whole wheat, regular width or thin, linguine, fettuccine, or my favorite, spaghetti rigati: spaghetti is long, smooth (with the exception of spaghetti rigati, which is ridged), and remains quite firm during cooking. Flat, long pasta is best suited for smooth sauces or where vegetables are finely chopped like Simple Tomato Sauce (page 186), Spaghetti Aglio e Olio (page 172), and Spaghetti Tofunese (page 176).

- **STUFFED PASTA.** Ravioli, tortelli, tortellini: hearty and nourishing stuffed pastas are the classic Italian comfort food. Tortellini and tortelli, a larger half-moon version, are available dried or frozen. Dried stuffed pasta is nice to have on hand especially for light soups or sauces, but I prefer them frozen because they're closer to what I used to get at the covered markets in Livorno, Italy. Tucked beside the open-air fruit and vegetable market, there were fresh pasta shops, bakeries, cheese vendors, butchers, and fish stalls, to name a few. The air was alive with the scent of coffee, bread, and coarse paper packaging. Scales swung and arms waved, all in the friendliest of manners, as people bartered with vendors for the best price. Some of my fondest food memories revolve around the sheer anticipation of walking through the crowded aisles, scouting out the perfect homemade ravioli stuffed with creamy ricotta, spinach, and a touch of nutmeg, or tortelli stuffed with savory pumpkin. While I no longer have these markets close by, I do make my own fresh stuffed pasta from time to time, and enjoy the process. The stuffed pastas from the Italian markets were smaller and the filling sparser, than their overstuffed cousins you find in America. With this in mind, I set about developing a lighter ravioli that everyone could enjoy, the result of which is Tofu Ravioli (page 181). Paired with its butter and sage sauce, or even Simple Tomato Sauce (page 186), these ravioli are heavenly.

How to Cook Pasta

BE SURE to cook your pasta in plenty of well-salted water—as salty as the sea, they say in Italy—until it's al dente, which means cooked but with a little bite. You shouldn't have to pry it out of your teeth, but you should feel the firmness.

Some of the benefits of properly cooked pasta include: slower digestion which in turn releases sugar into your bloodstream more slowly, extended energy, greater sense of satiation and, well, it's simply a delight to eat perfectly cooked pasta. Never add oil to the cooking water. This does nothing but waste oil and make your pasta too slippery so your sauce doesn't stick. Be judicious about serving size. In Italy, a pound of pasta feeds five people, but here a pound generally serves two or three. While pasta is quickly becoming a main course in Italy, especially at home, the portions are still significantly smaller than in the United States. Also, remember to dress your pasta with a light hand. Your sauce or vegetables should complement your pasta, not smother it.

PEPPER

Forget about those rusty tins of flat, lifeless, aromaless, preground pepper. The pepper you need is freshly ground peppercorns. The smell alone can bring a dish to life. Plus, the mere grind of the mill is the sort of small ritual upon which pleasurable cooking, and eating, is built. Peppercorns are widely available in black, green, or white and have different flavors and applications. I only use black for no other reason than it works well with everything I make. Cooking with pepper concentrates its flavor, therefore it's usually best to add fresh pepper just prior to serving your dish.

PORCINI MUSHROOMS, DRIED

If you're transitioning off meat or if you're a vegetarian who misses some of meat's textures and hearty nuances, try dried porcini. For a risotto or stand-alone mushroom dish, I recommend the Italian variety. They have larger caps, a meatier texture, and a mellower, richer flavor. But they can be pricey. So, for everyday use in stocks and soups, a good-quality Asian porcini works just fine. Quickly rinse the mushrooms, then soak them in warm water for 30 minutes to rehydrate. A few rehydrated porcini combined with common white button mushrooms can transform a recipe from bland to deep, wild, and woodsy. Be sure to save the "broth." Strain the soaking liquid through a fine-mesh sieve to get rid of any sand or tiny bits of dirt and use it in place of or in addition to stock or water called for in the recipe. You can also store the broth in a sealed container in the refrigerator to provide a delicious "beefy" flavor boost to soups, stews, and gravies.

Dried porcini are sold in bags ranging from less than ¼ ounce to up to ½ pound. If you don't have a scale handy, an ounce of porcini is roughly equal to 1½ cups loosely packed mushrooms. Fortunately, porcini broth is flexible and a little more or less of an accurate measure will still yield good results.

SALT

What we know as table salt has about as much connection to the sea as Tang does to oranges. Unadulterated sea salt is loaded with trace minerals and not only tastes bright and fresh, but is also good for our bodies. Table salt is refined with additives to prevent clumping and to retain its whiteness. As with any chemical process, all the nutritional value is stripped away when salt is refined. The only place I ever use this product is in boiling water and on my icy sidewalk.

There are a plethora of salts available today from seemingly every corner of the planet, each with its unique flavor and story. I'm fond of Maldon sea salt, which is harvested off the east coast of England, and kosher salt, which has a coarse grind. Both are inexpensive, widely available, and have a good texture. Texture is important because it allows you to control the amount of salt you're using more easily; you can grind it between your fingers, rather than just pouring it in and watching it disappear. It's this sort of tactile experience that will help you become an intuitive cook. Extremely coarse salt can be given a quick press in your mortar, as it will not dissolve properly without doing so. Finer sea salt is good to have on hand and is appropriate for baking.

SEAWEED

Seaweed, or sea vegetables, is a nutritious way to bring the flavor of the sea to vegetarian cooking. Toasted nori seaweed sheets are generally used for sushi rolls, but I use them whenever I wish to impart a briny ocean flavor. It adds the perfect touch to Mock Maryland Crab Cakes (page 196). A sprinkle of powdered dulse, another kind of seaweed, on salads, tofu, and in soups lends a mellow sea taste.

SEITAN (SAY-TAN)

Often called *wheatmeat,* seitan is a popular and extremely versatile meat alternative that is made from wheat gluten rather than soy. It has a pleasant chewy texture, absorbs flavors remarkably well, and is low in fat and high in protein. It takes well to roasting, grilling, frying, or broiling. Available in most supermarkets, seitan costs considerably more than its soy counterparts, but making it from scratch (see page 169) is easy, economical, and yields a far superior product in both flavor and texture.

SOY PRODUCTS

Soybeans are the most nutritious of all beans. And products made from soybeans are the perfect stepping stone for those transitioning off meat or dairy, and can serve as a cornerstone to a well-balanced vegetarian diet. Rich in minerals like iron and calcium, soy is also low in fat, has no cholesterol, and evidence suggests it can help reduce the risk of various cancers in both men and women. Because soy foods contain hormone-like substances called *phytoestrogens,* however, it's important not to overconsume them. As with all food, I recommend variety and moderation. Here are the most frequently used soy products.

■ **SOYBEANS/EDAMAME.** Plump, sweet, and tender, edamame (eh-dah-MAH-meh) are rapidly growing in popularity. These quick-cooking soybeans, have a mild nutty flavor and pleasant buttery texture, are inexpensive and chockful of vitamins, minerals, and protein. Absolutely delicious served as a snack, they also make a nutritious tasty addition to salads, soups, and stews. They are available in the pod or shelled in most supermarkets and health food stores, usually frozen.

- **MISO.** There are many varieties of miso, including brown rice, barley, and red rice. Miso is a fermented paste made from a mixture of soybeans, rice, wheat, or barley; some are fermented for more than two years. With a pleasant salty and deeply savory flavor, a spoonful or so of miso is a healthy addition to any dressing, soup, sauce, or noodle dish. Miso should not be boiled as this alters its flavor and destroys nutritional value. Therefore, add miso *after* your water, soup, or stew has boiled and is at a low simmer. Season the finished dish with additional miso to taste. Usually a teaspoon or two per cup of liquid does the trick. Lighter white miso is typically sweet and mild. Medium red miso is a bit richer and deeper, yet still mellow. Dark miso is dense and thick, with a more intense flavor suitable for savory and hearty soups and stews. Dark miso lacks the sweetness of the lighter varieties without being overly salty. For Miso Soup (page 108), and for most of my dishes, I use the medium. Miso is available in the refrigerated section of most mainstream markets or specialty shops. Once opened, miso keeps up to six months.

- **TEMPEH.** Available in the regular soy version or with the addition of brown rice, flax, grains, or vegetables, tempeh is one of my favorite soy foods. It's fermented, which boosts its nutritional value (high in protein, low in fat, and a good source of vitamin B), its digestibility, and its flavor. As with most fermented soy, like miso, tempeh doesn't have the same effect on the body as tofu or other soy products, so the suggested limitations in consumption need not be observed. I love the density, savory nutty undertones, and chewy texture. I also find that tempeh absorbs cooking flavors more readily than tofu. Fried, steamed, sautéed, baked, or grilled, tempeh is a flavorful addition to any dish. You can find tempeh in the refrigerated section of supermarkets, usually in 8-ounce plastic packages. Unused tempeh should be tightly wrapped and used within five days.

- **TEXTURED VEGETABLE PROTEIN.** TVP is used in soy burgers, vegetarian hot dogs, soy bacon, and chicken-style ready-made foods—to name just a few. While it convincingly mimics meat, it is heavily processed so the nutritional content drops considerably and the fat content rises. TVP products are convenient and can be prepared quickly, which is great for busy households. They can serve as transition foods for those moving away from

Tempeh Crumbles

- **MAKES ABOUT 1 CUP**

For a tasty stand-in for ground meat in any recipe, coarsely grind 4 ounces tempeh in a food processor with ½ cup toasted walnuts. Just brown in a little oil and mix in whatever you like.

eating meat—a vegetable burger, for instance, is far healthier than a cholesterol-laden meat one—but use them judiciously. Remember, variety and moderation.

- **TOFU.** If you're lucky enough to have an Asian market nearby that makes fresh tofu you're in for a real treat. But even if you don't, regular store-bought tofu is flexible and easy to use. Tofu is made much like a soft cheese. Soybeans are boiled, mashed, and strained, creating a milk. This milk is mixed with a coagulant to form curds. The curds are then pressed into blocks until set. Tofu is available in a variety of densities and textures. Soft and silken tofu are best suited for dressings, dips, desserts, cream sauces, and smoothies. Pour off excess water and use as is. Firm or extra firm tofu has a denser, drier texture that lends itself to slicing, grilling, cubing, burgers, cutlets, and desserts. Crumbled, it's also an excellent substitute for cheese, such as ricotta. Pour off excess water and blot dry. Some firm tofu is packaged without water and is extremely dry and chewy. For many people, this is more palatable, and even more meat-like in texture. This same chewy texture can be achieved by freezing water-packed tofu, unopened in its package, then defrosting it, gently squeezing it dry and frying or baking it.

SOY SAUCE

Made from fermented extract of soybean, soy sauce is not just for Asian cooking. Its rich salty brew lends depth of flavor to many dishes, sauces, and marinades. A good-quality soy sauce is affordable and readily available in grocery stores, Asian markets, and specialty stores. Be wary of some of the big name brands; they're watery, intensely salty, and full of additives. Asians don't even consider these to be true soy sauce. While traditional soy sauce is brewed for several months, sometimes even years, most big-name sauces are bottled after a couple of days or weeks, which compromises the flavor. Ironically, the imported Chinese brands are usually less expensive than their bland imitations.

Here are my three favorite types of soy sauce:

- **CHINESE SOY SAUCE.** Light Chinese soy sauce has a mild, delicate flavor that lends itself well to condiments, sauces, and stir-fries. Dark Chinese soy sauce can be syrupy with a robust, slightly fruity flavor. Often some measures of molasses, wheat, and sugar have been mixed in. This sauce works well in reductions and gravies. Two tablespoons perks up Porcini Gravy (page 107) without a salty aftertaste. The light and dark may be combined, each rounding out the flavor of the other.

- **SHOYU.** This Japanese soy sauce is a blend of soybeans and wheat. Traditionally aged in wooden casks, it can take one to three years to come to fruition and has a gentle, mellow flavor.
- **TAMARI.** As with shoyu, this sauce hails from Japan. Its fermentation can also take one to three years, but it's made solely from soybeans (ideal for those with wheat sensitivities). It has a mellow yet intensely deep flavor and is superb as a condiment or in recipes. I love it with the delicate flavor of tofu.

SPICES

I prefer whole spice seeds to preground, which tend to be flat and lifeless. Plus, if you look closely at the price-per-pound, you'll be amazed at what you're paying for the convenience of preground spices. Releasing the aromas of the seeds with a quick toasting or a grind in your mortar is a small ritual you may come to cherish. Basic dried spices to stock up on: caraway seeds, cardamom, cayenne, chili powder, chipotle pepper (ground), cinnamon, cloves, coriander, cumin (ground and seeds), fennel seeds, granulated garlic, ginger, nutmeg (whole), paprika (hot and sweet), poultry seasoning (which lends a traditional familiar flavor to dishes such as gravies, stuffings, and pot pies), red chile peppers, and saffron.

Garlic Salt

GARLIC SALT is widely available in the spice section of grocery stores. It's made with powdered garlic, salt, and anticaking agents to keep it free flowing. Some people find the flavor to be astringent and overly salty. Because I like the convenience of this blend, but not the artificiality, I often prepare my own, which lets me control the freshness, quality of the garlic, and amount of salt added. Crush 2 tablespoons organic dehydrated granulated garlic and add 1 teaspoon fine sea salt. Mix this well with your fingers and adjust the garlic and salt to suit your own taste. Store leftovers in a recycled spice container in your cupboard.

STARCH, CORN AND POTATO

Starches are thickening agents. Cornstarch and potato starch, in particular, make for smooth, satiny sauces and gravies. They're also great for fruit reductions. Europeans like to mix flour with cornstarch for a lighter cake batter. Cornstarch is gluten-free and a good substitute for flour in many recipes for wheat-sensitive people. Having said that, some people avoid corn and its byproducts for health and political reasons. In these situations, though it may take a bit of hunting to find, potato starch works well.

SUGAR

I prefer organic cane sugar. Its environmental impact is minimal—the cane fields are not sprayed with herbicides or synthetic fertilizers—and the growers support fair trade in an otherwise exploitive market. The sugar is not refined and no bleaching agents, chemicals, or artificial coloring are used. Also, this type of sugar is not processed through a bone char filter, made from the bones of cows, making it suitable for vegetarians and vegans.

What is Fair Trade?

FAIR TRADE is an international, market-based social movement by which workers are paid a fair price for their goods while a keen eye is kept on strict environmental standards. The movement focuses primarily on exports, such as coffee and chocolate, from developing countries to industrialized ones with the hope that the developing countries can move from a position of vulnerability to economic self-sufficiency and vibrancy. Fair trade contributes to sustainable development by securing the rights of otherwise marginalized producers and workers and by raising worldwide awareness of the importance of purchasing fairly traded products.

TOMATOES, CANNED

I keep a few cans of tomatoes on hand, my favorites being imported organic San Marzano tomatoes, whole or crushed, and domestic organic fire-roasted tomatoes. Regardless of the brand you buy, avoid those with added sugar. San Marzanos take their name from their hometown and are grown in the rich fertile volcanic soil surrounding Mount Vesuvius near Naples, which influences their taste. A variety of the familiar plum tomato, San Marzano tomatoes have a thinner shape, denser flesh, lower acid level, and deeper flavor, all without being overly sweet. Their unique taste and digestibility makes them worth the extra money. Many people comment on how great the food is, especially pizza, in Naples. It is, and a great deal of the credit goes to the San Marzano tomatoes. Italian tomatoes are grown under strict guidelines, much like our certified organic, and will carry the European Union's "DOP" emblem on the label. Look for this, otherwise you may be paying more for nothing.

There are also domestic varieties of San Marzano canned tomatoes available that are quite good. I even found some fresh one summer at our farmers' market in Portland, which was a delightful change from the usual Roma.

Fire-roasted tomatoes are just that: tomatoes roasted over fire. They have a rich smoky flavor that adds depth to soups, sauces, and stews.

TOMATO PASTE IN A TUBE

Popular in Europe for years now, these wonders have finally made their way to our shores. Squeeze what you need, cap and store the rest: these concentrates are economical and practical. No half-empty cans of tomato paste left sitting in the fridge. Regular tomato paste and sun-dried tomato paste are the two I have. Keep tightly capped in the fridge.

VANILLA

Vanilla is intensely aromatic with a sweet yet slightly bitter aftertaste. Pure vanilla is preserved in alcohol. When used in baking or cooking, the alcohol evaporates and the bitter edge disappears, leaving a creamy, rich flavor. Buy pure vanilla extract only: avoid artificially flavored brands. You can also purchase vanilla bean paste, which imparts flecks of vanilla seeds, or the whole vanilla bean, which you slice open and then scrape out the tiny seeds tucked inside. Vanillas from Madagascar and Mexico are considered to be the finest available. The tiny Mexican Melipone bee is the only insect uniquely equipped to fertilize the vanilla orchid. Although attempts were made to introduce this bee to areas outside of Mexico growing vanilla blossoms, the bee did not survive. Subsequently in 1836, a method of hand-pollinating the orchid blossoms was developed; all of which makes vanilla the second most expensive spice after saffron.

VINEGAR

The right vinegar can brighten up even the dullest dish. They're essential for salad dressings, and a few well-selected drops can bring out hidden flavor in soups and sauces. I say "well-selected" because there is quite a range of vinegars from which to choose. Fortunately, barring the Rolls Royce of vinegar—balsamic—they're generally inexpensive. Therefore, if possible, I'd encourage you to stock a few varieties.

- **APPLE CIDER VINEGAR.** I love the tartness of this vinegar. Its strong flavor is ideal for baking and marinades. Be sure to select the organic, unpasteurized type.
- **BALSAMIC VINEGAR.** Americans tend to view balsamic as the *piece de resistance* of vinegars (in Italy it's not used nearly as often). We love to drench anything and everything in it, to the point—in my mind at least—of being criminal. True, it has a taste that is complex and incomparable: dense and sweet, with a faint raisin undertone. Yet, this vinegar should be savored and appreciated for what it is: a fine condiment. A few precious drops—on fruits, ice cream, vegetables—can highlight flavors. Good thing moderation is key because a

bottle of the real thing starts pricing at about thirty dollars. Be mindful of cheap imitations which are simply vinegars spiked with balsamic flavors.

- **PLUM VINEGAR.** While this is not essential, or actually even a true vinegar, it's just plain nice. Plum vinegar is a brine made from pickling umeboshi plums and shiso leaves. On a whim, I once used it in a simple arugula-tomato salad and was delighted by its sweet, light, and slightly salty flavor. It's become a staple ever since.
- **RICE VINEGAR.** This Japanese vinegar is made from either brown or white rice. Both are lovely in soups, Asian dressings, rice dishes, and chili sauces.
- **SHERRY VINEGAR.** Produced in Spain, this vinegar has a subtle and lightly acidic flavor. A sprinkle puts a nice spin on vegetables, especially the more bitter ones, such as grilled radicchio, kale, and chard. Lovely with onions, squash, and tomatoes as well.
- **WINE VINEGAR, RED OR WHITE.** For common salad dressings or for a spike of flavor in soups and sauces, wine vinegars work well. Red tends to be a bit stronger than white. Many people are interested in making their own wine vinegar at home. It's actually quite an involved process, not one I can cover in this book, but I do want to note that leftover red or white wine does not miraculously turn into a great vinegar. Even if you pray a lot.

WORCESTERSHIRE, VEGETARIAN.

This sauce is great for marinades, boosting the tastiness of soups and stews, and is delicious on vegetable burgers. Vegetarian Worcestershire lacks the anchovies of its traditional counterpart, but none of its full-bodied flavor.

IN THE FREEZER

SOMETIMES YOU JUST can't get to the store to purchase fresh foodstuff. Here are some of the lifesavers I keep in the freezer for those times:

- **MIXED VEGETABLES.** Great for a fast minestrone or side dish. I keep on hand a bag or two of carrots, broccoli, hearty greens, and ethnic blends.
- **PETIT PEAS.** Use them in Cream of Green Pea Soup with Mint (page 110), tossed into roasted potatoes, or sprinkled over a lightly dressed pasta. I usually have more of these stocked up than any other vegetable.
- **PIZZA DOUGH.** Defrosts in about 3 hours, so you can have pizza or fresh hot flatbread with hardly a thought.

- **RAVIOLI OR TORTELLINI.** A great pasta option that serves as a meal. Use in soups or top with a simple sauce.
- **TOFU, FIRM OR EXTRA FIRM.** I always have some tofu stashed away in the freezer in case I forget to pick it up. Defrosted tofu has a great chewy texture and is handy in just about any entrée.
- **TORTILLAS, FLOUR AND CORN.** Fill with beans, vegetables, or eggs for a fast and healthy meal. Left in cupboards, these will get moldy.
- **TEXTURIZED VEGETABLE PROTEIN PRODUCTS.** Ready-made vegetable burgers, hot dogs, chicken-style strips, and sausage are nice to have on hand. Keep a variety for a quick-fix meal. Especially handy for households with kids.

LIGHT BITES

Appetizers, Dips, and Spreads

APPETIZERS, DIPS, AND SPREADS should be small, uncomplicated dishes that have the ability to move from the cocktail hour right through to dinner. I'm not into fussy canapés and pastries that require special ingredients and a lot of prep time. Don't get me wrong: I enjoy eating them at a party, but I hardly ever make them at home. There's a tendency these days at get-togethers to overdo appetizers, serving a wide array of heavy finger foods and filling cheeses.

Over the years, I've found that people prefer a few tasty things to nibble on while sipping a cocktail and milling around the kitchen in anticipation of the main course. My philosophy is to keep things light, and serve appetizers in moderation. I recommend preparing spreads and dips that might have a second life as leftovers, just in case you're lucky enough to have them. Pesto works beautifully as a pasta sauce, bruschetta as a base for pizza, and a salsa or dip can become the inspiration for a side dish, dressing, or an addition to a light supper.

Celebration Potstickers

MAKES 24

4 tablespoons or more canola or other vegetable oil

1 tablespoon sesame oil

1 bunch scallions (about 6), thinly sliced

2 garlic cloves, minced

1 medium head Napa or green cabbage, finely shredded

3 cremini mushrooms, finely chopped

1 to 2 tablespoons rice wine vinegar

1 tablespoon shoyu soy sauce

½ to 1 jalapeño pepper, finely minced (optional)

1-inch piece ginger, peeled and grated

1 medium carrot, finely grated

2 teaspoons minced cilantro or basil

24 wonton wrappers

Cremini Mushrooms

CLOSELY RELATED to common white mushrooms, earthy brown mushrooms like cremini or baby bellas are younger versions of robust portobellos. They're perfect when a more intense mushroom flavor is desired.

I USUALLY LEAVE *complicated Asian dishes to the experts, but when they're as easy to make as these dumplings are, I jump right in—especially since a little effort results in better (and healthier) potstickers than you could ever buy frozen or get from takeout. They are delicious as an appetizer with a cold beer, or served on a crunchy, green salad for lunch. If I prepare them while guests are hanging around the kitchen, they rarely make it onto the serving platter. Serve with Sweet Chili Dipping Sauce (below), if you like.*

To achieve the thinly shredded cabbage required for this recipe, an Asian mandoline works best. Wonton wrappers, which are square, unlike the round wrappers used for making dumplings or dim sum, can be found in both vegetarian (containing eggs) and vegan versions; for the latter I recommend Twin Marquis brand.

1. Heat 2 tablespoons of the canola oil and the sesame oil in a large skillet over medium-high heat. Add the scallions and sauté until they begin to soften, about 2 minutes, and then add the garlic. Sauté for a minute or so and then add the cabbage, mushrooms, vinegar, soy sauce, jalapeño, and ginger. Cook, stirring, until the cabbage is soft, about 3 minutes longer. Add the carrot and cilantro and remove from the heat. Transfer to a bowl to cool, about 10 minutes. Check for seasoning, and adjust as needed. If you're not using it right away, cover and place the filling in the refrigerator for up to 3 hours.

2. To assemble the wontons, lay a wrapper on a work surface and put about 1 tablespoon filling in the center. Rub a little water along two adjacent edges with your finger, then fold the wrapper over to make a triangle. Press and seal the edges. Fold in 2 points of the triangle to make a sailboat shape.

3. Heat a heavy skillet over medium-high heat until very hot. Add 2 tablespoons or more vegetable oil and follow with the potstickers Cook on one side—don't fiddle with them—until the bottom is a nice light brown. Shake the pan and when the potstickers become loose, add about ½ cup water to the pan. Quickly cover to allow the potstickers to steam for 3 to 4 minutes. Remove the cover and continue cooking until the water evaporates. Serve immediately.

Sweet Chili Dipping Sauce

■ **MAKES 3 TO 4 CUPS**

THIS RECIPE IS *courtesy of my friend, Chef Cathi DiCocco. The sweet-spicy sauce is good for finger foods such as Celebration Potstickers (page 48), but is equally delicious added to soups, stews, and marinades or as a basting sauce.*

2 cups rice wine vinegar
2 cups organic cane sugar
½ cup Lan Chi chili paste with or without garlic
¼ cup chopped garlic

1. Combine the vinegar, sugar, chili paste, garlic, and 2 cups water in a large saucepan and bring to a boil. Reduce the heat and gently simmer, uncovered, stirring occasionally, for about 2 hours, or until the sauce is reduced by half. Store in a covered container in the fridge for up to 6 months.

Golden Tofu Bites

SERVES 2 TO 4

½ cup (or more) canola or other vegetable oil for frying

One 14-ounce package firm tofu, frozen, then thawed, squeezed of water, and cut into bite-sized cubes

1 tablespoon tamari or soy sauce, or more to taste

1 to 2 tablespoons nutritional yeast, or more to taste (optional)

I ALWAYS KEEP *a package or two of firm tofu in my freezer in order to have a quick and healthy replacement for beef or chicken in any recipe. Freezing tofu completely changes its texture: it becomes more porous and spongy, so that you can easily squeeze out most of the water without it crumbling. Fried until it develops a golden crust and flavored with salty tamari and nutty nutritional yeast, tofu becomes a crisp, yet chewy, finger food. These disappear so quickly that I often double the recipe. They also keep well so you can make them a day or two in advance, then store in an airtight container in the refrigerator. Serve with pre-dinner cocktails or as part of a picnic lunch. Added to stir-fries, salads, pasta, or grains, children—often the pickiest of eaters—gobble them up.*

1. Pour the oil to about ½ inch deep in a wide, nonstick skillet and heat to 375°F over medium heat. Gently lower the tofu cubes into the hot oil with a slotted spoon, being careful not to crowd them. Since tofu has a high water content, even when squeezed, the oil will sizzle and spatter, so use a splatter screen over the skillet. Don't worry if the tofu sticks initially. Let the cubes develop a bit of crust on the first sides before turning them with a spatula. Once a crust develops, the cubes should loosen with little effort, and move freely about in the hot oil. Fry until the tofu is golden on all sides, 10 to 12 minutes. Drain on paper towels for a few seconds, then place in a bowl while still hot and toss with the tamari and sprinkle with yeast. Served hot, cold, or at room temperature.

Nutritional Yeast

NUTRITIONAL YEAST is not the same as brewer's yeast. While brewer's yeast is active, nutritional yeast is deactivated and is generally sold as flakes or powder. An excellent source of vitamin B$_{12}$ for vegetarians and vegans, nutritional yeast can be found in the bulk section of most natural food markets. I sprinkle nutritional yeast on pasta, popcorn, and anything normally topped with grated cheese. Store in the fridge for best results.

Marvelous Meaty Wontons

THESE "MEATY" BITES *are another fried treat that are usually gobbled up before they make it to the table in my house. Try serving them with an icy cold beer or a hearty red wine. The filling can be put together and refrigerated for a day or two, opening the door for an impromptu cocktail party. Serve these hot with one of your favorite dipping sauces, applesauce, or pepper jelly.*

1. In a bowl, crumble the sausage. Add the scallions, soy sauce, and sesame oil and blend well. Let the mixture stand for at least 30 minutes to allow the flavors to blend.

2. Spoon a heaping teaspoon or so of the "sausage" mixture into the center of each wrapper. Rub a little water along two adjacent edges with your finger, then fold the wrapper over to make a triangle. Press and seal the edges. Then fold in 2 points of the triangle to make a sailboat shape. (The wontons can be filled a few hours ahead of frying and serving, but avoid sogginess or stickiness by placing them on wax paper in a single layer and refrigerating.)

3. In a large heavy skillet, heat at least ½ inch of vegetable oil to 350°F. Carefully slide the wontons into the hot oil and cook until golden brown. Remove from the pan with a slotted spoon and drain quickly in a single layer on paper towels. Serve hot, but if you must wait, keep them warm in a low oven, covered with foil so they don't dry out.

One 8-ounce package vegetarian "sausage patties" (not vegetable links)

1 cup finely minced scallions

3 tablespoons soy sauce

½ to 1 teaspoon toasted sesame oil, to taste

24 wonton wrappers

¼ to ½ cup (or less) canola or other vegetable oil for frying

Mock Crab–Stuffed Mushrooms

3 dozen stuffing mushrooms, wiped clean, stems removed

½ recipe Mock Maryland Crab Cakes (page 196), prepared through the first step with very finely minced vegetables

½ cup panko (Japanese bread crumbs)

vegetable oil spray

I HAD SOME *leftover crab cake ingredients on hand and mushrooms just calling out to be stuffed, and I found that the crab cake mixture worked well repurposed as a stuffing, but with all the vegetables chopped much finer than for the cakes (where a chunkier texture is desired). Sometimes I like to bump up the filling's briny ocean flavor, so I'll add a shake or two of concentrated seaweed powder to the mix. Serve the mushrooms with a squeeze of lemon and a small dollop of Wasabi Mayonnaise (page 196). While the mushrooms make great appetizers, they're also hearty enough that if you drop a few onto a green salad, it is transformed into a light supper.*

1. Preheat the oven to 375°F. Place the mushrooms on a baking sheet. Fill each mushroom cap with about 2 tablespoons of the crab mixture. Bake for 8 to 10 minutes, until the mushrooms are softened. Preheat the broiler. Sprinkle each mushroom with panko and spray with a little vegetable oil spray. Broil 15 to 20 minutes, until the tops are crispy and hot.

Garlic Toasts

IN A SMALL *seaside trattoria along the coast of Livorno, I once had a light lunch of grilled Tuscan bread delicately rubbed with garlic and accompanied by sautéed bitter greens lightly dressed in olive oil. It was simple but delicious—my favorite combination—and I set out to recreate the flavorful toasts. They lend a garlicky crunch when served alongside any vegetable or pasta dish, or in a soup or stew— and it's a great way to add interesting bread to a meal without baking something from scratch.*

1. Grill, broil, or toast the bread until lightly browned, but not crunchy. While the bread is still hot, gently rub the surface with the garlic, concentrating on the outer crusty edges. The amount of garlic you rub will determine the depth of garlic flavor, so do this to your taste. Arrange the slices on a serving platter and drizzle with a little olive oil. Add a sprinkle of salt and serve.

1 day-old loaf Tuscan bread, cut into 1-inch-thick slices

1 or 2 garlic cloves, peeled and left whole

¼ to ⅓ cup (or less) extra virgin olive oil

Kosher salt, to taste

Greek Cheese Pie

SERVES 6 TO 8

12 ounces feta, crumbled until very fine

1 pint nonfat cottage cheese

2 large organic eggs, beaten well

3 tablespoons milk

3 tablespoons all-purpose flour

8 tablespoons (1 stick) unsalted butter or ½ cup olive oil

4 to 6 tablespoons extra virgin olive oil

1 pound organic phyllo, defrosted in the refrigerator

MANY TRADITIONAL GREEK *recipes call for large quantities of cheese, butter, and eggs. This one has been modified to eliminate some of the calories without compromising flavor. It still packs more fat than most of the dishes I make, so serve small portions with a fresh green salad and a bowl of salty Kalamata olives.*

When working with phyllo, some of the thin layers will break and tear. Don't worry, it happens to everyone, even experienced cooks. This recipe is very forgiving and torn sheets can be used within the layers; once it's baked you'll never know. Keep your dough frozen; thaw in the refrigerator for 24 hours before using. Have your filling ready before taking out the phyllo and exposing it to the air.

1. Preheat the oven to 350°F. Mix the feta, cottage cheese, eggs, and milk in a bowl until well combined. Stir in the flour until the consistency resembles lumpy cake batter, neither thick nor runny. Melt the butter in a small pan over low heat and stir in the oil; keep warm.

2. Remove the phyllo from the box, and unfold it; use the parchment it comes in to cover the stacked sheets of dough. Place a dampened cotton towel on top of the paper, covering the entire stack to keep the phyllo from drying out.

3. Using a pastry brush, lightly coat a jelly-roll pan with some of the butter-oil mixture. Remove the damp towel and place 2 sheets phyllo from the stack in the pan, overlapping in the center by 3 to 4 inches; allow about 1 inch overhang at the long sides of the pan. Lightly brush the sheets with the butter-oil mixture all the way around, including the edges. With the next two sheets, allow the phyllo to overhang an inch on the short sides of the pan. Continue alternating the overhang, maintaining a balanced assembly. Imagine you are creating an open box, with the overhang being the four flaps. The ends will be tucked in when the pita is assembled, creating a delicious crispy rolled crust. Be sure to cover the stack of phyllo with the damp towel when not using. Continue with layers of phyllo, completely brushing each sheet layer with the butter-oil, until you have used half the package (usually 10 sheets).

4. Evenly spread the feta mixture over the entire pastry surface. Continue layering and buttering each layer until you've used all the

sheets. Brush the top with more of the butter-oil, and using your fingers, tuck the edges down into the pan. The edges will appear broken and uneven, but once the pie is baked it will look perfect and the center seam will disappear. One last brush of butter along the edges and you're done.

5. Bake for about 40 minutes, until the top is a deep, rich, golden color. Remove the pie from the oven and let cool for 10 minutes. Cut with a knife into squares or triangles and serve right away.

Tomato and Basil Bruschetta

SERVES 2 TO 4

6 ripe Roma tomatoes

Handful of basil leaves

1 tablespoon plus ¼ cup extra virgin olive oil

Salt and freshly ground black pepper, to taste

1 loaf day-old rustic Italian or French loaf

1 large garlic clove, peeled and left whole

ITALIANS ARE INGENIOUS *at getting the most out of leftovers, and bruschetta is a perfect example of this: day-old bread—topped with a bit of choice ingredients—is transformed into a marvelous appetizer or light main dish. My version uses summer's juiciest, ripe Roma tomatoes and fragrant fresh basil. When local tomatoes are out of season in Maine, I substitute cherry tomatoes from the grocery store because they have a sweetness that other midwinter hothouse tomatoes can't match. I sometimes throw a tablespoon of capers into the tomato mixture for a salty-acidic touch or place thin slices of fresh mozzarella onto the grilled bread before topping with the tomato-basil mixture. Serve with a robust wine. Don't worry, you won't have any leftover bread after this one.*

1. Cut the tomatoes in half, scoop out the insides, and chop into ¼-inch dice. Place in a bowl. Rub the basil leaves between your hands to release the aroma, slice into thin ribbons, and add to the chopped tomatoes. Drizzle 1 tablespoon of the olive oil over the tomato-basil mixture and sprinkle with salt and a grinding of black pepper. Let the mixture marinate at least 15 to 30 minutes while you prepare the grilled bread.

2. Slice the bread into ½-inch-thick slices. Grill or toast lightly on both sides. Rub the garlic over one side of the warm toasts, concentrating on imparting garlic essence to the edges and over the middle. Pour ¼ cup of the olive oil onto a medium plate to create a very shallow puddle. Holding a toast by its edge, press into the oil, garlic side down. Place oiled side up onto serving platter. Repeat with the remaining toasts.

3. Spoon the marinated tomato-basil mixture onto the prepared toasts. Add an additional sprinkle of salt and a drizzle of olive oil, if desired.

The Scent of Herbs

TO ENHANCE the flavor of fresh leafy herbs such as basil, sage, tarragon, and rosemary, rub the leaves together in your hands lightly before chopping. This technique of gently bruising the leaves helps release the aromatic oils in herbs.

Bean and Basil Bruschetta

SERVES 2 TO 4

BRUSCHETTA IS ONE *of my most satisfying dishes: it's simple and begins with bread, my favorite thing. If I'm not eating it as an appetizer, I'll team up this cannellini-basil version with soup, salad, fresh fruit, and a robust wine for a light and satisfying main meal. Top the bean mixture with grilled radicchio or seared baby spinach for even more nutritional punch.*

For this recipe I always use fresh cannellini beans that I've cooked from dried. They hold their shape and texture much better than canned, but if you only have canned, be sure to rinse them well, and fold very gently. Canned cannellinis in particular have a creamy texture and, if roughly handled, tend to turn into a mash.

1. In a bowl big enough to accommodate all the ingredients, combine the olive oil, vinegar, and pepper flakes. With a small whisk, mix rapidly to emulsify into a creamy dressing, about 15 seconds (this insures that the dressing will coat the beans). Add the garlic, then fold in the beans and basil chiffonade, reserving a little of the basil for garnishing. Add salt and pepper to taste. Pile onto the grilled or toasted bread. To finish, drizzle with any remaining dressing from the bowl and sprinkle with a basil garnish.

5 tablespoons extra virgin olive oil

5 tablespoons good-quality balsamic vinegar

1 teaspoon crushed red pepper flakes

1 to 2 garlic cloves, thinly sliced

2 cups cooked cannellini beans

3 tablespoons chiffonade basil leaves (see below)

Salt and freshly ground black pepper, to taste

4 slices day-old rustic bread, grilled or toasted

Chiffonade

THE CHIFFONADE technique is simple. Take any leafy green and stack the leaves, roll the stack tightly, and then cut across with a knife to create long, thin strips. Sometimes for a tossed salad, I'll chiffonade the various greens. I love the way the salad looks when piled high on a plate.

Gorgonzola and Pear Bruschetta

SERVES 2 TO 4

1 to 2 ripe firm Bartlett pears, quartered, centers and seeds removed

Vegetable oil

1 loaf day-old French baguette or Tuscan bread

1 small garlic clove, peeled and left whole

¼ pound Gorgonzola dolce

½ cup walnuts, toasted (see page 86) and chopped

1 tablespoon extra virgin olive oil

GORGONZOLA, AND ITS *creamy, younger version called Gorgonzola dolce, complements the caramelized flavor of grilled pears. Made from cow's milk, Gorgonzola can be served with fruit, spread on a cracker, or added to sauces. Spread it on grilled bread that has been rubbed with a bit of fresh garlic for this easy bruschetta that works as an appetizer or accompaniment to a salad. If you can't find Bartlett pears, don't despair; try Bosc or any other firm pear, like sweet little Seckels.*

1. Heat a grill pan over medium heat. Thinly slice the pears, brush with a little vegetable oil, and grill in batches, oiled side down, until just slightly softened and showing grill marks.

2. Slice the bread into ½-inch-thick pieces. Grill, broil, or toast the bread until golden. Immediately rub the toasts around the outer edge of each slice with the garlic. Use a light hand—you're aiming to add just a hint of garlic. Working quickly while the bread is still warm, spread the Gorgonzola thinly on each toast. Sprinkle with the walnut pieces; finish with the grilled pear slices and a drizzle of olive oil.

Fried Polenta Squares

IN MANY RESTAURANTS in Italy, these piping hot, crunchy squares are served while you peruse the menu. You'll be amazed how something so simple can be so delectable. I enjoy them plain, but they're also great as a substitute for crackers or flatbreads with dips and spreads. Unlike frying with a neutral tasting vegetable oil, frying in fruity olive oil adds to the exceptional sweet corn–salty flavor of this appetizer.

2 cups extra virgin olive oil

Creamy Polenta (page 129), cooled and cut into small squares about ¼ inch thick (or thinner for a crispier texture)

Kosher salt, to taste

1. Heat the olive oil in a deep pan or fryer until hot (about 340°F). In batches, carefully slide the polenta pieces into the hot oil with a slotted spoon; they may spatter somewhat so use caution. Fry until the pieces are crispy and golden, then transfer to paper towels to drain. Sprinkle immediately with salt and serve hot.

Fresh Figs with Gorgonzola

SERVES 2 TO 4

12 fresh figs

Salt and freshly ground
black pepper, to taste

¼ pound (or less)
Gorgonzola dolce

1 tablespoon honey

2 tablespoons
sherry vinegar

FIGS ARE TOO *often underrated. The entire fruit is edible: incredibly sweet yet savory, mild, chewy, with tiny delicate crunchy seeds. Fresh figs are available from June to September. Look for ones that are plump with firm stems and in shades ranging from light green to deep purple. They should have a sweet fruity fragrance. Occasionally, you'll find a fig or two lurking at the bottom of the package with broken skins or on the verge of going bad. Compost those and store the remaining fruit in a single layer on a paper towel–lined plate in the refrigerator, keeping them covered to retain valuable moisture. Sometimes, due to seasonality, figs may be under-ripe. If so, simply place them in a single layer on a plate and keep at room temperature for a day or two. For a vegan dish, omit the cheese and honey dressing and broil the figs as directed; when cool, sprinkle with toasted walnuts and drizzle with a good-quality balsamic or fig balsamic vinegar.*

1. Preheat the broiler. Wash, and then slice the figs in half lengthwise. Remove the stems. Lay the figs in a shallow baking dish skin side down. Sprinkle with a little salt and pepper. Broil only until the tops of the fruit begin to bubble. With a demitasse spoon or the tip of a butter knife, scoop a small amount of Gorgonzola into the center of each fruit and press in gently. Broil until the cheese bubbles. Let cool slightly. Mix the honey with the vinegar, drizzle over the warm figs, and serve.

Gorgonzola Dolce

GORGONZOLA DOLCE is milder than the more common aged variety. Because it's a younger cheese it's also softer and more spreadable. I find Gorgonzola dolce at my local Italian grocery store, but if you don't have such a grocery store nearby, check any food specialty or gourmet store, or you could try putting in a suggestion at your neighborhood supermarket to stock it. In a pinch, use regular Gorgonzola, but don't add as much since it's more pungent than Gorgonzola dolce. A creamy Stilton also works well in the recipe.

Roasted Chickpeas

ROASTED AND CRUNCHY, *savory chickpeas make a nutty treat for snacking. I adore their sweet creamy centers and slightly crisp outer shells. Have these on hand during cocktail hour or at a picnic as an innovative replacement for the standard bowl of nuts. Because I love an extra kick of garlic, I sometimes toss in 1 or 2 minced cloves at the end. I've also been known to add a squeeze of lemon juice or a sprinkling of chipotle powder, curry powder, or ground cumin to add spice. These tend to disappear fast, so if you're making them for party finger food, I suggest doubling the recipe.*

2 to 3 tablespoons extra virgin olive oil, plus additional for serving

One 15½-ounce can chickpeas, rinsed and drained

3 garlic cloves, unpeeled

3 to 4 sage leaves

Coarse kosher salt

1. Preheat the oven to 425°F. Heat the oil in a large cast-iron or other oven-proof skillet over medium heat. Add the chickpeas and garlic and sauté for 1 to 2 minutes, until you can smell the garlic. Add the sage, toss, and remove from the heat. Roast in the oven for 15 to 20 minutes, until the chickpeas begin to brown. To help the beans roast evenly, give the pan a shake every few minutes. Let cool. Sprinkle with additional olive oil and kosher salt to bring out the sage and garlic accents. Serve at room temperature.

Garlic Confit

MAKES 2 CUPS

3 to 4 heads fresh garlic, cut in half horizontally (through the belly, not stem to end)

About ½ cup extra virgin olive oil

3 to 4 whole branches thyme or lemon thyme

20 whole peppercorns

MY FRIEND, CHEF *Cathi DiCocco—who owns Cafe DiCocoa, nestled in the beautiful mountain town of Bethel, Maine—turned me on to this recipe while filming one of the show's early episodes. Roasting garlic produces a complete change in flavor—the "bite" of raw garlic magically transforms into a mellow sweetness. I often roast up to half a dozen garlic heads at a time and then use as a spread or mash in dressings. A few cloves along with a generous drizzle of some of the reserved cooking oil add an incredible deep rich flavor to simple dishes like mashed potatoes and steamed vegetables. These also keep well—a month or more in the fridge—although you're likely to find yourself using them so often, they don't last that long. To prepare roasted garlic without the addition of herbs or seasonings, see Roasted Garlic (pg 98).*

1. Preheat the oven to 300°F. Set the garlic cut side down in a small glass baking dish (glass or ceramic dishes work best since metal tends to absorb flavors). Cover the garlic about halfway with olive oil and drop in the herbs and peppercorns. Roast the garlic for about 1 hour, until the heads look golden and are caramelized. The garlic will slide out of the skins smoothly. Be sure to strain and save the oil—it's packed full of mellow garlic flavor.

Hummus in a Hurry

HUMMUS IS SO *easy and inexpensive to make, there's no good reason to spend four dollars on a small container produced in a factory. Of all the canned beans available, chickpeas are the best at retaining their texture and flavor, and their convenience means I can get adequate protein at a moment's notice. Hummus is a well-loved healthy dip that goes great with Spicy Pita Crisps (page 68) and Garlic Toasts (page 53), along with pretzels and baked potatoes. Replace the chickpeas with whole black beans, add ¼ cup minced scallions, ¾ teaspoon cumin, and a dash of cayenne and spoon onto warmed corn tortillas to take the spread south of the border.*

2 garlic cloves, minced and then mashed

One 15- to 19-ounce can chickpeas, drained and rinsed

¼ cup tahini

2 tablespoons freshly squeezed lemon juice

2 to 3 tablespoons fruity extra virgin olive oil, plus more for drizzling

Sprinkle of ground cumin, or more to taste

Fine sea salt

Paprika

1. Combine the mashed garlic and chickpeas in a food processor and pulse until finely ground. Add the tahini, lemon juice, olive oil, cumin, and up to ¼ cup hot water (hot water makes the dip smooth and fluffy, add more if desired). Process the hummus until smooth, then add salt to taste. Spoon the dip into a serving dish, drizzle with a little olive oil, and sprinkle with paprika.

Cannellini Bean Spread

MAKES 2 CUPS

1 garlic clove, chopped

Salt, to taste

2 tablespoons untoasted pine nuts

One 15-ounce can cannellini beans, drained and rinsed

2 to 3 tablespoons extra virgin olive oil

2 tablespoons chopped parsley (optional)

Squeeze of lemon

Freshly ground black pepper, to taste

Paprika

THE CREAMY TEXTURE *of this smooth mellow spread makes it an appetizing alternative to butter. It's delicious smoothed on bagels or toast, or used as a dip for vegetables. The basic recipe is fairly neutral, but add ¼ cup chopped sun-dried tomatoes cured in oil and 1 tablespoon of the oil from the jar and you get a creamy spread with a deep, rich tomato tang that's even perfect over pasta. With our without additions, it's great paired with Spicy Pita Crisps (page 68), garlic bread, toast, crackers, crudités, and baked potatoes or spooned over sautéed dark leafy greens such as Sesame-Garlic Kale (page 209). When in season, I like to add fresh tarragon, thyme, or parsley. I've also thrown in chopped Kalamata olives which adds an earthy salty twist and a bit of extra texture.*

1. In a food processor, combine the garlic, a pinch of salt, and the pine nuts and pulse for a few seconds. Add half the beans and the olive oil. Process until fairly smooth; the mixture will be a little dry. Add the remaining beans and 2 to 3 tablespoons hot water and process until smooth and creamy. If necessary, add more hot water. If using parsley, add and pulse until just combined. Stir in the lemon juice (which adds a nice lift and brightens the flavor of the beans). Season with salt and pepper, sprinkle on the paprika, and let stand for at least 1 hour. Serve at room temperature.

Season as You Go

ALWAYS ADD ingredients and seasonings in small increments and taste; add more as you go along, until you reach the desired flavor.

Tzatziki

MAKES 2 CUPS

TZATZIKI, THE GARLICKY *Greek sauce, usually involves complicated preparations: first draining yogurt of its water, and then making sure that the peeled, seeded, and grated cucumber is dried well. By substituting the denser, drier kefir cheese for the drained yogurt, both of these steps are eliminated. I use this sauce as a creamy dip with crudités or Spicy Pita Crisps (page 68), a topping for baked—sweet or regular—potatoes, and with falafel in a rollup. You can also thin some tzatziki with milk, soy milk, or water and use as a dressing for green salads. The garlic flavor intensifies over time, so make sure you let it rest for a while before serving.*

No mint on hand? Substitute chives, scallions, or parsley; each herb imparts a different flavor to the creamy, garlicky sauce. Experiment and discover which you prefer. Vegans can substitute 2 cups Tofu Sour Cream (page 147) for the kefir leban; the garlic, olive oil, and cucumber are very assertive flavors and work well with tofu. If kefir leban is unavailable, Greek yogurt may be substituted.

1. Combine all the ingredients and allow to them sit for at least a couple hours in the refrigerator.

¼ to ½ cup extra virgin olive oil

2 cups kefir leban or plain Greek-style yogurt

1 small cucumber, peeled, seeded, and grated

2 to 3 garlic cloves, mashed with ½ teaspoon fine sea salt

2 tablespoons chopped mint

Kefir

KEFIR IS an ancient cultured milk product closely resembling yogurt. It's available in many styles, from a smooth and creamy liquid to a drier, denser, thick cheese called *kefir leban*. Kefir has a slightly effervescent tang and is easily digestible even for those people with lactose sensitivity.

Mashing Garlic

INSTEAD OF processing garlic through a press, try mashing it with a little coarse salt in a mortar and pestle. I love using hand tools like this and slowly mashing the garlic with salt brings out the sweetness of the bulb in a way you can't duplicate with a hard, metal press. It's like the difference between a quick blast in the microwave or slow oven roasting.

Roasted Eggplant Caviar

1 medium eggplant

¼ cup chopped red onion

2 to 3 garlic cloves

1 plum tomato,
seeded and diced

2 tablespoons extra
virgin olive oil

3 tablespoons lemon juice

3 tablespoons parsley,
coarsely chopped

2 tablespoons basil,
coarsely chopped

Salt and freshly ground
black pepper, to taste

WHEN I'M DEVELOPING *recipes for the show, I'll usually have an informal tasting where friends and colleagues can sample my works-in-progress. This dip was gone within minutes on its trial day. Serve it spooned over vegetables, with toasted pita or pumpernickel bread, or even as a light pasta sauce. A drizzle of flavorful oil (such as nut, sun-dried tomato, or truffle) adds a lovely finish. I've learned the flavor improves overnight, so if you can keep it from the hungry hordes, this is a dish to make a day ahead of use.*

1. Roast the eggplant according to the directions on page 180. After the eggplant has cooled, remove the flesh—retaining the seeds—and place in the food processor. Add onion, garlic, tomato, olive oil, lemon juice, parsley, basil, and salt and pepper and process until fairly smooth. Serve at room temperature.

Red Pepper–Tofu Dip

MAKES ABOUT 2 CUPS

THIS DIP IS *traditionally made with sour cream and cream cheese, but I find the texture of tofu to be lighter—and it stands up nicely to the assertive flavors of roasted peppers and lemon. Fresh roasted peppers are best, but for a quick dip or sauce, store-bought peppers packed in water work well. Serve as a dip for crackers, chips, or raw vegetables. I also use it as a sandwich spread, add it to soups, and spoon it over potatoes or other cooked vegetables like green beans and carrots.*

1. Combine the tofu, olive oil, lemon juice, vinegar, and salt in a food processor. Process until smooth and creamy. Transfer to a serving bowl. Process the peppers in the food processor until fairly smooth but still retaining some chunky texture. Stir the peppers into the tofu mixture. Garnish with the parsley before serving.

One 14-ounce package firm tofu, drained and dried on paper towels

⅓ cup extra virgin olive oil

¼ cup lemon juice

1 tablespoon cider vinegar

1 teaspoon fine sea salt

One 8-ounce jar roasted red peppers packed in water, or 2 medium red peppers, roasted (see below), skinned, and seeded

Chopped parsley

Roasting Peppers

VIRTUALLY ANY pepper can be roasted but red, orange, and yellow peppers are the sweetest and most digestible. Green peppers are picked before they are fully ripe and tend be tough and somewhat bitter. Peppers can be roasted over an open flame, a grill, under the broiler, or in the oven. I prefer to roast them under the broiler. To begin, move your top oven rack to its highest position, then preheat the broiler. Place 4 to 6 peppers on a foil-lined baking sheet. When the broiler is hot, slide in the sheet. Broil the peppers on one side until they are nicely browned and beginning to blacken. Turning the peppers, continue broiling each side until each entire pepper is darkened and starts to collapse. This should take 15 to 20 minutes. When the peppers are evenly charred, remove the sheet from the oven and immediately pull up the sides of the foil over the peppers and crimp closed, creating a sealed package. Let the peppers rest for an hour or until they are cool enough to handle. The peppers will be soft and slippery. Slide off the loosened skins and pull away the stems, ribs, and seeds.

Some chefs like to clean roasted peppers under running water, but in Italy it is believed by many, me included, that some of the sweet roasted flavor also goes down the drain. Slice the peppers into strips or dice, toss with a little olive oil, and store in a covered jar or container for up to 10 days. One average-size pepper, roasted, peeled, and seeded, will yield about ⅔ cup.

Spicy Pita Crisps

½ teaspoon garlic salt, or
more to taste

½ teaspoon dried oregano or
Italian blend seasoning

½ teaspoon dried basil

½ teaspoon paprika (sweet,
smoked, or hot)

¼ teaspoon crushed red
pepper flakes, or more to
taste

⅛ teaspoon freshly ground
black pepper

4 pita breads,
each cut into 16 triangles

¼ cup extra virgin olive oil

ONE FEATURE THAT *distinguishes pita bread from most other flatbreads is its two layers, which when baked, create a hollow center, or pocket. Slice the pita down the middle and you have a starting place for a stuffed sandwich; leave it whole and you've got the base for a quick pizza. Now available in a wide variety of grains, from white and whole wheat to soy and spelt, pita keeps very well in the freezer and, because it's flat, takes up little space. Make your own spicy crisps using pita bread to pair with Roasted Eggplant Caviar (page 66) or Cannellini Bean Spread (page 64). You can also use them for scooping up salsa or pesto, or for adding spicy crunch to soup or salad. To make these tasty triangles even lower in fat, lay them on a baking sheet and lightly spray with vegetable oil spray (in place of the olive oil) before sprinkling on the spice mix. Because the crisps contain oil they are best when served right after baking, but they can be made a day ahead and stored in an airtight container.*

1. Preheat the oven to 375°F. Combine all of the spices in a small bowl. Brush the pita triangles with the olive oil. Using your fingers, sprinkle the spice mixture evenly over all. Bake for about 8 minutes, until just crisp and lightly browned. Watch carefully while baking as they can easily burn if forgotten.

Cashew Pâté

THIS WAS ONE *of the first pâté recipes passed on to me when I became a vege-tarian. Tasty and full of great texture, the best part is how easy this dense nutty spread is to make. For a more traditional pâté flavor, I add cognac, but it's just as delicious without. Serve with crackers or toasted baguette rounds.*

1. Heat the oil in a large skillet over medium-high heat. Add the onion and sauté until lightly browned. Transfer to a food processor and add the cashews, beans, and lemon juice. Pulse until the mixture is smooth but still retains some texture (you don't want to make cashew butter). Stir in the cognac, if desired, and season with salt and pepper. Serve at room temperature.

2 tablespoons canola or other vegetable oil

1 medium onion, diced

1 cup cashews, toasted (see page 86)

1 cup frozen French-style string beans, defrosted

1 tablespoon lemon juice

1 tablespoon cognac (optional)

Salt and freshly ground black pepper, to taste

Tomato Salsa

4 to 6 red ripe tomatoes, seeded and diced small

1½ medium white onions, chopped

2 scallions, chopped

1 to 3 poblano peppers, or any other hot pepper such as jalapeño, chopped

⅓ cup chopped cilantro

1 lime, juiced with pulp

¼ cup jarred picante sauce, or to taste

Salt to taste

THIS CLASSIC TABLE *sauce is a perfect complement to any Mexican-influenced menu. Just a spoonful delivers a burst of spicy tomato flavor. Try adding other chopped vegetables like cucumber or jicama to add crunchy texture, or fruit such as pineapple or peaches for sweet-savory juiciness. I like to serve salsa with warmed corn tortillas; it also pairs nicely with vegetable fajitas, bean tostadas, or your favorite tortilla chip. For a hearty meal, mix in a can of rinsed pinto beans and serve over Creamy Polenta (page 229). I also love mixing leftover salsa with tofu or eggs for a spicy, tomato-y breakfast omelet.*

1. Combine all the ingredients in a bowl and let stand for at least 30 minutes.

Green Salsa Picada

½ medium yellow onion, coarsely chopped

½ to 1 cup cilantro, chopped

1 lime, juiced

Few pinches chipotle powder

Few pinches kosher salt

SOME PEOPLE HAVE *a true sensitivity to cilantro, in which case this picada might be too potent for them. I know of other people, however, who thought they hated cilantro, but this chunky topping passed their scrutiny because it's so light and tart with lime. Serve as a topping to liven up any dish with fresh, bright crunch. I particularly like it spooned over fragrant basmati or jasmine rice, egg dishes, and baked or fried potatoes.*

1. Mix all the ingredients in a bowl and let stand for 15 to 30 minutes.

Chunky Avocado Salsa

I'M PARTIAL TO *a hearty, rustic salsa; one that scoops onto a tortilla chip instead of simply coating it with tomato juice, half of which winds up down the front of your shirt. All the friends and viewers who've tried this salsa agree that the buttery warmth of the avocado is perfectly enhanced by in-season, juicy, tart tomatoes, a squirt of refreshing lime, and just a few pinches of smoky spice. Try it on tacos, as an accompaniment to rice dishes, or even tucked into a warm roll up with any of your favorite vegetables. The jalapeño adds just the right spicy kick. Be aware that lime juice has a tendency to bring out the salty flavor in food, so use a light hand.*

1 ripe but firm Hass avocado, peeled and coarsely chopped

½ medium yellow onion, coarsely chopped

½ pint cherry tomatoes, quartered or halved depending on the size

3 to 4 tablespoons chopped cilantro

Few pinches chipotle powder, cayenne, fresh chopped jalapeño, or crushed red pepper flakes

Salt and freshly ground black pepper, to taste

1 to 2 tablespoons fresh lime juice

1. Gently mix the avocado, onion, tomato, cilantro, chipotle powder, salt, and pepper in a bowl. Add the lime juice and stir to combine. Let stand for 15 minutes to allow the flavors to blend. Just prior to serving, recheck seasonings and adjust to taste.

RECIPE COURTESY OF HEIDI VALENZUELA.

Artichoke Pesto

MAKES ABOUT 2 CUPS

1 garlic clove, halved

½ cup freshly grated Parmesan or Pecorino, or both (optional)

One 14-ounce can artichoke hearts, or defrosted frozen artichokes hearts

¼ to ½ cup extra virgin olive oil

2 teaspoons or more lemon juice

1 tablespoon chopped parsley

Salt and freshly ground black pepper, to taste

I THINK OF *this pesto recipe as an artichoke canvas: its very simplicity allows it to be adapted in many ways. Double the garlic for an extra boost of flavor and an immune system kick; or add finely chopped vegetables, like orange or red peppers, scallions, and jalapeño; or throw in some capers; or try it with chopped nuts and a nice handful of fresh basil. Serve as a spread with bread or crackers, or use as a wonton filling or a pasta sauce. For a more rustic pasta topping, back off on the oil and add the artichokes last, pulsing only a few times. Or add 1 to 2 tablespoons of sun-dried tomatoes packed in oil and substitute 1 tablespoon of the sun-dried tomato oil for the olive oil.*

1. Combine the garlic and the cheese in a food processor. Add the artichokes and pulse a few times to blend. Add the olive oil while continuing to pulse, to ensure slow blending. After adding ¼ cup of oil, check consistency and, if desired, add more; stop when the pesto is smooth but still retains some texture. Stir in the lemon juice and parsley and season with salt and pepper.

Fresh Is Best

I ALWAYS USE freshly grated cheese, which wins out over commercially grated cheese in every respect. But if you're using commercially grated cheese, because of its powdery consistency and stronger flavor, use half the amount called for.

Dried Tomato Pesto

THE DENSE TOMATO tang of this pesto is delicious mixed into hot pasta or spread on toasted rustic bread. The flavor is intense, deep, and rich—so a little goes a long way. I'll sometimes mix this pesto with goat cheese for a starter with crisp crackers. I also love it added to dressings or sauces. Even if you don't follow all the measurements exactly, there's no way to ruin the recipe. I use the oil left in the pan from making Garlic Confit, but you can use regular extra virgin olive oil.

1. Combine the dried tomatoes, roasted garlic, chopped garlic, and basil in a food processor. Process, drizzling in oil a little at a time, just until the mixture becomes cohesive but not oily. Season with salt and pepper and serve.

6 Oven-Dried Tomatoes (page 206) or store-bought sun-dried tomatoes

1 roasted garlic clove (see page 98)

1 garlic clove, coarsely chopped

Handful of basil

1 to 2 tablespoons oil from Garlic Confit (page 62) or extra virgin olive oil

Salt and freshly ground black pepper, to taste

Cilantro-Mint Pesto

2 cups cilantro leaves and stems

1 cup mint leaves and tender stems (remove tough stems)

1 bunch scallions (about 6), coarsely chopped

1 small jalapeño pepper, chopped

Juice of 2 lemons

1 to 2 tablespoons extra virgin olive oil

Salt and freshly ground black pepper, to taste

THIS LIGHT PESTO *picks up a hint of heat from the jalapeño and brightness from the fresh lemon. It works beautifully as a topping for pasta or as an addition to salsas, dressings, or any dish you want to infuse with a fresh burst of flavor. For a more traditional pesto consistency, add additional olive oil.*

1. Place all the ingredients in a food processor and process until smooth.

RECIPE COURTESY OF CATHI DiCOCCO

SALADS AND DRESSINGS

SALADS ARE FINDING their way to becoming main dishes for good reason: they're hearty, healthy, and the combinations are endless. Gone (almost) are the days of flavorless iceberg lettuce with a smattering of watery tomatoes and a fat-laden dressing. Today's salads are thoughtfully prepared with fresh greens of all types, cabbages, fruits, nuts, crispy vegetables, and beans that offer a mouthwatering variety of nourishing options. A little good olive oil, lemon juice or quality vinegar, and some fresh herbs can make a simple salad sensational.

Be sure that lettuces are washed, dried, and chilled before dressing. Use a bowl that's large enough for the salad to be tossed well. To avoid becoming soggy, salad greens should be lightly dressed just prior to serving. Salads with beans or pasta, and those made with crisp vegetables like cabbage, carrot, or celeriac, benefit from macerating in the dressing.

Vegetarian Caesar Salad

SERVES 2 TO 4

2 ounces cubed Parmesan or grated vegan Parmesan, plus more for serving if desired

2 garlic cloves, peeled

1 cup silken soft tofu, cubed

1½ tablespoons Dijon mustard

1½ teaspoons white wine vinegar

1¼ teaspoons vegetarian Worcestershire sauce

Kosher salt and freshly ground black pepper

2 tablespoons extra virgin olive oil, or more if needed

1 head romaine lettuce, tough ribs removed, broken into bite-sized pieces.

2 handfuls Savory Croutons (page 115)

THIS SALAD'S CREAMY, *egg-free, anchovy-free Caesar dressing gets its kick from fresh garlic, pungent Parmesan, and spicy Dijon mustard.*

1. Starting on the lowest speed of your blender, chop the Parmesan cubes until well grated. Add the garlic and chop until minced. Add the tofu, mustard, vinegar, Worcestershire sauce, pinch of salt, and pinch of pepper. Process until smooth. While the processor is running, drizzle in the olive oil, just enough until an emulsion forms. You may need more than 2 tablespoons but that amount usually works well. Transfer the dressing to a jar or bottle and shake well before using. The dressing will keep for up to a week in the fridge.

2. Place the lettuce in a roomy bowl and top with croutons. Pour the dressing around the salad, ¼ cup at a time, and begin tossing, lightly coating all the leaves. Serve immediately with a generous grind of black pepper and a little additional cheese if desired.

Insalata Pomodoro

WHEN FRESH JUICY *tomatoes, aromatic basil, and sweet baby spinach are in season, there's little else that beats this Mediterranean combination. With its vibrant color and bright flavor, the recipe works overtime as a salad, an uncooked pasta sauce, and, of course, since I'm compelled to put virtually everything on toast, a delicious bruschetta topping. Baked tofu has a cheese-like texture and flavor and is a nutritious substitute for mozzarella cheese.*

1. Combine the spinach, tomatoes, onion, tofu, and basil in a medium bowl. Toss the nuts into the salad. In a small bowl, whisk together the oil and vinegar until emulsified. Pour the dressing over the salad and toss lightly. Season with salt and pepper and serve immediately.

½ cup baby spinach

2 cups cherry tomatoes, cut in half

½ small red onion, thinly sliced

½ cup diced baked tofu or diced fresh mozzarella

Handful of chiffonade basil (see page 57)

½ cup pine nuts, toasted (see page 86)

2 to 3 tablespoons extra virgin olive oil

1 tablespoon red wine vinegar

Salt and freshly ground black pepper, to taste

Salad Dressing Ratio

AS A RULE of thumb, when mixing dressing for tossed green salads, use 3 tablespoons oil to 1 to 1½ tablespoons of acid (i.e., vinegar or citrus juice).

Caribbean Cabbage and Carrot Salad

SERVES 4

½ medium head green cabbage, shredded

2 carrots, grated

½ celeriac bulb, julienned

½ cup lemon juice

¼ to ½ cup chopped cilantro

Salt and freshly ground pepper, to taste

WHILE VISITING THE *Cayman Islands, I sampled this slaw-like salad at one of the local food stalls. The well-balanced flavors and textures stuck with me and when I returned home I set about making my own version. Mix things up by tossing in some cherry tomatoes, sliced red onion, or diced avocado. This is delicious on or with Jamaican Jerk Tempeh (page 160).*

1. Place the cabbage, carrots, and celeriac in a bowl and toss to combine. Add the lemon juice and cilantro and toss again. Season with salt and pepper. Serve chilled.

Cabbage Slaw with Tomatoes and Ginger

SERVES 4

ON MY FIRST *visit to Veggie Planet, chef Didi Emmons's restaurant in Cambridge, Massachusetts, we prepared this slaw to accompany her Kasha Krunch Burgers (page 191). The contrast of spicy and earthy flavors dramatically altered my view of cabbage salads forever. So much so, I eat it at least once a week. You can put aside moderation with this one and serve up a bowlful, tossing in extra spinach and tomatoes if you like. The peanuts and coconut add the perfect finishing touch. This salad is best served immediately after assembling and dressing.*

1. Chop the watercress, including the remaining stems, into 1-inch pieces. Place in a large bowl and add the cabbage, tomato, peanuts, and coconut.

2. In a small bowl, combine the lime juice, ginger, sugar, and salt, stirring until the sugar dissolves. Stir in the hot sauce if using. Pour the dressing over the salad and toss well until the vegetables are coated. Sprinkle the salad with the sesame seeds. Serve at room temperature, or refrigerate up to 2 hours and serve chilled.

1 small bunch watercress, trimmed, discarding the bottom ½ inch of the stems

2 cups very thinly sliced green cabbage (about half a large head)

1 large, ripe tomato (or 2 plum tomatoes), cut into ½-inch cubes

¼ cup unsalted roasted peanuts, chopped

2 tablespoons shredded or grated unsweetened dried coconut

¼ cup fresh lime juice (about 3 limes)

3½ tablespoons minced ginger

1 tablespoon light brown sugar

2 tablespoons kosher salt, or to taste

Good squeeze of hot sauce (optional)

2 tablespoons toasted sesame seeds

Fennel-Cabbage Slaw

SERVES 4 TO 6

¼ cup distilled white vinegar

1 tablespoon extra virgin olive oil

1 tablespoon organic cane sugar

2 teaspoons anise seed

3 cups shredded green cabbage (1 small head or ½ large head)

2 cups shredded fennel bulb (1 to 2 bulbs)

½ medium red onion, halved and thinly sliced into half moons

1 large carrot, grated

Kosher salt and freshly ground pepper, to taste

DIDI EMMONS IS *a regular guest on* Totally Vegetarian, *and, in addition to cooking at her restaurant, Veggie Planet, she serves as a personal chef. She developed this slaw recipe for a family on a low-salt diet. If fennel really isn't your thing, you can make this without and just add a bit more shredded cabbage. This recipe can be prepared and refrigerated up to 2 days, but I recommend you don't add the onion until just before serving as its flavors become too intense with storage. While this is delicious prepared without salt, if you do decide to salt it, wait until serving time, as the salt will cause the vegetables to leach water and the dressing will become diluted and bland.*

1. Whisk together the vinegar, oil, sugar, and anise seed in a large bowl. Add the cabbage, fennel, onion, carrot, and salt and pepper. Toss until the vegetables are evenly coated with the dressing.

Minty Tomato-Fennel Salad

SERVES 4

1 pound cherry tomatoes, halved

½ small red onion, chopped

½ fennel bulb, finely diced

¾ cup mint leaves, plus a few leaves for garnish

¼ cup extra virgin olive oil

Juice and grated zest of 1 lemon

Salt and freshly ground black pepper, to taste

TYPICALLY MADE WITH *basil, I enjoyed a version of this salad in Rome. I was pleasantly surprised by my substitution of mint; I prefer the lighter, more complementary brightness that fresh mint imparts to raw fennel. For the dressing, I use lemon juice in place of a more acidic wine vinegar; the lemon enhances the combination of fresh tomatoes, subtle red onion, and the mild anise taste of the fennel. Serve the salad as soon as it is dressed, before the juicy tomatoes make it watery.*

1. Combine the tomatoes, onion, fennel, and mint in a large bowl. In a separate bowl, whisk the oil and lemon juice. Add dressing to taste to the salad and toss to combine. Season with a little salt and pepper. Garnish with mint leaves and a little zest and serve immediately.

Edamame and Apple Salad

SERVES 4

KIDS LOVE EDAMAME, *especially when mixed with sweet apples. You can also toss some nutritional raisins or nuts into this salad for an even more kid-pleasing dish. The cilantro here is optional and the jicama may be replaced with radish or omitted entirely. Most of the salad can be made up to a day ahead and stored in an airtight container; just add the freshly diced apple prior to serving.*

1. Bring 5 cups water to a boil. Add the edamame, return to a boil, and cook for 5 minutes. Drain and rinse well with cold water. Let cool for 10 minutes.

2. Mix the oil, vinegar, and salt and pepper in a large bowl. Add the edamame, apple, jicama, and cilantro. Toss to coat and serve immediately.

1 pound frozen shelled edamame

1 tablespoon canola or other vegetable oil

¼ cup seasoned sushi rice vinegar

¼ teaspoon fine sea salt

⅛ teaspoon freshly ground black pepper

1 Granny Smith apple, cored and cut into ¼-inch dice

One 8-ounce jicama, peeled and diced small

½ to 1 cup lightly packed chopped cilantro

Boiled Edamame Pods

■ **SERVES 4**

I FIRST TRIED *edamame pods as an appetizer at a Japanese restaurant, and I've been in love with the bright color, sweet flavor, and crisp texture of the cooked soybeans ever since. Their attributes are all things that kids love too—steamed or boiled in their shells, they make a protein-packed, salty after-school snack. In my house, we make edamame instead of popcorn for movie-watching.*

1 pound frozen or fresh edamame pods
Coarse sea salt

1. Bring 3 cups water to a boil in a medium saucepan and add the salt and edamame. Cook for 5 to 10 minutes, until tender but still firm. Drain, place in a large bowl, and add another sprinkle of sea salt. Enjoy hot or chilled.

2. To eat the beans and not the inedible pod, squeeze the pod partially open, then gently suck the salty pod while scraping it between your teeth—the beans will pop right out.

Orange-Jicama Salad

1 medium jicama, peeled and cut into a small dice

2 oranges, peeled and sliced into wedges, reserving the juices

¾ cup canola or other vegetable oil

½ cup fresh lime juice (3 to 4 limes)

1 garlic clove, crushed

1 shallot, minced, or ¼ cup minced red onion

½ to 1 teaspoon fine sea salt

1 teaspoon chile powder

¼ cup finely chopped cilantro

2 tablespoons unsalted peanuts, chopped (optional)

Few pinches crushed dried red pepper flakes

JICAMA HAS A *crunchy texture and fresh flavor similar to that of water chestnuts. I often add jicama to salsas or use it in salads like this one where its sweetness is enhanced by tart citrus fruits, crunchy nuts, and a smoky spicy dressing. No matter how you slice it, jicama never loses its pleasing mild crunch.*

1. Combine the jicama and the oranges and their juice in a medium bowl. In a small bowl, whisk together the oil and lime juice until emulsified, then add the garlic, shallot, salt, and chile powder. Pour the dressing over the jicama and oranges and combine. Chill for 30 minutes. Toss again, garnish with cilantro, peanuts (if using), red pepper flakes, and serve.

Cucumber-Dill Salad

MY MOTHER IS *a cucumber enthusiast so I've had cucumbers prepared just about every way imaginable. But no matter how many cucumber salads she tries, this is her favorite. It's a refreshing hot-weather dish, which is perfect because that's when cucumbers are in abundance at farmers' markets. The sugar is optional, but worth a try if you feel in the mood for a little sweetness.*

1. Wash the cucumbers and pat dry. Peel by running a vegetable peeler down the length of each cucumber, spacing it out to create stripes. Slice the cucumbers fairly thin and lay the slices in a shallow bowl. Toss in the dill.

2. Into a small bowl, squeeze the lemon and pull out any seeds. If using sugar, dissolve it into the lemon juice. Slowly whisk the olive oil into the juice, until emulsified. Pour the dressing over the cucumbers and toss to coat evenly. Cut cucumbers tend to exude a lot of water when standing, so I like to serve this immediately at room temperature.

2 medium cucumbers

2 to 3 tablespoons minced dill

1 lemon

Few sprinkles organic cane sugar (optional)

½ to 1 tablespoon extra virgin olive oil

Spinach Salad
with Chutney Dressing

⅓ cup extra virgin olive oil

¼ cup sherry vinegar

1 tablespoon Major Grey's chutney

1½ teaspoons curry powder

Dash dry mustard

Salt and freshly ground black pepper, to taste

2 bunches fresh spinach, washed, dried, and stemmed

2 crisp apples, any variety, cored and diced

½ cup chopped scallions, white part only (about 3-4 scallions)

⅔ cup Fresh Roasted Peanuts (see next page)

½ cup raisins

THE RECIPE FOR *this salad is written on a well-worn card in my recipe box, although I have no idea where it came from. Regardless of its origins, spinach provides a hearty canvas for fragrant curried chutney dressing, crisp sweet apples, and raisins. The peanuts add some crunch. For a variation, substitute toasted walnuts or pine nuts for the peanuts, dried apricots for the raisins, and garnish with some fried tempeh.*

1. Whisk the oil and vinegar together in a bowl until emulsified, then whisk in the chutney, curry powder, and mustard until well blended. Season with salt and pepper.

2. Combine the spinach, apples, scallions, peanuts, and raisins in a large bowl. Whisk the dressing again, add to the salad, and toss. Serve immediately.

Nuts to You

DRY ROASTED PEANUTS provide 7 grams of protein per ounce and nearly 3 grams of fiber (a vital part of a healthy diet that animal protein can't provide). Peanuts also contain important B vitamins, (B_1, B_2, B_3, and trace amounts of B_6), niacin, folic acid, calcium, magnesium, potassium, iron, copper, and zinc. Loaded with heart healthy fats, peanuts contain about 165 calories per one ounce serving. Nutritionists recommend consuming an ounce or two of nuts every day. Abiding by the 2-ounce rule will help keep your energy up and your waistline in check.

Fresh Roasted Peanuts

■ **MAKES 4 CUPS**

PEANUTS ARE NOT *nuts—they are legumes. Because of this, in many parts of the world they are added to soups, stews, and other main dishes the way we would add beans. Loaded with protein and fiber, peanuts are a great source of vitamins, minerals, and cholesterol-lowering, unsaturated fats. And nothing beats the bite, flavor, and nutrition of fresh, dry roasted peanuts. Not only that, roasting them at home couldn't be easier. I love them plain or sprinkled with just a bit of coarse salt. These freshly roasted peanuts can also be added to salads, main dishes, stir-fries, cereals, and even desserts to add tasty crunch and nutritional punch.*

4 cups blanched peanuts

1. Preheat the oven to 350°F. Place the peanuts in a single layer on a baking sheet. Roast for 20 to 25 minutes, until the peanuts take on a rich, golden brown color. Cool and store in an airtight container. Larger amounts may be frozen up to 4 months.

Arugula Salad with Figs

SERVES 4

2 to 3 tablespoons extra virgin olive oil

1 tablespoon lemon juice

Salt and freshly ground black pepper, to taste

½ pound arugula, washed and torn

6 to 8 fresh figs, quartered

¼ cup toasted nuts (see below), such as walnuts or pine nuts (optional)

¼ cup feta or Stilton, crumbled (optional)

PEPPERY ARUGULA AND *sweet fresh figs just belong together. While I usually use sweeter baby arugula for most of my dishes, here I prefer the mustardy sharp flavor of the more mature greens.*

1. Whisk together the oil, juice, and salt and pepper in a salad bowl. Add the arugula and figs and fold gently to combine. Divide the salad among 4 salad plates. Top each serving with nuts and cheese if you like. Serve immediately.

Toasting Nuts

TOASTING OR roasting releases the rich depth of flavor in nuts that's sometimes lost during storage. To toast nuts, heat a small dry skillet over medium heat. Add the nuts and begin tossing by shaking the pan. Nuts have a high oil content and can burn easily, so it's essential to keep the pan moving. As soon as the nuts become a nice golden color, remove them from the pan. I toast only what I need. Nuts may also be roasted in the oven on a foil-lined baking sheet at 350°F, until aromatic and golden in color. Again, keep an eye on them since they roast and burn quickly.

Arugula, Pear, and Celeriac Salad

SERVES 2 TO 4

CELERIAC, ALSO CALLED knob celery and celery root, has a great crisp texture—much like jicama—with a mild celery taste; this makes it a perfect match for robust and sweet flavors such as arugula, beets, apples, and walnuts. It's often served in Europe dressed in mustard and mayonnaise. In this recipe, the celeriac is nicely accented with peppery arugula, mellow sweet pear, crunchy nuts, and the lightest of dressings—just a few shakes of vinegar and a drizzle of olive oil. I keep the cheese at a minimum and use lots of fresh black pepper. An Asian mandoline comes in very handy for the salad, allowing you to put it together in a matter of minutes.

1. Lay the pears out flat and slightly overlapping around the edges of 1 large or 2 medium plates. Leave the center open for the greens. Set the arugula in the center and sprinkle the celeriac slivers over all. Dress with a little olive oil and a sprinkling of vinegar. Season to taste with salt and black pepper. Top with the walnuts and a few small shavings of cheese, if you like, and serve immediately.

1 ripe Bosc pear, cored, cut in half, and sliced into thin half moons (don't peel)

2 handfuls of arugula, washed and dried

½ celeriac bulb, peeled and julienned

Extra virgin olive oil

Sherry vinegar

Salt and freshly ground black pepper, to taste

⅓ cup walnuts, halved and toasted (see page 86)

Parmigiana Reggiano or Pecorino Toscano, shaved into long ribbons (optional)

Julienne

JULIENNE REFERS to the technique of cutting food, usually vegetables, into matchstick-size strips. To julienne vegetables like carrots, jicama, celeriac, and potatoes, first cut into ⅛-inch-thick slices. Stack the slices, then cut those into ⅛-inch-thick strips. Trim the strips to the desired length. For vegetables like jicama or celeriac with a round shape, trim the bottom so it sits flat without rolling around and then begin slicing.

Black-Eyed Pea and Arugula Salad with Honey Vinaigrette

SERVES 4 TO 6

¼ cup extra virgin olive oil, plus more for sprinkling

1 tablespoon sherry vinegar

1 generous teaspoon honey

2 teaspoons dried oregano, more or less to taste

One 15-ounce can black-eyed peas, rinsed and well-drained; frozen may be used

1 bunch scallions (about 6), thinly sliced

1 small red onion, finely diced

4 large Roma tomatoes, diced

4 to 6 cups baby arugula

I REALLY MAKE *an effort to incorporate a variety of protein-rich beans and grains into my diet, but for many years, black-eyed peas remained something only served with ham hocks or bacon. I'm happy to say I figured out ways to enjoy them: here, their creamy flavor is accented with a bright, lightly sweetened dressing and served on a bed of baby arugula. You may substitute endive, spinach, watercress, or baby beet greens for the arugula or combine greens to suit your own taste. Serve with hearty crusty bread.*

1. In a large bowl, combine the olive oil, vinegar, honey, and oregano and whisk until emulsified. Add the peas, scallions, onion, and tomatoes. Fold gently until well coated. Fill individual plates or a serving platter with the arugula. Spoon on the vegetable mixture and top with a sprinkle of olive oil.

Black Bean, Tomato, and Corn Salad

WHEN TOMATOES AND *sweet corn are in season, I'm always looking for new ways to prepare them. In this summer salad, the black beans add just the right touch of creaminess, and the lime, cilantro, and jalapeño give it a south-of-the-border feel. Serve the salad on its own, as a side dish, or spoon some on top of cooked rice, quinoa, orzo, or over a crisp bed of greens. Sometimes I add a little ground cumin and roll the salad up in tortillas, or mix it with rice for a burrito.*

1. Whisk together the lime juice, cilantro, and scallions in a large salad bowl. Continue whisking while slowly adding the olive oil until emulsified. Fold in the beans, corn, avocado (if using), tomatoes, and jalapeño. Let stand for 15 minutes for the flavors to meld. Season with salt and pepper.

½ cup lime juice

½ cup chopped cilantro

3 scallions, thinly sliced

½ cup extra virgin olive oil

One 32-ounce can black beans, drained and rinsed

1 cup fresh corn kernels, cooked (about 2 ears)

1 firm ripe avocado, diced (optional)

½ pound quartered cherry tomatoes or diced fresh tomatoes

1 small jalapeño pepper, minced

Salt and freshly ground black pepper, to taste

Mexican Sweet Potato–Black Bean Salad

SERVES 6

Dressing

2 canned chipotle chiles

2 garlic cloves

¼ cup Sweet Chili Dipping Sauce (page 49) or prepared sweet chili sauce

¾ cup fresh lime juice about 6 limes)

1 cup canola or other vegetable oil

Salad

8 medium sweet potatoes, peeled and cut into ¾-inch chunks

3 to 4 tablespoons canola or other vegetable oil

1 tablespoon ground coriander

1 tablespoon chile powder

1 tablespoon ground cumin

1 tablespoon fine sea salt

4 cups corn (about 6 ears or 1 pound frozen)

4 cups cooked black beans; or two 15½-ounce cans black beans, drained and rinsed

1 bunch scallions (about 6), white and green parts, thinly sliced

1 cup chopped cilantro

THIS SOUTHWESTERN-INSPIRED *dish is an often requested at Cafe DiCocoa, and I was absolutely delighted to have Cathi DiCocco appear on my show and share her recipe. Roasted sweet potatoes, velvety black beans, and sweet corn get an extra punch from her zingy lime-infused chipotle dressing. With its kaleidoscope of bright colors and complex flavors, this protein-rich tangy salad is perfect as an accompaniment to burgers, tempeh, and tofu dishes, or scooped up with warm tortilla chips. The salad keeps well and makes a great take-along lunch. Serve with a generous dose of freshly chopped cilantro.*

1. **TO MAKE THE DRESSING:** Combine the chiles, garlic, chili sauce, and lime juice in a blender. Turn the blender on and slowly add the oil, until the dressing is creamy and emulsified. Makes about 3 cups. Leftover dressing can be stored in the refrigerator for up to 2 months.

2. **TO MAKE THE SALAD:** Preheat the oven to 375°F. In a large bowl, toss the potatoes with the canola oil to coat. Sprinkle with the coriander, chile powder, cumin, and salt, and toss again. Arrange the potatoes in a single layer on a baking sheet and roast until golden and just tender, 15 to 20 minutes. Transfer to the large bowl and let cool.

3. Microwave the corn in a small amount of water for 3 to 5 minutes. Drain and place in the bowl with the potatoes. Add the beans, scallions, and cilantro. Gently toss with ½ cup of the dressing (or more to taste) to moisten the salad. Let the salad marinate for 15 to 30 minutes. Serve at room temperature. Store any leftover salad in a covered container in the fridge for up to 5 days.

Orzo, Basil, and Sun-Dried Tomato Salad

ORZO, RICE-SHAPED *pasta, is combined with slivered sun-dried tomatoes and their oil, buttery pine nuts, and bright fresh basil for a light salad. I sometimes add grilled zucchini and eggplant or serve the salad on a bed of arugula or baby spinach. This salad is at its best when its assertive flavors meld together for at least an hour before serving at room temperature.*

1. Bring a medium pot of salted water to a boil and cook the orzo until just a minute before al dente.

2. Meanwhile, combine the scallions, tomatoes, and 1 cup of the basil in a large bowl and toss to combine. In a small bowl, whisk together the mustard, vinegar, and tomato oil.

3. Drain the orzo well and add to the bowl of vegetables along with the pine nuts. Add the dressing and mix well. Add the remaining 1 cup basil and season with salt and pepper. Let the salad rest for 1 hour. Serve at room temperature.

1 pound orzo

4 scallions, white and green parts, chopped

½ cup sun-dried tomatoes packed in herbed oil, slivered, plus ½ cup of the oil

2 cups loosely packed finely slivered basil leaves

3 to 4 teaspoons Dijon mustard

2 to 3 tablespoons red wine vinegar

1 cup pine nuts, toasted (see page 86)

Salt and freshly ground black pepper, to taste

Pasta Salads

WHEN MAKING pasta for salad it's important that the pasta be a little underdone. Pasta of any kind plumps up and softens when it's cooled and dressed; slightly undercooking it prior to dressing ensures it will maintain the perfect al dente texture.

Curried Lima Bean and Rice Salad with Tempeh

SERVES 4 TO 6

1 cup plain nonfat or soy yogurt

2 tablespoons minced garlic

3 teaspoons extra virgin oil

1 cup basmati rice

1½ teaspoons curry powder

1 teaspoon turmeric

1 teaspoon fine sea salt

One 10-ounce package frozen lima beans

¼ cup chopped scallions

Topping

2 to 3 tablespoons canola or other vegetable oil

Half 8-ounce package tempeh, cut into ½-inch cubes

1½ cups diced tomatoes

½ cup diced onion

⅓ cup chopped cilantro

1 tablespoon seeded and minced jalapeño pepper

I OFTEN REACH *for lima beans, also called* butter beans, *when a recipe asks for fava beans. The flavors and textures are quite similar, but fava beans, though prominent in Italian markets, are typically harder to find. Here, lima beans combined with a tempeh-tomato topping makes a salad that is a light but substantial supper. You'll have some of the garlicky dressing left over—it makes a wonderful condiment for potatoes, vegetables, or pita crisps and stores well in the fridge for up to a week.*

1. Mix the yogurt and 1 tablespoon of the garlic in a small bowl. Cover and refrigerate for 1 hour.

2. Heat 1 teaspoon of the olive oil in heavy medium saucepan over medium heat. Add the rice and stir to coat with the oil, 2 minutes. Stir in the curry powder, turmeric, and remaining 1 tablespoon garlic and cook for 1 minute. Add 2 cups water and the salt and bring to boil. Add the frozen lima beans and reduce the heat to medium-low. Cover and simmer until the rice is tender and water is absorbed, about 15 minutes. Transfer the bean-rice mixture to a large bowl and let cool slightly. Stir in the remaining 2 teaspoons olive oil and season with salt and pepper.

3. Meanwhile, make the topping: Heat a shallow skillet over medium heat and add 2 tablespoons vegetable oil. Add the tempeh and cook, turning, until golden and crispy, 5 to 7 minutes. Add additional oil if the mixture becomes too dry. Drain the tempeh on paper towels for about 5 minutes. In a small bowl combine the tempeh, tomato, onion, cilantro, and jalapeño. Spoon the tempeh topping over the rice and garnish with ¼ cup of the yogurt mixture and the scallions. Serve at room temperature.

Blue Waldorf Salad

DIDI EMMONS CREATED *this new classic version of a favorite salad for my show's third season. Waldorf salad traditionally includes a lot of mayonnaise to hold it together, but this version is lighter—and has a sprinkling of blue cheese. It's perfect for fall, when the apples are local, crisp, and tart. Prepare the salad components, except the apple, up to 24 hours ahead of time, but combine everything just before serving. Store the dressing in a jar with a lid in the fridge, and store the vegetables in a separate container.*

1. Stir together the lemon juice, olive oil, and honey in a small bowl and mix well. In a large bowl, combine the apple, celery, walnuts, and raisins. Toss the salad with the dressing, then add the blue cheese, onion, and cilantro. Toss again to combine. Serve immediately.

2 tablespoons lemon juice

3 tablespoons extra virgin olive oil

1 tablespoon honey

1 large Fuji or Gala apple, cored and chopped into ¼-inch dice

4 stalks celery, chopped

1 cup walnuts, toasted (see page 86) and coarsely chopped

⅓ cup yellow raisins, soaked in hot water for 10 minutes and drained

3 ounces crumbly blue cheese, such as Great Hill or Maytag

1 small red onion, chopped

1 bunch cilantro or parsley, chopped

Spicy Chickpea Salad

SERVES 2 TO 4

One 15½-ounce can chickpeas, drained and rinsed

2 tablespoons finely chopped red onion

½ cup red or yellow chopped bell pepper (mix red and yellow for added color)

¼ cup pine nuts, toasted (see page 86)

¼ cup basil, cut into ribbons

2 tablespoons extra virgin olive oil

1 tablespoon lemon juice

1 teaspoon chili paste

Salt and freshly ground black pepper, to taste

BECAUSE CHICKPEAS ARE *so versatile, satisfying, and healthy, I always keep a few cans in my pantry. When we finished shooting our second season of the show, at the last minute we realized that we were short one segment. Out came the chickpeas and this recipe was born; its simplicity born of necessity has made it a personal favorite. With their firm and creamy texture, chickpeas really shine alongside the crispy peppers, fragrant basil, and spicy chili paste. Pine nuts, another pantry staple, are toasted, and add a soft buttery taste. Enjoy the salad with a hearty slice of bread to sop up the juices.*

1. In a medium bowl, combine the chickpeas, onion, bell pepper, pine nuts, and basil. In a small bowl, whisk together the oil, lemon juice and chili paste until emulsified. Add the dressing to the chickpea mixture and toss well to combine. Season with salt and pepper and serve.

Toasted Sesame Noodle Salad

SERVES 4 TO 6

PERFECT FOR A *party, picnic, or as an accompaniment to sandwiches or burgers, this tangy pasta salad is also substantial enough to qualify as a main dish. Use whole wheat linguine as I do, or substitute Asian soba noodles. Sometimes I'll add additional vegetables, like cherry tomatoes, shelled edamame beans, roasted sweet potatoes, green beans, or peas. Really any vegetable you like works, which is why I rely on this recipe so often. Make it a few hours in advance of serving to ensure that the flavors marry. A sprinkle of crispy fried tofu adds protein and texture. Leftover dressing is terrific on green salads and sautéed hearty greens, or makes a delicious dipping sauce for wontons.*

1. Bring a large pot of salted water to boil. Add the pasta and cook following package instructions until al dente.

2. Meanwhile, combine the tamari, chili sauce, ginger, sesame oil, and garlic in a small bowl. Mix well or place in a jar and shake to blend.

3. Drain the pasta and combine with the dressing in a large bowl. You may not use all the dressing, taste as you go along. Add the scallions, cilantro, and sesame seeds and toss again. Serve at room temperature. Leftover dressing may be stored in the refrigerator for up to 2 weeks.

1 pound organic whole wheat linguine or soba noodles

½ cup tamari soy sauce

¼ cup sweet chili sauce

2 teaspoons finely grated ginger

⅓ cup toasted sesame oil

1½ tablespoons minced garlic

4 scallions, white and green parts, chopped

½ to ¾ cups chopped cilantro

3 tablespoons toasted sesame seeds, white or black or both

Soba

SOBA IS a popular Asian noodle made from buckwheat. Available in most supermarkets, soba is delicious in cold salads or hot soups. To maintain its pleasant texture, be sure not to overcook it. After boiling in water, drain well, but don't rinse. Use it as you would linguine.

Red Bliss Potato Salad

3 pounds small
Red Bliss potatoes

Fine sea salt and freshly
ground black pepper, to taste

1 cup regular or vegan
mayonnaise

¼ cup buttermilk, or an
additional ¼ cup vegan
mayonnaise mixed with 1
teaspoon lemon juice

2 tablespoons Dijon mustard

2 teaspoons organic
cane sugar

1 tablespoon cider vinegar

½ cup chopped dill

1 crisp apple, any variety,
cored and diced

½ to ¾ cup chopped celery

½ cup chopped yellow
or red onion

THE SECRET TO *great potato salad is to not overcook the potatoes; they should have a firm bite. To improve the flavor, let the vegetables and creamy dressing meld together for a few hours or even overnight before serving. Serve with spicy dishes such Barbequed Tempeh (page 159) or as an accompaniment to a sandwich of Marinated Portebello Mushrooms (page 202) on a toasted kaiser roll.*

1. Place the potatoes and 1 tablespoon of salt in a large pot of water. Bring the water to a boil, reduce the heat, and simmer for 15 to 20 minutes, until the potatoes are just tender when pierced with a knife. Drain the potatoes in a colander, then set the colander with the potatoes over the empty pot or in the sink.

2. In a small bowl, blend the mayonnaise, buttermilk, mustard, sugar, vinegar, dill, salt, and pepper. When the potatoes are still warm but cool enough to handle, pull the peels off, if desired, and cut into quarters or in half, depending on their size. Place the warm potatoes in a large bowl and add the dressing, apple, celery, onion, salt, and pepper. Toss well. Cover and refrigerate for 1 to 2 hours. Serve cold or at room temperature. Store in a covered container in the fridge for up to 3 days.

Panzanella

ONLY THE ITALIANS *could turn stale bread into something this wonderful; it's one of the best examples of why I love Mediterranean cooking. For a true Tuscan panzanella, the bread must be unsalted and very dry, but bread with salt works just fine. The lovely red, white, and green bread salad can be savored within minutes of being dressed. I prefer the tame, softer flavor of red onions, but white or yellow will do just as well. This is another recipe best made when tomatoes are at their peak.*

1. Break the bread into pieces and place in a bowl. Add 1 cup warm water and soak the bread for 3 to 5 minutes, until softened. Squeeze the bread dry using your hands and crumble into a serving bowl. Arrange the tomatoes, garlic, onion, and basil over the top of the bread. In a separate small bowl, combine the olive oil, vinegar, salt, and pepper. Whisk and pour over the salad. Season with additional salt and pepper if desired, and serve immediately.

One 8-ounce loaf very dry unsalted Italian bread

3 to 4 large ripe tomatoes, seeded and cut into cubes or wedges

3 to 4 garlic cloves, minced

1 medium red onion, thinly sliced

⅓ to ½ cup coarsely chopped basil

⅓ cup extra virgin olive oil

2 tablespoons red wine vinegar

¼ teaspoon fine sea salt, or more to taste

¼ teaspoon freshly ground black pepper, or more to taste

Herbed Garlic Balsamic Vinaigrette

MAKES ¾ CUP

1 to 2 garlic cloves, crushed, or 4 cloves Roasted Garlic (below) or Garlic Confit (page 62)

Fine sea salt

2 tablespoons balsamic vinegar

1 tablespoon lemon juice

2 to 3 tablespoons chopped herbs like basil, cilantro, mint, or parsley

4 to 5 turns of freshly ground black pepper

½ cup extra virgin olive oil

I BEGAN MAKING *this dressing after my friend Cathi DiCocco suggested adding some mellow roasted garlic to my favorite herbed vinaigrette. Alternatively, fresh raw garlic adds a delicious crisp bite to the dressing, so if I'm in the mood for that, I'll use half the amount of roasted garlic. Great on salads, tempeh, tofu, or vegetables, this dressing can also be used to "dress up" a simple pasta salad. Add some grated cheese, red pepper flakes, mustard, or even chopped shallots in place of half the garlic to create a dressing that suits you.*

1. Place the garlic in a small bowl and mix it with ¼ teaspoon salt, creating a paste. Add the vinegar, lemon juice, herbs, pepper, and salt to taste. Slowly whisk in the oil until the dressing is well blended.

2. Stored in a jar in the refrigerator, the dressing will keep for a few weeks. The recipe doubles quite well.

Roasted Garlic

ROASTING BRINGS out garlic's inherent sweetness and cuts its astringent bite. I put aside the aromatic herbs of Garlic Confit (page 62) for this recipe and enjoy the pure flavor of simple roasted garlic with a drizzle of olive oil. I spread mashed roasted garlic on toasted baguette rounds and add to dressings, sauces, soups, and just about anything where a sweet garlic undertone is desired. I like to roast three to four entire heads at a time.

Preheat the oven to 400°F. Tear off a piece of foil about 15 inches long and then cut or tear into four individual squares. Peel away the papery outer layers of 4 heads of garlic, leaving the bulbs and remaining skin intact. With a knife, trim ¼ inch from the tops of the bulbs (the pointed ends), just exposing the individual cloves. Reserve these trimmed ends for adding to stock. Set each bulb in the center of a square of foil, drizzle about a teaspoon of olive oil over each exposed bulb, rubbing it gently to be sure to evenly coat the head of garlic. Sprinkle with a little kosher salt and wrap the bulbs in the foil.

Set the bulbs in a baking dish and roast for 35 to 40 minutes, until the garlic feels soft when pressed. Let the garlic cool until you can comfortably handle. Using a knife, a small fork, or your fingers, ease the garlic out of the skin. Store in a small jar or container in the fridge for up to 2 weeks.

Tarragon Vinaigrette

MAKES ½ CUP

INFUSED WITH HINTS *of anise, this all-purpose dressing can be paired with any salad, bean dish, or, my favorite, over sautéed mushrooms on a bed of mixed greens, as tarragon and mushrooms complement each other well.*

1. In a small bowl, mix together the vinegar, mustard, shallot, salt, and pepper. Whisk in the oil in a thin stream until the dressing is nicely emulsified. Add the tarragon and whisk again. Store in a lidded container or jar in the fridge for up to 2 weeks. Give a good shake before serving.

¼ cup sherry vinegar

1½ teaspoons Dijon mustard

1 tablespoon finely minced shallot

1½ teaspoons fine sea salt

Scant 1 teaspoon freshly ground black pepper

¼ cup extra virgin olive oil

2 tablespoons finely minced tarragon

Mustard-Lemon Dressing

MAKES 1 CUP

DELICIOUS ON ROBUST *earthy greens, cauliflower, beans and bean salad, and potato salad, this piquant dressing also makes a delightful sandwich dressing. Add a bit of fresh yogurt for a creamy variation.*

1. In a small bowl, combine the lemon juice, mustard, salt, pepper, and cilantro if using. With a small salad whisk, whisk in the oil until nicely emulsified. The dressing can be stored in a container in the fridge for up to 2 weeks.

⅓ cup lemon juice

2 tablespoons Dijon mustard

1 teaspoon fine sea salt

1 teaspoon freshly ground black pepper

1 tablespoon chopped cilantro (optional)

⅔ cup extra virgin olive oil

Lemon-Honey Dressing

MAKES ½ CUP

¼ cup lemon juice

2 tablespoons organic honey, Italian or Greek

2 tablespoons extra virgin olive oil

HERE IS A *simple all-purpose dressing that works especially well with salads that contain fruit, avocado, or delicate peppery greens.*

1. Combine the juice and honey in a bowl. Stir to dissolve the honey, and then whisk in the oil. Store any leftover dressing in the refrigerator in a jar for up to 2 weeks. Give a good shake before using.

Orange, Jalapeño, and Cilantro Dressing

MAKES 1 CUP

1 cup fresh orange juice

2 tablespoons canola or other vegetable oil

2 jalapeño peppers, seeded and chopped

6 garlic cloves, chopped

2 teaspoons black peppercorns

1 cup coarsely chopped cilantro leaves and stems

Zest of 1 lime

Salt, to taste

THIS DRESSING/MARINADE *is as light as it is versatile. Use it as a sauce on cooked tofu or tempeh, and as a dressing for roasted sweet potatoes, sandwiches or burgers, white beans and onions, orzo, rice, and even citrus salad. It's especially good on tacos. This can be spicy, so adjust the jalapeño to suit your taste.*

1. Combine ¾ cup of the juice, the oil, jalapeños, garlic, and peppercorns in a blender and blend until the peppercorns are pulverized. Add the remaining ¼ cup juice, the cilantro, and lime zest. Process until smooth. Season with salt. Use immediately or store in the fridge for up to a week.

Chipotle Dressing

FROM CAFE DICOCOA in Bethel, Maine, this dressing gives potatoes, beans, and just about any vegetable a spicy hit. Chipotle chiles are simply smoked jalapeño peppers. They are often sold packed in a deep red-brown piquant sauce called adobo, which is made from herbs, ground chiles, and vinegar. Leftover adobo sauce from the chipotles makes a spicy addition to barbeque sauces, marinades, or soups.

1. Combine the lime juice, sweet chili sauce, chiles, and garlic in a blender and begin processing. Slowly add the oil until creamy and emulsified. Use immediately or store in a container in the fridge up to 2 months.

¾ cup fresh lime juice (about 6 limes)

¼ cup Sweet Chili Dipping Sauce (page 49) or prepared Thai sweet chili sauce

2 canned chipotle chiles

2 garlic cloves

1 cup canola or other vegetable oil

Tofu-Lime Dressing

3 garlic cloves, peeled

2 tablespoons coarsely chopped ginger

⅓ cup lime juice (about 3 limes)

8 ounces silken tofu

2 to 3 tablespoons organic cane sugar

¾ cup canola or other vegetable oil

Salt and freshly ground black pepper, to taste

SMOOTH AS SILK, *this dressing—courtesy of Chef Didi Emmons—gets its zip from fresh ginger, garlic, and lime juice. Try it over thinly sliced red cabbage, potatoes, red onion, grated carrot, or shelled edamame.*

1. Combine the garlic and ginger in a food processor and pulse until finely chopped. With the machine running, add the lime juice, tofu, and sugar, followed by the oil poured in a slow steady stream. Season with salt and pepper to taste. Transfer to a container and chill until ready to use. The dressing keeps for up to a week, covered, in the fridge.

Lime-Ginger Dressing

3½ tablespoons finely minced ginger

¼ cup fresh lime juice (about 1-2 limes)

1 tablespoon light brown sugar

2 tablespoons kosher salt, or to taste

Good squeeze of hot sauce (optional)

LIGHT AND DELICIOUS, *this dressing, courtesy of Didi Emmons, goes with her Cabbage Slaw with Tomatoes and Ginger (page 79) or on any salad of your choice. Tart and fat-free, I serve it over a salad of spinach, cherry tomatoes, and chopped nuts.*

1. Combine all the ingredients in a bowl and blend well with a fork or whisk. Be sure the sugar is dissolved before serving. Store in a jar or lidded container in the fridge for up to a week.

Creamy Curry Dressing

MAKES 1½ CUPS

THIS IS A *creamy, tart dressing for roasted beets, assorted vegetables, or even with a salad. If you like the flavor of cilantro, enhance it by adding a few inches of the stems—which are loaded with sweet flavor—with the other ingredients.*

1. Mix the lemon juice, yogurt, mayonnaise, curry powder, and garlic in a bowl. When everything is well combined, whisk in the oil until emulsified. Stir in the cilantro. Store in a container in the fridge for up to a week.

3 tablespoons lemon juice

2 tablespoons plain yogurt

2 tablespoons mayonnaise

4 teaspoons Madras curry powder

2 garlic cloves, crushed

10 tablespoons extra virgin olive oil

1/4 cup chopped cilantro

Curry Powder

CURRY POWDER is a turmeric-based blend of as few as five and up to twenty savory spices, which may include curry leaves, cumin, coriander, fenugreek, chiles, cinnamon, nutmeg, pepper, and cloves. Curry spice blends have a deep golden color and range in flavor from mild to hot. There are many unique blends and they vary greatly from region to region in India. My favorite is the mild, all-purpose Madras curry powder. The warm intensity of any curry spice is at its finest when added at the beginning of a recipe or to hot oil, which releases its incredible aromas. Curry powders may also be used in moderation to liven up toasted grains or creamy dressings. Garam masala, a spice blend without turmeric, is a good substitute for curry powder. To my palate, it's a bit spicier and I think best when added near the end of cooking. All are available in supermarkets or specialty food shops and will store well in airtight containers for up to 2 years.

Tahini Dressing

MAKES 1 CUP

⅓ cup tahini, well mixed

3 garlic cloves, chopped

¼ cup lemon juice

½ to ¾ teaspoon fine sea salt

WITH ITS BUTTERY, *toasted sesame flavor, this basic all-purpose tahini dressing is good on sandwiches, Eggplant Meatballs (page 214), Baked Tofu Meatballs (page 148), salads, and vegetables. Sometimes I add more lemon or garlic for a bit of kick. You can also add a little honey or sugar for a sweeter taste.*

1. Be sure the tahini is mixed and as smooth as possible. Place all the ingredients in a food processor or blender and blend with ¼ cup warm water until smooth and creamy.

Tahini

TAHINI IS a smooth paste made from ground hulled or unhulled sesame seeds. I purchase tahini made from hulled seeds since the unhulled variety has a distinctly bitter flavor. Widely available in most grocery stores or ethnic markets, it's typically sold in jars, plastic tubs, or cans. Tahini will often separate from the oil and requires mixing or blending before using in dips, sauces, and spreads. Stored in the refrigerator, tahini will keep for up to a year or more.

SOUPS AND STEWS

I GREW UP eating soup or stew a few times a week: hearty stews packed with rustic cut vegetables and served with potatoes or rice; nourishing soups simmered with beans, greens, and lentils, some delicately pureed, others based on rich stock. Despite their differences, they were all economical, fragrant, and comforting. No doubt because of this abundant lineage, they were some of the first foods I learned to cook. When I started compiling recipes for my television show, I assumed pasta dishes would far outnumber soups, but it was the other way around. I attribute that to the challenge of getting wider varieties of vegetables into my family's meals; something a pot of aromatic soup or a thick stew easily accomplished. Don't make your soups and stews as an afterthought, preparing them only to use up vegetables on the verge of mummification. Plan ahead, shop with quality in mind, and savor slow-cooked food at its best.

Vegetable Stock

8 celery stalks

2 medium carrots

2 medium onions, quartered

1 daikon radish
(about ½ pound)

1 bunch scallions
or 1 large leek

4 dried shiitake mushrooms

Few sprigs parsley or cilantro

3 garlic cloves

2 bay leaves

20 peppercorns

Kosher salt

Homemade stock is one of the easiest and most economical things to make, yet so few people take the time. A good stock is essential for great soup and makes a flavorful base for vegetarian gravy. I save the washed vegetable tops and trimmings and then add them to the basic ingredients for extra flavorful stock. Depending on what the stock will be used for, you can also add thyme, fresh fennel, or tomatoes.

For a deeper, richer stock, first roast the vegetables in a 375°F oven for 40 minutes. When done, add ½ cup water to the pan and stir to loosen the caramelized bits at the bottom of the pan. Let the vegetables rest for 5 minutes before transferring to a stockpot with the rest of the water and herbs. Cook as instructed below. However you choose to prepare it, this stock keeps in the fridge for a week. For longer storage, pour stock into ice cube trays (for 2-tablespoon portions) or in individual lidded containers—either way it will keep frozen for up to 3 months.

1. Place the celery, carrots, onions, daikon, scallions, mushrooms, parsley, garlic, bay leaves, peppercorns, and salt in a 6-quart stockpot. Add 3 quarts cold water and bring to a boil. Reduce the heat and simmer, covered, for 45 minutes to 1 hour. Let cool for about 30 minutes. Strain through a fine mesh strainer or cheesecloth. The stock should be very clear.

Using Store-Bought Broth

IF YOU are using store-bought canned vegetable broth instead of homemade stock in these recipes, dilute it a bit as it is very concentrated. This holds true for broth made with bouillon as well. Watch the salt.

Porcini Stock

DRIED PORCINI MUSHROOMS *are one of the most intensely flavorful ingredients available to vegetarian cooks. These woodsy mushrooms are a wonderful addition to many dishes, and can be made into an intense porcini stock—one that rivals any dark beef stock as a foundation for gravy to ladle over mashed potatoes or polenta.*

Make this at least a day in advance since it should rest overnight to bring out the strong flavors. When I use the stock, I remove the porcinis, chop or puree them, and add them to gravy; the meaty mushrooms and stock can also add another layer of flavor to sauces, soups, or stews. I often freeze this in 2-cup portions, so it's available at a moment's notice.

1 ounce dried porcini, picked over to remove stones or bits of wood

3 bay leaves

¼ cup Madeira wine

2 tablespoons dark Chinese soy sauce

1 teaspoon kosher salt

1. Place the mushrooms in a 3½-quart or larger stockpot and cover with 8 cups warm water. Add the bay leaves, Madeira, soy sauce, and salt and gently bring to a simmer. Reduce the heat to very low and cook for 2 hours. Let the stock cool in the pot overnight.

2. The next day, the mushrooms will have settled to the bottom of the pot. Divide the stock and mushrooms and freeze in 4 freezer-safe storage bowls, or use at once.

Porcini Gravy

■ **MAKES 3 CUPS**

I ALWAYS HAVE *a box of cornstarch on hand, in part because of how easily it creates a light, smooth, silky sauce in an instant. Because this gravy is not bound as tightly as a flour-based sauce, it's best used immediately.*

3 cups Porcini Stock
2 tablespoons cornstarch blended with 2 tablespoons cold water

1. Bring the stock to a low boil in a saucepan. Reduce the heat and slowly whisk in the cornstarch mixture. The gravy will immediately begin thickening. Continue stirring and add just enough of the cornstarch mixture until you reach the desired consistency. The gravy should be glossy and smooth. If it becomes too thick, add additional stock or water, a few tablespoons at a time. Serve immediately.

Spinach and Tofu Soup

2 tablespoons canola
or other vegetable oil

8 ounces fresh spinach,
washed, stems removed,
dried, and chopped

1 teaspoon sea salt

3 to 4 ounces firm tofu, cut
into small dice

2 tablespoons light soy sauce,
or more to taste

1 teaspoon toasted
sesame oil

Freshly ground
black pepper, to taste

I THROW TOGETHER *this quick-and-easy soup when I'm craving a clear, light, uncluttered soup. It's mellow, so if you want to perk things up a bit, add a dash of Thai hot chile pepper. Serve in small cups accompanied by some Marvelous Meaty Wontons (page 51) and Sweet Chili Dipping Sauce (page 49).*

1. Heat the oil in a saucepan over medium heat. After a minute, add the spinach and stir-fry until soft. Add the salt and 2½ cups water. Bring to a boil, reduce the heat, and add the tofu and soy sauce. Cook for 2 to 5 minutes. Remove from the heat, stir in the sesame oil, season with more salt and black pepper, and serve hot.

Miso Soup

6 cups Vegetable Stock
(page 106) or water

7 ounces red miso

4 ounces tofu (firm, medium,
or soft), cut into
¼- or ½-inch dice

2 or 3 drops toasted
sesame oil

1 scallion, thinly sliced
into rings

TRY MISO SOUP *as a pick-me-up in place of a cup of tea, especially in the middle of a dreary day. Made from fermented soybeans, miso imparts a pleasant salty and savory flavor to soups, stocks, and vegetable dishes. Although I often serve miso soup before a meal or as a quick lunch soup accompanied by a sandwich, my favorite way to enjoy it is to ladle into a cup so I can sip it. The sesame oil adds a toasty, nutty flavor but may be omitted if desired. For added nutrition and color, garnish with some chopped fresh spinach.*

1. Bring the water or stock to a boil in a small heavy pot and reduce to a simmer. Whisk in the miso. When the miso is blended, almost thickening a little, remove from the heat and add the tofu and sesame oil. Let the soup rest a minute or two. Serve in small cups, garnished with scallion.

Hot and Sour Soup

TRADITIONALLY PREPARED WITH *beef or pork, you won't miss either one in this vegetarian hot and sour soup. Reconstituted dry shiitakes lend a more concentrated mushroom flavor than fresh, but fresh may be substituted. Sambal oelek is a favorite red pepper sauce, but the same amount of crushed red pepper flakes or Tabasco may be substituted. In keeping with the Asian theme, I serve the soup piping hot, garnished with chopped scallions and accompanied by Celebration Potstickers (page 48) or Marvelous Meaty Wontons (page 51).*

1. Bring the stock to a boil in a large pot and reduce to a simmer. Add the tofu, mushrooms, water chestnuts, bamboo shoots, and chile and simmer for about 5 minutes. Add the vinegar, soy sauce, and cornstarch. Raise the heat to a boil; the soup will begin thickening. Stir in the scallions, oil, and sambal oelek. Cook for an additional 5 minutes. Remove from the heat, add the cilantro, season with salt and pepper, and serve.

6 cups Vegetable Stock (page 106)

6 ounces firm tofu, cut into 2-inch strips

8 dried shiitake mushrooms, reconstituted in hot water for about 15 minutes, drained, stems removed, cut into quarters

Half 4-ounce can sliced water chestnuts, drained

One 8-ounce can bamboo shoots, drained and cut into matchsticks

1 Thai red chile or jalapeño pepper, diced

2/3 cups unseasoned rice vinegar

3 tablespoons light soy sauce

3 tablespoons cornstarch dissolved in 3 tablespoons water

6 to 7 scallions, white and green parts, finely chopped

1½ tablespoons toasted sesame oil

1 to 2 tablespoons sambal oelek, to taste

1 to 1½ cups chopped cilantro

Salt and freshly ground black pepper, to taste

Cream of Green Pea Soup
with Mint

One 16-ounce package frozen peas or 1 pound fresh peas

2 to 3 cups Vegetable Stock (page 106) or water, or 1 vegetable bouillon cube dissolved in 2 cups water

¼ cup milk or plain soy coffee creamer (optional)

Salt and freshly ground black pepper, to taste

¼ cup fresh chopped mint

MY FAVORITE TIME *to make pea soup is in the summer when peas are at their peak of freshness in Maine. Frozen petit peas also work well, and because they're available year-round, economical, and retain their snappy texture and sweet flavor, I can make this soup in less than half an hour any day of the year. For a more formal presentation, I add milk. Accompany this with robust Gorgonzola and Pear Bruschetta (page 58) or crispy Garlic Toasts (page 53).*

1. Combine the peas and stock in a medium saucepan. Bring to a boil, reduce the heat, and simmer for 15 minutes. Remove from the heat and let cool for 10 minutes. Transfer to a blender in small batches and blend until smooth and creamy (or use an immersion blender—you can process the soup in the pan immediately). If desired, add milk while blending. Season with salt and pepper, top with fresh mint, and serve hot.

Chilled Avocado Soup

COOL AND CREAMY, *this chilled soup is perfect for a light summer supper or Sunday brunch. Avocados are extremely rich in vitamins C and E and contain a significant amount of monounsaturated fats that are reputed to have a beneficial effect in lowering blood cholesterol. I adore the soft buttery flavor and texture of avocado and add it often to my salads, sandwiches, and salsas. This recipe came to me by way of a friend in California where avocados are in abundance year-round.*

1. Combine half the stock, the avocado, garlic, lime juice, yogurt, and pepper paste (if using) in a blender and blend until smooth. Add the remaining stock and blend for about a minute. Season with salt and pepper. Chill the soup for 1 hour or longer before serving. Garnish each serving with cilantro, tomato, scallion, a sprinkle of cumin, and a little dollop of sour cream.

3½ cups Vegetable Stock (page 106)

2 to 3 ripe avocados, halved, pitted, flesh scooped out, and cut into cubes

2 garlic cloves, crushed with a pinch of kosher salt

1 tablespoon fresh lime juice

3 tablespoons plain yogurt (optional)

1 teaspoon hot red pepper paste (optional)

Salt and freshly ground black pepper, to taste

2 tablespoons cilantro, chopped but not minced (optional)

1 fresh tomato, seeded and chopped

1 scallion, green part only, cut into long thin strips

Ground cumin

Sour cream

Celeriac, Garlic, and Ginger Soup

SERVES 4

1 medium celeriac bulb, peeled and cut into 1-inch dice

1 large carrot, peeled and cut into 1-inch dice

1 medium potato, any variety, peeled and cut into 1-inch dice

12 to 15 garlic cloves, peeled and left whole

2-inch piece ginger, cut into thirds

6 cups Vegetable Stock (page 106)

Salt, to taste

½ cup milk, cream, or soy milk (optional)

Chopped parsley or cilantro

Freshly ground black pepper, to taste

WHETHER SERVED COOKED *or raw, celeriac (or celery root) imparts a delicate hint of celery flavor laced with mild anise undertones. It's delicious roasted, boiled, and mashed with a little butter and salt; fried; or slivered raw into salads. And, in soups. The amount of garlic in this recipe may seem like a lot, but with cooking, garlic becomes almost sweet. Loaded with vitamin C, this nutritious soup is especially satisfying and uplifting when you're feeling under the weather. Serve with a sprinkling of chopped parsley or cilantro and a drizzle of fruity olive oil. If you have some on hand, a good-quality, herb-infused oil adds a nice flavor dimension.*

1. Combine the celeriac, carrot, potato, garlic, and ginger in a 3-quart saucepan. Cover with the stock, add a sprinkle of salt, and bring to a boil. Reduce the heat and simmer for about 35 minutes, until all the vegetables are soft when pierced with a fork. Let cool for 10 minutes.

2. Transfer the soup to a blender and puree for 2 minutes, just until the soup is smooth and creamy. (Or blend with an immersion blender.) If the soup becomes too thick, add water, about ½ cup at a time. Return the pureed soup to the pot and stir in the cream if using. Season with salt and pepper, garnish with fresh parsley, and serve hot.

Parsnip-Carrot Ginger Soup

SERVES 2 TO 4

COOL-WEATHER PARSNIPS *are among my favorite root vegetables. Available in farmers' markets, they are best after the first frost when their otherwise starchy, potato-like flesh becomes sweet, mellow, and creamy. They're delicious roasted, pureed, and mashed with just a hint of butter—and in this soup where their flavor is enhanced by the peppery heat of fresh ginger. Garnish simply with chopped scallions or chives and serve with Marvelous Meaty Wontons (page 51)*

1. Heat the butter in a saucepan over medium heat until it begins to foam. Add the ginger and gently sauté for a minute or two to release its aroma. Reserve some of the scallions for garnish. Add the remaining scallions, the parsnips, carrots, and stock to the soup. Bring to a boil, reduce the heat, and simmer for 15 to 20 minutes, just until the parsnips and carrots are fork tender. Let cool for 10 minutes.

2. Transfer the soup to a blender and blend until smooth and creamy (or use an immersion blender). Return the soup to the pot and reheat for a minute or two. Season with salt and pepper, garnish with the reserved scallions, and serve.

1 tablespoon unsalted butter or soy margarine

3-inch piece ginger, peeled and thinly sliced

1 bunch scallions (about 6), coarsely chopped

1 pound parsnips, sliced into ½-inch pieces

2 medium carrots, sliced into ½-inch pieces

3½ cups Vegetable Stock (page 106)

Salt and freshly ground black pepper, to taste

Fresh Ginger

NEVER SUBSTITUTE dried powdered ginger when fresh is called for. When buying fresh ginger, try to buy only what you need. Look for firm ginger with taut smooth skin. If ginger is very fresh, you can even skip the peeling process.

Roasted Pumpkin Bisque

SERVES 4

One 2-pound sugar pumpkin

2 tablespoons extra virgin olive oil

1 large yellow onion, diced

1 large carrot, diced

1 tablespoon minced fresh ginger

1 to 2 teaspoons rosemary leaves

Fine sea salt and freshly ground black pepper, to taste

4 cups Vegetable Stock (page 106)

2 teaspoons organic cane sugar or honey

½ to 1 cup 2% milk, light cream, or soy milk

¼ to ½ cup chopped chives

Sprinkle of nutmeg (optional)

FESTIVE AND COLORFUL, *this soup makes a perfect holiday meal; or on quieter occasions, a comforting winter supper served with hearty braised greens, a salad, or a sandwich. Use fresh ginger as it lends a peppery warmth that powdered simply can't deliver. Butternut, buttercup, or acorn squash can stand in remarkably well for the pumpkin. Garnish with chopped scallions and crisp croutons.*

1. Preheat the oven to 425°F. Cut the pumpkin in half across the equator, not stem to bottom. Remove the seeds and strings with a spoon. Place the pumpkin cut side down on a foil-lined baking sheet and roast until tender, about 40 minutes. Set it aside until cool enough to handle. Scoop out the pulp and place in a bowl; discard the shell.

2. Heat the olive oil in a 3- to 4-quart heavy pot over medium-high heat. Add the onion, carrot, ginger, and a sprinkle of salt. Sauté until the onion is translucent and the carrots begin to soften, about 10 minutes. Add the pumpkin, rosemary, and 2 teaspoons salt. Stir well and sauté for about 5 minutes. Add the stock and bring to a low boil. Reduce the heat and simmer for about 10 minutes, until the pumpkin is soft. Remove from the heat and stir in the sugar. Let cool 10 minutes.

3. Transfer the soup to a blender and blend, slowly adding the milk a little at a time. You may need to do this in two batches. Check the texture, which should be smooth and dense, you may not need to add the entire cup of milk, so do this to your taste. When the soup is whipped and creamy, return to the pot and heat through. Stir in the chives, season with black pepper, sprinkle with nutmeg if using, and serve hot.

Savory Croutons

■ **MAKES ABOUT 6 CUPS**

HOMEMADE CROUTONS ARE *a good way to use up day-old bread. This recipe calls for one medium loaf rustic bread, seasoned to taste: do as I do and sample the croutons as you go along and make them as savory or spicy as you wish. Croutons may be served immediately while warm or stored in an airtight container. They store well in any type of container, just be sure they are thoroughly cooled— usually a few hours—before packing.*

½ to 1 loaf day-old rustic loaf (boule, ciabatta, focaccia, or similar)
3 to 4 tablespoons extra virgin olive oil
1 to 2 teaspoons dried oregano
1 teaspoon fine sea salt or prepared garlic salt
½ teaspoon sweet paprika
Freshly ground black pepper, to taste

1. Preheat the oven to 350°F. Cut the bread into 1-inch cubes and place in a roomy bowl. Drizzle the olive oil over the cubes and add the oregano, salt, paprika, and black pepper. If you're using a half loaf of bread adjust the amount of oil and seasonings accordingly. Toss with your hands to be sure the cubes are evenly coated. Spread the croutons in a single layer on a baking sheet. Bake until golden and toasted, 10 to 12 minutes, depending on the moisture in bread.

Roasted Red Pepper and Leek Soup

SERVES 4

2 tablespoons extra
virgin olive oil

2 tablespoons unsalted butter
(or substitute additional 2
tablespoons olive oil)

4 cups chopped leeks,
white parts only

5 large red bell peppers,
roasted (see page 67),
seeded, and chopped;
or one 24-ounce jar
roasted red peppers

4 to 5 cups Vegetable Stock
(page 106) or water

½ to 1 cup coconut milk
(optional)

Salt and freshly ground
black pepper, to taste

I HAD AN *extremely rich version of this soup at a tavern while traveling up the coast of Maine. Its bright red color was absolutely stunning, and I enjoyed the combination of the sautéed sweet leeks and smoky roasted red pepper. But the whopping half pound of Brie and cup of heavy cream I could do without, so when I returned home I was determined to whip up a lighter version. When I am in the mood for extra creaminess, I add coconut milk. Garnish with fresh herbs such as parsley, cilantro, or tarragon and accompany with a side of crusty bread. For a bigger meal, serve with the Tempeh Club Sandwiches (page 197).*

1. Heat the oil and butter in a large pot over medium-high heat. Add the leeks and peppers and sauté until the leeks are soft, about 10 minutes. Add the stock and bring to a simmer. Reduce the heat and simmer for 30 minutes, or until the vegetables are very soft. Let cool 10 minutes. Transfer to a blender and puree until smooth. Return the soup to the pot and stir in the milk, if using. Season with salt and pepper, heat through, and serve hot.

Watercress-Potato Soup

VALUED AS A *cleansing tonic, the perky little watercress plant is packed with 15 essential vitamins and minerals and contains significant cancer-fighting properties. Usually served raw in a salads or sandwiches, watercress can also be eaten cooked; either way, it should be consumed a few times a week, especially during the cold and flu season. Watercress works well with salty and sweet foods and its peppery undertones are tamed when paired with bland foods like white beans, potatoes, mushrooms, tofu, and rice. For this soup, I blend watercress with creamy potatoes, onions, and water; the beautiful pale green emulsion almost qualifies as a tonic: its flavor is deep, bright, and earthy. Watercress stems are loaded with flavor and only the bottoms should be trimmed. A generous dose of fresh black pepper is a must. This soup is best served the same day it's prepared as reheated watercress takes on a slightly bitter flavor. I serve alongside colorful Tomato and Basil Bruschetta (page 56), Bean and Basil Bruschetta (page 57), or hot crispy Garlic Toasts (page 53).*

3 tablespoons unsalted butter or vegetable oil

1 medium yellow onion, diced

Salt, to taste

3 small potatoes, any variety, peeled and cut into rough 1-inch pieces

6 to 7 cups Vegetable Stock (page 106) or water

4 to 5 cups watercress (1 bunch)

Freshly ground black pepper, to taste

1. Heat the butter in a stockpot over medium heat. Add the onion and a sprinkle of salt. Cook, stirring often so the onion doesn't brown, until translucent, about 5 minutes. Add the potatoes and stir well to coat. Add the stock and half of the watercress, mix, and bring to a low boil. Cook until the potatoes are tender and almost breaking apart, about 20 minutes. Add the remaining watercress and cook for 5 minutes. The goal is to have the remaining cress retain its bright green color. Let cool 10 minutes.

2. In batches, transfer the soup to a blender and blend until smooth; the watercress should be reduced to flecks of green. Return the soup to the pot and season with salt and a generous grating of black pepper. Serve hot.

Jerusalem Artichoke and Potato Soup

2 tablespoons canola
or other vegetable oil

1 small onion,
coarsely chopped

3 small potatoes,
scrubbed and diced

1 pound Jerusalem artichokes,
scrubbed and cut into
2-inch dice

1 celery stalk, chopped

3 garlic cloves, minced

6 cups Vegetable Stock
(page 106) or water or a
combination of both

Salt and freshly ground
black pepper, to taste

JERUSALEM ARTICHOKES, SOMETIMES *called sunchokes, are small knobby root vegetables related to sunflowers. Despite their coarse appearance, these tubers have a mild flavor that becomes sweet and nutty when sautéed or roasted. If you're able to find organic chokes, the flavors are even richer. These little guys can be a bit of a pain to peel, so I find a good scrubbing with a stiff brush suffices. Accompany with Minty Tomato-Fennel Salad (page 80) and a side of crispy Garlic Toasts (page 53). If you have some on hand, a light drizzle of herb-infused oil makes a delightful finish.*

1. Heat the oil in a Dutch oven. Add the onion, potatoes, Jerusalem artichokes, and celery and sauté over a fairly high heat, stirring frequently, until lightly browned, 8 to 10 minutes. Add the garlic and sauté a few minutes more. Add the stock and bring to a boil. Reduce the heat and simmer for about 25 minutes, until the potatoes and chokes are tender. Remove from the heat and either mash the vegetables or let the soup cool 10 minutes and blend in a blender just until smooth, about a minute. Serve hot.

Potato-Leek Soup

SERVES 4

I AM QUITE *partial to the subtle onion flavor of leeks, and this soup is a wonderful way to showcase them. Although it is ready in less than an hour, it has a simmered-all-day flavor. Children enjoy the soup's mild flavor, especially when it's blended to a smooth consistency and topped with crispy oyster crackers. Be mindful not to overprocess in the blender since the potatoes will quickly transform from warm and creamy to starchy and sticky. Serve hot, garnished with chopped chives and a generous grinding of fresh black pepper.*

2 tablespoons canola or other vegetable oil

3 to 4 medium leeks, white parts only, washed and sliced into rings

Kosher salt

1 vegetable bouillon cube, crumbled, or 2 teaspoons powdered bouillon

1 large baking potato or 2 medium Yukon Gold potatoes, peeled and diced

½ cup milk or soy milk (optional)

Freshly ground black pepper, to taste

1. Heat the oil in a heavy stockpot over medium-high heat for 1 minute. Add the leeks and sauté 5 minutes. Add a sprinkle of salt and sauté for another 5 minutes, until the leeks begin to lightly brown and caramelize. Add the bouillon, sauté for a minute or so, then add 1 cup hot water. Continue cooking for 5 minutes. Add the potato and 4 cups hot water. Bring to a boil and reduce the heat to a simmer. Cover and cook until all the vegetables are soft and cooked through, about 25 minutes. Add the milk, if desired. Let cool 10 minutes.

2. Transfer the soup to a blender and blend to the desired consistency, adding a little water if necessary. (Or blend with an immersion blender.) Season with salt and pepper and serve hot.

Leeks

LOOK FOR leeks on the smallish side with their roots intact. Leeks are layered in such a way that soil and grit tends to hide inside the top layers of leaves making meticulous cleaning essential. Slice off the root and remove the tough, damaged outer leaves, and cut away most of the woody dark green tops, a little more than halfway. Save those for making vegetable stock. Slice the pale green parts of the leeks into thirds or quarters (the bottoms are closed so there's no hidden dirt there), slice in half lengthwise, and begin fanning out the tops, pointed downward under cold running water to wash away hidden dirt. Alternatively, I rinse the trimmed leeks, chop them to my desired cut, then place in a colander under running water and rinse well, tossing them around to ensure all the dirt washes away.

Black Bean and
Fire-Roasted Tomato Soup

¼ cup extra virgin olive oil

2 medium yellow onions, chopped

2 celery stalks, chopped

1 medium carrot, chopped

2 to 3 medium jalapeño peppers, seeded and diced

Kosher salt

Three 15½-ounce cans black beans, rinsed and drained

8 cups Vegetable Stock (page 106) or water or a combination of both (or less for a thicker soup)

One 15½-ounce can fire-roasted tomatoes, chopped

1 tablespoon ground cumin

2 to 3 tablespoons chipotle powder, to taste

1 cup chopped cilantro, plus more for garnish

Freshly ground black pepper, to taste

Dollop of sour cream, plain yogurt, or Tofu Sour Cream (page 147)

1 lime, cut into wedges

BLACK BEANS IMPART *a deep, velvety purple hue to this rich, smoky soup. In the summer months, I serve it topped with fresh tomatoes, sweet Vidalia onions, and creamy avocado. During the cooler months when I crave something more substantial, I reduce the liquid, leave the vegetables in larger pieces, and don't bothering pureeing—it's delicious served as a hearty stew spooned over rice or day-old corn bread. Garnish with cilantro, a dollop of the cream of your choice, and some lime wedges.*

1. Heat a large Dutch oven over medium heat and add the oil. After a minute, add the onions, celery, carrot, jalapeño peppers, and a bit of salt. Cook, stirring occasionally, until the vegetables are tender, about 10 minutes. Add the beans, stock, and tomatoes. Bring to a boil, reduce the heat, and simmer for about 1 hour.

2. Add the cumin and chipotle powder and continue cooking for 10 minutes. Using an immersion blender or potato masher, blend the soup until it is creamy but still retains some whole beans. Or transfer half the soup to a blender and blend for less than a minute, then return to the pot. This partial blending makes the soup thick and creamy. Stir up any beans that may have sunk to the bottom of the pot. Stir in the cilantro and season with salt and pepper. Top with cilantro and a dollop of cool sour cream and serve hot with lime wedges for squeezing.

Pasta e Fagioli

THE ITALIAN SIDE *of my family in America always prepared this thick dense soup with a rich tomato base. When I moved to Italy, I was struck by how different the Italian version was; they were utilizing the same basic ingredients, but in different increments at different stages, resulting in a lighter version. This is my mother's version, and my favorite. The thick soup of beans and pasta can be put together in minutes, making it perfect for a last minute supper or quick hearty lunch. I usually add short tubular pasta like ditalini, but if I don't have that on hand, broken spaghetti makes a respectable replacement. Serve with freshly grated Parmesan, a few turns of black pepper, and a drizzle of fruity olive oil.*

3 to 4 tablespoons extra virgin olive oil

1 medium yellow onion, finely diced

1 celery stalk, finely diced

1 carrot, finely diced

Salt, to taste

2 garlic cloves, chopped

1 teaspoon minced rosemary

3 sage leaves, minced

½ teaspoon dried oregano

One 15½-ounce can cannellini beans, drained and rinsed

1 cup canned San Marzano tomatoes, crushed

2 cups cooked pasta, such as ditalini

Freshly ground black pepper, to taste

1. Heat the oil in a stockpot or Dutch oven over medium-high heat. Add the onion, celery, carrot, and a pinch of salt and sauté for 5 minutes. Add the garlic and cook, stirring, until the carrots are firm-tender. Add the rosemary, sage, and oregano and blend. Add the beans, tomatoes, and 3 cups water. Bring to a boil and quickly lower to a simmer. Cook for 15 to 20 minutes, until the vegetables are tender. I use my immersion blender and partially puree the soup to add thickness and body, but this isn't necessary. Season with salt and pepper, spoon the hot soup over the cooked pasta, and serve hot.

Perking Up Canned Beans

TO LIVEN the taste of canned beans, bring 3 cups of water to a boil. Rinse the canned beans, add them to the boiling water, and boil for 3 to 4 minutes. Drain, rinse with cold water and use according to your recipe.

Potato-Chard Stew

3 tablespoons extra virgin olive oil

2 medium yellow onions, diced

Salt, to taste

1 medium sweet potato, cut into 2-inch pieces

1 medium Yukon Gold potato, cut into 2-inch pieces

½ red pepper, rib and seeds removed and cut into ½-inch dice

4 garlic cloves, finely chopped

1 tablespoon finely minced ginger

1 serrano pepper, minced with seeds

1 teaspoon ground coriander

½ teaspoon turmeric

¼ teaspoon cayenne pepper (optional)

One 14-ounce can full-fat coconut milk

1 bunch rainbow chard, washed, tough center ribs removed, leaves coarsely chopped

Juice and grated zest of 1 lime

¼ cup chopped cilantro or parsley (optional)

THIS CREAMY, COLORFUL *stew is the perfect winter dish: hearty potatoes and robust chard are bathed in sweet coconut milk along with some lemony coriander and warming serrano chiles. Serve this over a scoop of jasmine rice, quinoa, or millet. Finish with a squirt of fresh lime, a bit of grated zest, and, for added flavor and crunch, garnish with toasted sliced almonds. For this recipe, I use colorful mixed or rainbow chard, but any sturdy green may be substituted.*

1. Heat a large saucepan over medium-high heat and add the oil. Add the onions and sprinkle with a bit of salt to sweat them. Cook, stirring, until translucent but not brown, about 5 minutes. Add the sweet potato, Yukon Gold potato, red pepper, garlic, ginger, serrano pepper, coriander, turmeric, and cayenne (if using) and sauté for a minute or two. Add the coconut milk and 2¼ cups water and bring to a boil. Cover, reduce the heat, and simmer for 15 to 20 minutes. Add the Swiss chard and continue cooking for 5 to 8 minutes, just until the chard is tender but still has a little bite. Top with a squeeze of fresh lime, grated zest, and chopped cilantro (if using) and serve hot.

Lentil Stew

FRENCH PUY (PRONOUNCED *PWEE) lentils have a sweet earthy flavor, a pleasant firm texture, and a vibrant blue-green color that goes with sturdy greens like spinach and chard. I serve this stew on a blank canvas of creamy polenta, but any grain may be substituted. Try adding 2 cups of coarsely chopped cremini mushrooms to the onion/celery sauté just prior to adding the lentils; this lends more substance and depth as will broccoli florets or a splash of Marsala or Madeira wine or salty soy sauce. If you prefer a thinner consistency, stir in more stock.*

1. Heat a heavy stockpot or Dutch oven over medium-high heat and add the olive oil. After a minute, add the onion and celery. Sauté gently until translucent, 5 to 7 minutes. Add the garlic and sauté for a few minutes longer. Add the parsley and stir well to combine. Add the lentils and stock and bring to a boil. Immediately reduce the heat and gently simmer until the lentils are tender, about 30 minutes. Just before serving, season with salt and pepper, a good squeeze of lemon juice, and a grating of fresh lemon zest to taste. Spoon the stew over a bed of fresh spinach if you like, and top with chopped cilantro. Serve hot.

3 tablespoons extra virgin olive oil

1 large yellow onion, chopped

2 celery stalks, diced

2 garlic cloves, finely chopped

½ cup chopped parsley

1½ cups lentils (preferably Puy), rinsed and picked over for stones

4 cups Vegetable Stock (page 106) or water

1 lemon

2 to 4 cups baby spinach, torn (optional)

Chopped cilantro, mint, or additional parsley, to taste

Pumpkin-Bulgur Chili

SERVES 6

One 2-pound sugar pumpkin

1 cup medium grain bulgur wheat

1 tablespoon canola or other vegetable oil

1 large yellow onion, chopped

2 garlic cloves, minced

2 tablespoons chile powder

1 tablespoon curry powder

½ teaspoon ground cinnamon

6 plum tomatoes, chopped

½ cup green pumpkin seeds, toasted

½ cup chopped cilantro leaves and stems

Salt and freshly ground black pepper, to taste

THIS AUTUMNAL CHILI *was created by Didi Emmons for the third season of my television show. Didi never ceases to inspire and surprise me with her healthy, creative combinations of vegetables. The best part about her recipes is that every dish tastes so darn good. For this far-from-traditional chili, the pumpkin is roasted to bring out its sweetness. Chewy, fiber-rich bulgur mimics the texture of ground meat and the dish is finished off with protein-packed toasted pumpkin seeds. Aromatic and comforting, this is a meal, according to Didi, that both she and her cat, Henry, thoroughly enjoy.*

1. Preheat the oven to 375°F. Cut the pumpkin in half with a large knife, such as a cleaver. Scoop the seeds out with a large spoon. Place the pumpkin cut side down on a foil-lined baking sheet and bake until the flesh is soft, 50 to 60 minutes. Spoon out the flesh and set aside.

2. Meanwhile, in a medium bowl, combine the bulgur and 2 cups warm water. Let stand for 15 to 30 minutes.

3. In a large, heavy-bottomed saucepan or stockpot, heat the oil over medium heat. Add the onion, garlic, chile powder, curry powder, and cinnamon. Cook, stirring frequently, for about 5 minutes, or until the onion is soft.

4. Drain the bulgur, then scoop it into your hands and squeeze out the excess water. Add to the pot along with the tomatoes and 2 cups water. Bring to a simmer. Add the pumpkin flesh and cook for about 20 minutes, adding more water if necessary, ¼ cup at a time, to attain a chili-like consistency. Just before serving, add the pumpkin seeds and cilantro. Season with salt and pepper and serve.

BREADS AND PIZZA

Breads

FOR ME, BREAD is irresistible. I may try to fool myself by slicing my bread paper-thin, but I've learned that thirty thin slices do a half loaf make. We're extremely lucky to have a few outstanding organic and European-style bakeries here in southern Maine, and I frequent all of them. Sometimes I walk in with the intention of taking a few deep breaths of bread-scented air, but I always wind up with a warm loaf of something under my arm.

Because I'm busy and have great bread readily available to me from local bakeries, I don't bake a lot of bread, but I've included a few of my favorites. These breads are easy, reliable, and well worth the time taken to bake from scratch because they're so delicious. In just a few hours, you can make homemade focaccia gently bathed in a little olive oil with a sprinkling of coarse salt and fragrant rosemary. If you're in a hurry, mix up a quick corn bread that bakes to golden perfection in 30 minutes. The trick is getting the fresh, hot bread to the table before everyone indulges in countertop samples. When I bake bread at home, the warm, yeasty aroma permeates the house with comfort. When the kids come in, no matter what else is on the menu— it could be anything, literally—a mere whiff of the baking loaf transforms the mood from moderately uninterested to highly anticipatory.

Pizza

FOR MORE THAN twenty years, I invested in and wrestled with special pans, pizza peels, pizza ovens, and pizza stones, hoping to discover the secret to crispy, homemade pizza. While living in Italy, I learned how to hang and stretch the dough but the essential challenge remained: how to achieve that perfect crust without a bona fide wood-fired oven.

After watching exactly how the pizza was made in one of my favorite Italian neighborhood haunts, I realized that there is a two-step process to getting that crunchy crust, and it has nothing to do with special equipment or magic hands. First, the dough goes into a very hot oven, naked, and is allowed to bake for a minute or so. It is then taken out, topped, and returned to the hot oven to bake until crisp and bubbling. My method is an adaptation that takes you through these two steps. All you really need is a hot pizza stone, plus a little practice to get that crispy crust you're craving—and all in about the same amount of time it takes to get a pizza delivered, at half the cost to your pocketbook and your health.

Pizza is one of my favorite foods and preparing it at home allows me to create the perfect pizza that highlights the integrity of individual ingredients while keeping pizza a healthy food choice. Whether you choose to make your own or use a ready-made dough for convenience, my two-step method will give you the best results possible.

Basic Bread

1 ounce fresh yeast or two ¼-ounce packages active dry yeast

3 tablespoons honey or organic cane sugar

7 to 8 cups unbleached all-purpose flour

2 tablespoons fine sea salt

KEEP IN MIND *that bread making is not an exact science and the results can be affected by weather, humidity, altitude, and temperature, so don't be afraid to adjust wet or dry ingredients and baking times; make your adjustments in small increments and you'll be fine. Once you make this bread a couple of times, you'll become familiar with the texture and will be able to do it by "feel." Check the date when buying yeast to make sure it hasn't expired. If you prefer, substitute whole wheat flour or semolina flour for half of the all-purpose.*

1. Combine the yeast, honey, and 1 cup warm water in the bowl of a stand mixer with the dough hook attached. Let rest for 5 to 10 minutes, until it begins to puff and bubble. In a separate bowl, mix 7 cups of the flour with the salt. Turn the mixer on low and begin adding the flour, about a cup at a time. As the dough comes together, add 1¼ cups warm water, then slowly continue adding flour. The goal is a dough consistency that's smooth and elastic but not too sticky or dry. If necessary, add small increments of the remaining cup of flour and additional water, and continue kneading with the mixer. I like to hold back on some flour. Remember you can always add a bit more flour or water but you can't subtract it once it's added. Continue kneading the dough for 5 to 8 minutes, until smooth and elastic.

2. Shape the dough into a round or oblong loaf about 10 inches in diameter. Place the loaf on a baking sheet and carve an X across the top with a knife, just grazing the surface to prepare the dough for the first rise. Place the bread in a warm, draft-free place and cover with a lint-free cotton towel. I use my oven set to warm. Let rise until doubled in size, 45 minutes to 1 hour.

3. Place the dough on the board and "punch" it down by pushing the air out of the dough. Using your fists or the heels of your hands, knead the dough, continuing to push out all of the air, for 1 or 2 minutes. Reshape the loaf and place it back on the baking sheet. If you wish to make two smaller loaves, cut the dough in half and shape into rounds or oblong loaves. Let rise until doubled in size again, about 30 minutes.

4. Preheat the oven to 400°F. Gently place the baking sheet with the loaf or loaves in the oven and bake for 20 to 25 minutes, until golden brown and the bread sounds hollow when tapped on top.

5. Cool on a wire rack for at least 20 minutes, or, as we do at my house, start slicing. Keep in mind that bread sliced hot out of the oven is only advisable if you have a very sharp bread knife. Otherwise, you risk crushing the hot loaf.

Corn Bread

1 cup unbleached
all-purpose flour

1 cup organic cornmeal,
fine or medium

1 tablespoon baking powder

½ teaspoon fine sea salt

8 tablespoons (½ stick)
unsalted butter or soy
margarine, melted

¼ cup organic cane sugar

1 large organic egg

1 cup 2% milk
or soy milk

2 tablespoons unsalted butter,
softened, for topping
(optional)

LIGHT AND MOIST, *this corn bread—a good companion for spicy soups and hearty stews—is best when eaten hot out of the oven. A light, fine crumb results from the eggs here; for an eggless vegan version, see the Vegan Corn Bread recipe that follows.*

1. Preheat the oven to 375°F. Grease an 8-inch square glass or terra-cotta baking dish. Mix the flour, cornmeal, baking powder, and salt in a medium bowl. Add the melted butter and sugar, stirring just until the mixture resemble a coarse crumble. In a small bowl, mix the egg and milk until well combined. Gently fold the egg mixture into the dry ingredients and mix just until moistened. Be careful not to overmix as this will make the bread heavy.

2. Spoon the batter into the prepared baking dish and bake 25 to 30 minutes, just until the bread feels firm to the touch and a toothpick inserted into the center comes out clean. If you like, pierce the top of the hot corn bread all around with a skewer and spread the butter over the top. Serve hot.

Tomato and Basil Bruschetta, page 56
Bean and Basil Bruschetta, page 57

Caribbean Cabbage and Carrot Salad, page 78

Celebration Potstickers, page 48

Minty Tomato-Fennel Salad, page 80

**Spicy Chickpea
Salad, page 94**

Toasted Sesame Noodle Salad, page 95

**Simple Tomato
Sauce,** page 186

Tofu Ravioli with Butter and Sage, page 181

Seared Tofu, page 146

Tempeh and Cabbage, page 164

Tempeh Club Sandwiches, page 197

No-Egg Salad Sandwiches, page 194

Stuffed Sugar Pumpkins, page 215

Eggplant Meatballs, page 214

Grilled Asparagus with Lime, page 203

Mock Maryland Crab Cakes, page 196

Chickpea Crepes, page 132

Cucumber and Radish Sandwiches, page 238

Loaded Bagel, page 243

Basmati Rice Pudding, page 252

Tofu Cannoli, page 250

Tofu Coconut Cream Pie, page 251

Vegan Corn Bread

DON'T EXPECT THE *high rise of a corn bread made with eggs here, but do expect lovely, golden squares that are moist and flavorful. Serve with soup or chili, or split the squares in half horizontally and add any taco filling. For variation, add chopped scallions or chives to give an onion flavor. Sometimes I add a tablespoon of chopped jalapeño pepper. Leftover corn bread, toasted and smothered in fruit jam, is a breakfast treat. Masarepa, or white grits, is widely available in supermarkets and helps balance the coarse texture of the cornmeal for a smother softer crumb.*

1 cup unbleached whole wheat or all-purpose flour

½ cup organic yellow cornmeal, fine or medium

½ cup white grits or masarepa (fine white cornmeal)

2½ teaspoons baking powder

¼ cup canola or other vegetable oil

3 tablespoons organic cane sugar

1 teaspoon fine sea salt

Soy margarine, softened

1. Preheat the oven to 350°F. Grease a 9-inch pie dish, a 9-inch cast-iron skillet, or an 8 × 8-inch square baking pan. Mix the flour, cornmeal, grits, and baking powder in a bowl. In a separate bowl, whisk together 1 cup plus 1 tablespoon warm water, the oil, sugar, and salt (and any additional flavorings, like scallions or jalapeños). Add the liquid ingredients to the dry and mix by hand with a wooden spoon just until everything is well incorporated. Be careful not to overmix as that will create dense, heavy bread.

2. Pour the batter into the prepared pan and bake for about 30 minutes, or until a skewer inserted in the center of the corn bread comes out clean; overbaking will make it dry and crumbly

3. While the bread is hot, poke small holes across the top with a knife or barbeque skewer and spread with margarine, allowing it to melt into the bread. Serve warm or at room temperature.

Chickpea Crepes

MAKES 12 TO 15

1 cup chickpea
(garbanzo bean) flour

1 cup unbleached
all-purpose flour

1 tablespoon sesame oil

1 tablespoon extra
virgin olive oil

½ teaspoon fine sea salt

CREPES ALWAYS LOOK *as though you went through a great deal of work to make them, when they're actually no trouble at all. Keep in mind though that there's a rule when cooking crepes: The first crepe never works. Just toss it. Don't give up; practice and you'll soon get the hang of it. Because I make them frequently, I invested in a high-quality crepe pan, which is flat with shallow sides. Crepe pans can range widely in price, but any 7- to 10-inch well-seasoned or nonstick flat pan will turn out decent crepes.*

I replaced half of the all-purpose flour of a traditional egg-and-white-flour recipe with chickpea flour to make the crepes more nutritious and lower in fat. Chickpea flour, also called garbanzo bean flour, can be found in natural foods and specialty markets as well as many supermarkets. Bob's Red Mill is a well-known brand sold in many outlets and easily obtained online at www.bobsredmill.com.

These crepes can be wrapped in foil and kept warm in the oven until you're ready to fill them. They can also be frozen; simply separate the crepes with wax paper then wrap in foil. For a savory dish, I sprinkle with a little olive oil and black pepper or stuff with Rosemary-Roasted Winter Vegetables (page 212). I also use them in place of pasta for cannelloni. For dessert, fill dessert crepes with chopped fresh fruit or jam, roll up, and drizzle with pure maple syrup, or spread the crepes with Nutella and a shower of confectioners' sugar.

Dessert Crepes

TO MAKE CREPES that are suitable for desserts, dissolve 1 to 2 tablespoons organic cane sugar in ¼ cup water and then stir into the remaining 3 cups water. Prepare as above, except use 2 tablespoons canola or other vegetable oil in place of the sesame oil and olive oil.

1. Heat a nonstick crepe pan over medium heat while making the batter. In a bowl, whisk the chickpea flour, all-purpose flour, 3¼ cups water, the sesame oil, olive oil, and salt together into a smooth batter. Strain through a fine-mesh sieve to remove any lumps. Pour ⅓ cup batter onto the hot crepe pan; tip the pan to spread the batter evenly over the surface, you want fairly thin coverage. Let the crepe cook until it's loose when you shake the pan. Flip with a spatula or use your fingers—just be careful not to burn yourself. Cook the other side for about 15 seconds. The crepe should slide right out of the pan. Depending on how you to serve them, either fill as you go or continue cooking and stacking for filling later.

Focaccia

MAKES ONE 12 X 17-INCH BREAD

UNTIL RECENTLY, FOCACCIA *was only found in North America in old-line Italian bakeries and eateries. That's all changed, as has how most people make it. Traditional focaccia is made with a* biga *(starter) and can take hours to proof and rise, but I'm in the camp that's for a quicker recipe that delivers traditional results in a fraction of the time—this recipe, start to finish, takes less than 90 minutes. I use my stand mixer with the dough hook attachment to make this, but it can be done by hand—which gives you a bit of an upper-body workout to boot. Make sure the water added to the dough is very warm or you may not obtain the chemical reaction you need for the rise, 115°F is perfect; use an instant-read thermometer if necessary. Though it has a higher rise and softer bread-like texture than traditional pizza dough, focaccia can double as a crust for pizza. Experiment by adding Kalamata olives, sun-dried tomatoes, or fresh sage to the dough before baking.*

4½ to 5 cups unbleached all-purpose or whole wheat flour

Two ¼-ounce packages quick-rising yeast

¾ to 1 teaspoon fine sea salt

1 tablespoon honey or organic cane sugar

2 to 3 tablespoons extra virgin olive oil, plus more for topping

¼ cup coarsely chopped rosemary

Coarse sea salt, to taste

1. Blend 2½ cups of the flour with the yeast and fine salt in a large bowl. Add the sugar, if using (but not the honey). If you're kneading by hand, rub your hands with a little olive oil before beginning. If you're using an electric mixer, start at a very low speed. Once the dry ingredients are well mixed, add 2 cups very warm water, the oil, and honey, if using. Slowly add the remaining 2 to 2½ cups flour, just enough so that the dough pulls together and looks smooth and silky. Turn the mixer up to the next speed for a slow and steady knead. If you're kneading by hand, you'll look for the same silky, smooth dough that isn't too dry or flaky. Using the mixer should take about 5 minutes; by hand, 8 to 10 minutes. Once the dough is easily formed into a smooth ball, set it on a board or in a bowl, cover with a lint-free towel, and let rise for 10 to 15 minutes, until doubled in size.

2. While the dough is rising, preheat the oven to 350°F. If you have a pizza stone, set the top rack in the middle of the oven and put the stone on it (you'll set the pan directly on the stone when you bake the focaccia). Coat a 12 × 17-inch jelly-roll pan with a little olive oil.

3. Once the dough has doubled in size, gently stretch it onto the prepared pan. Spray the towel with a little water to dampen it slightly and cover the dough completely. Set the pan in a warm, draft-free location and let rise for 25 or 30 minutes, during which time it should double in size.

4. Just prior to baking, use your knuckles to dimple the entire surface of the dough at 1- to 2- inch intervals, without breaking through to the bottom. Brush on or sprinkle the dough with additional olive oil, so it settles into the dimples. Sprinkle the surface with the rosemary and coarse salt. Place the pan directly on the stone or in the oven.

5. Bake for about 10 minutes or so, then open the oven and mist the focaccia with warm water. Close the oven and continue baking until the focaccia is golden brown and sounds hollow when tapped, another 10 to 15 minutes.

6. Allow to cool for 10 minutes. Slice and serve warm. Any leftovers, and I never have leftovers, can be wrapped, stored, and reheated.

    NOTE: Jelly-roll pans come in varying sizes from 9 × 13 inches to 12 × 17 inches. If your pan is a little smaller than what I've suggested, don't worry, the recipe will turn out beautifully no matter the size.

Grilled Focaccia

MAKES 6 FLATBREADS

CHEWY AND SOFT *beneath the grilled crust's crunch, these semolina focaccia rounds can be eaten right off the grill without adornment, or spread with mellow roasted garlic, or topped with grilled eggplant or zucchini. The trick with grilling bread—or anything else for that matter—is not to be reverent about it. If you have a hot spot on your grill, bread may burn, but don't worry, just move the focaccia away and keep going. Grilling isn't about haute cuisine, it's about excellent food, eating al fresco, and connecting with one of our primal comforts: fire. So relax, throw the dough on the barbee, and watch what happens. If you've never made bread before, this is the recipe for you.*

1½ tablespoons (about 1½ packages) active dry yeast

2 tablespoons extra virgin olive oil, plus more for brushing

6 to 8 cups unbleached all-purpose flour, or half all-purpose and half whole wheat

1 cup semolina flour

1 tablespoon fine sea salt

1. Combine the yeast and ¼ cup warm water in a small bowl and let sit until it is bubbly and smells yeasty. Place 3 cups warm water and the olive oil in a large mixing bowl and add the yeast mixture. Combine the all-purpose flour, semolina flour, and salt. Add the flour a cup at a time to the yeast mixture and, by hand or using an electric mixer, mix with each addition until you have a soft dough. Knead about 10 minutes or until the dough is no longer sticky. Cover the dough and let rise about 30 minutes. Punch down the dough, and divide into 6 pieces, each about the size of an orange. Shape and stretch each piece of dough into a 10-inch round (or larger or smaller if you like).

2. Meanwhile, heat the grill. It should be quite hot when you're ready to grill the bread.

3. To grill the focaccia, gently brush the dough rounds with olive oil. In batches if necessary, carefully flip the rounds, oiled side down, onto the hot grill. Brush more oil on the top. Cover the grill for about 1 minute or so, and then take a peek: Using tongs, gently lift the edges of the rounds. If they're somewhat firm and wearing grill marks, they're ready to flip over. Flip and slide the rounds to the edges of the grill over more indirect heat and cover again. Keep your eye on them but let them cook a few minutes more, until they're golden and cooked through. Eat hot right off the grill.

RECIPE COURTESY OF CATHI DiCOCCO

Quick Mini Pizzas

MAKES TWELVE 6-INCH PIZZAS

One ¼-ounce package active dry yeast

1½ teaspoons organic cane sugar

2 tablespoons extra virgin olive oil

1¾ cups unbleached all-purpose flour

1½ teaspoons fine sea salt

Toppings, such as fresh mozzarella, chopped basil, sautéed garlic and onions, etc.

THIS DOUGH COMES *together quickly and works perfectly for mini or medium pizzas. I often dress the crusty rounds with just a little olive oil, salt, and pepper, but they can also be finished with any toppings of your choice. My kids like to get creative with the toppings—peanut butter and jelly pizza? Why not? The pizzas are good hot or at room temperature and they also make a special (but easy) bring-along for a potluck dinner or party gathering. The recipe can easily be doubled and the rounds can be made smaller if desired.*

1. Dissolve the yeast in ¾ cup warm water (105° to 115°F). Whisk in the sugar and let the mixture sit for 10 minutes, until the yeast begins to bubble. Add the oil. In a large bowl, combine ¾ cup of the flour and the salt. Pour in the yeast mixture and blend with a wooden spoon until the flour is mixed in. Add another ½ cup flour and stir until the dough starts pulling together. Place on a wooden board and knead by hand for 5 minutes. If the dough is very sticky, add the remaining ½ cup of flour a tablespoon at a time, just enough so the dough feels smooth and silky, neither too wet nor too dry. Let the dough rest for a minute or two.

2. Sprinkle a little flour onto a cookie sheet. Divide the dough into twelve pieces. Moisten your hands with a bit of olive oil and roll the pieces into balls, placing them on the cookie sheet as you go, making sure they don't touch one another. Cover the pan tightly with plastic wrap to keep it from drying out. Let the dough rise for 40 minutes.

3. Preheat the oven to 450°F. Remove the plastic wrap from the dough. Using your hands, shape and stretch each ball into a 6-inch round, or smaller if desired. Lay the rounds on a large baking sheet and add your toppings. Bake for 10 to 15 minutes, just until the crust is golden brown and crispy.

4. Alternatively, you may bake these directly on a preheated pizza stone. Preheat the stone for 30 minutes in a 475°F oven. Prepare the pizzas, slide a floured spatula gently under each, and lay directly onto the stone. Bake for 8 to 10 minutes, or just until the crust is golden brown and crispy.

Homemade Pizza Dough

MAKES ENOUGH FOR TWO 12-INCH PIZZAS

One ¼-ounce package active dry yeast

5½ to 6 cups unbleached all-purpose flour

4 teaspoons fine sea salt, plus more for sprinkling

Extra virgin olive oil

1. Combine the yeast and 2 cups lukewarm water in a large bowl. Let stand for 5 to 10 minutes, until bubbly and foamy. By hand with a wooden spoon or with an electric mixer, add 1 cup of the flour and the salt and mix well. Add enough of the remaining flour, 1 cup at a time and working in the flour with your hands, to form a dough that is smooth but not sticky. If the dough feels too sticky, add additional flour a few tablespoons at a time. Remove the dough from the bowl and shape it into a ball. Place in a lightly oiled bowl and turn to coat the whole dough ball. Cover with plastic wrap and let the dough rise in a warm place for 1 hour, until doubled in size.

2. Punch the dough down and divide into 2 balls. Place the balls back into the bowl and let the dough rise again for 45 minutes, until doubled. Use immediately or wrap in plastic and refrigerate overnight. For longer storage, the dough may be wrapped tightly in plastic and frozen for up to 4 weeks.

3. If you made the dough earlier and it's frozen, defrost completely. If it's refrigerated, let stand at room temperature for a few minutes. You want to work with dough that's cool, but not cold because it will shrink. Likewise, you don't want it too warm—the dough will break, develop holes, and stick.

4. Place the top oven rack in the middle of the oven and place a pizza stone on the rack. Preheat the oven at 500°F for 45 minutes.

5. Have salt and olive oil, along with any toppings, sauce, seasonings, and cheese, prepped and ready to use. Lay one dough disk on a lightly floured surface. Working from the center, press outward with your fingers, making your way toward the outer edges and turning the disk in a circular motion as you press, which will expand the surface area. Pick up the dough and, with your fists just off the center, let the dough hang. Gently stretch the dough outward in opposite directions for a few seconds, turning it as you stretch. Using this technique, the dough should begin thinning in the middle and become quite pliable. Move your fists to the outer edges, and let the weight of the dough hang off your loose fists with the bottom edge close to the board. Moving quickly, gently hang and stretch the dough this way, while

turning it in a circular motion. Focus on stretching the dough but also maintaining an all-around, even thickness. Lay the dough back down on the board and finish stretching with your fingers, pressing and flattening the thicker areas into a uniform disk the approximate circumference of your pizza stone.

6. After the dough is shaped into an even disk, you're ready for the pre-bake. I'm comfortable walking my dough over to the oven, but some people feel more confident using a peel. I find pizza peels to be cumbersome and, frankly, I don't have any storage space that will accommodate the long handle. If you like the peel, use it. If you don't have one, just use your hands.

7. First, open the hot oven and slide out the rack with the hot stone so you're ready. Pick up your dough and quickly and evenly lay it on the stone. The dough will instantly stick to the hot stone, but that's fine because it won't slide or shrink as you gently and carefully pull and press the crust out to meet the edge of the stone before it starts to set; take care not to touch the stone and burn yourself. After the dough is stretched, quickly drizzle olive oil across the dough's entire surface, prick the crust all over with a fork, sprinkle with a little salt, and slide the pizza back into the hot oven to bake.

8. Check it in 3 to 5 minutes. The crust should be a little puffy and light gold in color. Carefully tap the edge to make sure it isn't sticky. This indicates the pizza is partially baked and ready to be topped. If you like your pizza very well done, let the dough bake until the outer crust becomes more golden brown, another 5 minutes or so. Add toppings and bake 5 to 7 minutes more, to desired doneness or as directed in the recipes that follow.

9. To remove the pizza from the oven, slide it onto a round pizza pan, cookie sheet, or large wooden board. The pizza should lift off the stone easily. If you're using a pizza peel to remove the pizza, be sure to set the pizza on a board or pan for cutting. You never want to score a pizza peel with knife marks. Wait a minute or two for your pizza to rest, then slice and serve.

Pizza Margherita

MAKES TWO 12-INCH PIZZAS, SERVING 4

HERE IS MY *all-time favorite pizza—what we in America call* plain, *and I call* delicious. *This classic features the colors of the Italian flag: ripe red tomatoes, fresh white mozzarella, and fragrant green basil. For a vegan option, use soy or rice cheese, but don't add it until the last few minutes of baking as nondairy cheese hardens and becomes inedible if overcooked.*

1. Place the top oven rack in the middle of the oven and place a pizza stone on the rack. Preheat the oven at 500°F for 45 minutes.

2. Pull out the rack with the stone and place a dough round on the stone. Sprinkle with olive oil and some salt. Bake for 3 to 4 minutes, until the surface looks a little dry and begins to puff a bit. Slide the crust out and add the toppings: half of the tomatoes, cheese, and basil, and salt and pepper. (Dot the pizza with cheese, but do not cover it completely.) Bake the pizza until browned at the edges, about 7 minutes or longer. Crunchy crust is the preferred texture and it's a heck of a lot less messy to eat. Transfer the pizza to a pizza pan or board for slicing, and then top with olive oil and fresh black pepper. Repeat to make the second pizza.

2 pounds store-bought pizza dough or Homemade Pizza Dough (page 137), shaped and stretched into two 12-inch rounds

Extra virgin olive oil

Salt and freshly ground black pepper, to taste

1½ cups crushed tomatoes, fresh or canned

½ pound fresh mozzarella (not water-packed), sliced and patted dry

Handful of basil

Salad Pizza

4 cups mixed fresh arugula, baby spinach, and baby romaine, torn into bite-sized pieces

Extra virgin olive oil

Red wine vinegar

Salt and freshly ground black pepper, to taste

2 fresh Roma tomatoes, cut into ¼-inch-thick slices

Handful of Kalamata or other black olives, pitted

2 pounds store-bought pizza dough or Homemade Pizza Dough (page 137), shaped and stretched into two 12-inch rounds

Crushed red pepper flakes

½ teaspoon dried oregano

½ cup freshly grated Pecorino or Parmesan (optional)

I FIRST HAD *salad pizza in a little trattoria in Rome. Thin-crusted and draped with lightly dressed, peppery arugula and baby lettuces, I was delighted by how delicate it was. Though you can use any salads on this pizza, underdress the greens and don't pile them on too heavily or the crust will become soggy and collapse.*

1. Place the top oven rack in the middle of the oven and place a pizza stone on the rack. Preheat the oven at 500°F for 45 minutes.

2. In a large bowl, combine the salad greens and drizzle with a little olive oil and a few sprinkles of vinegar. Do this to taste, free hand; it's much easier than fussing with mixing the oil and vinegar in a separate bowl. Be sure the salad is very lightly dressed and tossed well. Taste the salad and season with salt and pepper, then place it in a cool spot away from the hot oven. Place the tomatoes and olives in bowls so you're ready to dress the pizza once it's prebaked.

3. Pull out the rack with the stone and lay a dough round on the stone. Drizzle with olive oil and sprinkle with salt and a few pinches of red pepper. Bake for 5 minutes. Slide the rack out and sprinkle on the oregano and the cheese, if using. Slide the pizza back into the oven and continue baking until a deep golden brown and crispy, about 7 minutes. Remove from the oven, sliding the baked pizza onto a flat pan or wooden board.

4. While the pizza is still warm, arrange half of the tomatoes on the crust in a circular pattern and dot half the olives among the tomato slices, reserving a few for the top. Lightly pile half the dressed salad on top of the tomato and olive layer. Let the pizza rest for 5 minutes, then slice and serve with a sprinkling of additional olives and freshly ground black pepper. Repeat to make the second pizza.

Mushroom Pizza

MAKES TWO 12-INCH PIZZAS, SERVING 4

HOW MANY TIMES *have you ordered a mushroom pizza at a restaurant and been served a soggy pie? By searing and sautéing fresh button and cremini mushrooms with a few dried porcini before baking the pizza, excess water is eliminated from the topping. Alternatively, just prior to baking the pizza, sliced mushrooms may be tossed with a sprinkle of salt and pepper, spread on a foil-lined baking sheet, and oven-dried for 10 to 15 minutes.*

1. Place the top oven rack in the middle of the oven and place a pizza stone on the rack. Preheat the oven at 500°F for 45 minutes.

2. While it's warming, heat a large skillet over medium-high heat and add the olive oil. Add the button and cremini mushrooms and sauté 5 minutes, stirring often to prevent burning. Add the chopped, reconstituted porcini and sauté until the mushrooms are cooked down but still retain their chewy texture. If the mixture becomes too dry, add some of the reserved porcini broth, a tablespoon or less at a time. The goal is to make sure the water expressed from the cooking mushrooms evaporates, leaving a silky coating of moisture but virtually no water in the bottom of the pan. When the mushrooms are just about soft, remove the pan from the heat, and add half the cubanelle pepper.

3. Pull out the rack with the stone and place a dough round on the stone. Sprinkle with olive oil and some salt. Bake for 3 to 4 minutes, until light and golden. Slide the crust out and top with an additional sprinkle of olive oil over the entire surface, a sprinkling of red pepper flakes, and half of the crushed tomatoes. Using the back of a wooden spoon, spread the tomatoes into a thin layer. Slide the rack back into the oven and bake until the tomatoes are steaming, 3 to 4 minutes. Slide out again and top with half of the cooked mushroom-pepper mixture. Bake until the crust is a deep golden brown, with a nice crispy bottom, another 10 to 12 minutes. I like my pizza fairly well done, so I'll often let it go 15 minutes. Transfer the pizza to a pizza pan or board for slicing. Top with half of the uncooked pepper pieces, a drizzle of olive oil, and half of the parsley. Repeat to make the second pizza. Slice and serve hot.

2 pounds store-bought pizza dough or Homemade Pizza Dough (page 137), shaped and stretched into two 12-inch rounds

2 tablespoons extra virgin olive oil, plus more for sprinkling

8 ounces button mushrooms, thinly sliced

10 to 12 ounces cremini mushrooms, sliced

2 ounces dried porcini mushrooms, soaked in ¼ cup warm water, chopped, broth reserved

1 cubanelle pepper, cut in half, seeded, and sliced into thin half moons

Salt, to taste

Few sprinkles of red pepper flakes, to taste

½ cup canned crushed San Marzano tomatoes

½ cup chopped parsley

Roasted Eggplant Pizza with Olives, Capers, and Arugula

MAKES TWO 12-INCH PIZZAS, SERVING 4

1 cup Roasted Eggplant Sauce (page 180)

Generous handful of pitted Kalamata or black olives of choice

2 tablespoons salted capers, rinsed and drained

¼ cup crumbled feta (optional)

3 cups loosely packed arugula

2 pounds store-bought pizza dough or Homemade Pizza Dough (page 137), shaped and stretched into two 12-inch rounds

Extra virgin olive oil

Salt and freshly ground black pepper, to taste

SWEET EGGPLANT SAUCE *and peppery arugula blend beautifully with the robust, salty flavors of olives, feta, and capers. Feel free to substitute torn baby spinach for the arugula or use a mix of the two greens.*

1. Place the top oven rack in the middle of the oven and place a pizza stone on the rack. Preheat the oven at 500°F for 45 minutes. Place the eggplant sauce, olives, capers, feta, and arugula in bowls so they are ready to put on top of the pizza.

2. Pull out the rack with the stone and place a dough round on the stone. Sprinkle with olive oil and some salt. Bake for 3 to 4 minutes, until the surface looks a little dry and begins to puff a bit. Slide the crust out and add half of the toppings, spreading over the entire surface of the dough: the sauce first, then the olives, capers, cheese (if using), and salt and pepper. Slide the rack back into the oven and bake until the pizza is nicely golden around the edges, about 5-8 minutes. Pull out the rack and lay on half of the arugula leaves. Continue baking another 5 to 8 minutes, until the pizza is bubbling and the crust is a dark golden brown around the edges. A little well-done is the preferred texture. Remove from the oven, top with a drizzle of olive oil and a generous grinding of fresh black pepper. Repeat to make the second pizza.

Potato-Sage Pizza

THIS CHEESELESS PIZZA bianca, *or white pizza, is a favorite street food in Italy. I serve it at room temperature for Sunday brunch. For dinner, accompany the pizza with Insalata Pomodoro (page 77) and a chilled, dry white wine. Leave the skin on the potatoes if you like—they add visual texture and are loaded of vitamins. While nothing beats the flavor of sage with potatoes, rosemary works nicely if you can't find fresh sage.*

1. Place the top oven rack in the middle of the oven and place a pizza stone on the rack. Preheat the oven at 500°F for 45 minutes.

2. Meanwhile, place the potatoes in a pot of salted water and bring to a boil. Lower the heat and cook for 8 to 10 minutes, until the potato pieces can be pierced with a knife. Rinse immediately with cold water to stop them from cooking further. When cool enough to handle, slice the potatoes into thin rounds. When ready to assemble the pizzas, have your potatoes, olive oil, sage, salt, and pepper ready at hand.

3. Pull out the rack with the stone and place a dough round on the stone. Sprinkle with olive oil and some salt. Bake for 3 to 4 minutes, until the surface looks a little dry and begins to puff a bit. Slide the crust out on the rack and arrange half of the potatoes in a circular pattern, overlapping them just a bit. Sprinkle with half of the chopped sage, drizzle olive oil over the entire surface, and season with salt and pepper. Slide the pizza back into the hot oven and bake for 10 minutes or so, until the edges are nicely browned. Transfer the pizza to a pizza pan or board for slicing. Repeat to make the second pizza. Serve hot or cold.

3 medium Yukon Gold potatoes, peeled if you like and halved

Extra virgin olive oil

¼ cup coarsely chopped sage

Salt and freshly ground black pepper, to taste

2 pounds store-bought pizza dough or Homemade Pizza Dough (page 137), shaped and stretched into two 12-inch rounds

Pan-Fried Pizza

1 pound store-bought pizza dough; or Homemade Pizza Dough (page 137), prepared through the second rise and punched down

2 tablespoons extra virgin olive oil

½ to 1 cup canned crushed plum tomatoes

4 ounces fresh mozzarella, thinly sliced and patted dry

¼ cup basil, leaves torn

1 tablespoon capers, rinsed well

THESE PIZZAS ARE *first flash-fried in fruity olive oil, topped with savory fresh tomato sauce, fresh mozzarella, and capers, and then finished in the oven. It's deliciously juicy and incomparably crusty and tasty.*

1. Place the top oven rack in the middle of the oven and place a pizza stone on the rack. Preheat the oven at 500°F for 45 minutes.

2. Heat a 10-inch cast-iron griddle or skillet over medium-low heat on the stovetop. Stretch one-third the dough into a 10-inch round. When the pan is hot but not smoking, sprinkle enough olive oil to cover the bottom in a thin layer and lay the dough in the pan. It will shrink a little when it hits the hot surface, and that's fine. Fry the dough lightly on one side until it's crispy and very light brown. Sprinkle a bit more oil over the entire top surface and, using large tongs, lift and flip the dough.

3. Quickly add one-third of the toppings: tomatoes, cheese, basil, and capers. Cook for 2 minutes, until the toppings are just beginning to heat. Remove the pan from the stove and place directly on the pizza stone in the oven. Bake until the bottom of the pizza is crispy and brown when lifted, 5 to 7 minutes. Repeat to make 2 more pizzas. Slice and serve hot or at room temperature.

TOFU

COMMONLY KNOWN AS bean curd, tofu was the first soy food I was exposed to and, for many years, the one I utilized least. I was under the mistaken impression that it would take nothing short of magic to convert this cheese-like block of soy into anything appetizing. After opening my mind and my cupboards, I've learned that the opposite is true. Tofu is one of the easiest soy foods to work with, yet it has a undeserved reputation for being bland and lacking texture. Once you learn a few preparation techniques, you'll realize this isn't true.

Below are a few good-to-know, put-together-in-a-snap, basic tofu recipes. Moving from breakfast right through to dessert, tofu is versatile and can be flavored any way you like. There are so many varieties and brands available that I recommend you experiment to find which you like best. Firm and extra-firm styles offer the most flexibility, while silken or soft are dead-ringer substitutes for dairy in cream sauces or dressings. Tofu is perishable, however, and must be kept refrigerated. Check the expiration date on the package and use it within a week of the "best used by" date.

Seared Tofu

SERVES 2 TO 4

One 14-ounce package extra-firm tofu, drained and pressed

3 tablespoons canola or other vegetable oil

2 tablespoons tamari

Kosher salt

HERE IS ONE *of my favorite ways of preparing tofu, resulting in crisp—yet tender—nuggets. Extremely versatile, pan-seared tofu lends itself well to any number of dishes. I like to top it with a big handful of chopped parsley or cilantro. It's also great with rice, quinoa, or millet, with scallions and roasted peanuts scattered on top. And it adds wonderful flavor, protein, and texture when tossed into a salad or pasta dish. When I don't have tamari, I'll substitute vegetarian steak sauce or vegetarian Worcestershire sauce. Firm or extra-firm tofu has the best texture for searing (cooking over high heat).*

1. Cut the tofu into slabs, cubes, or chunks. In a well-seasoned cast-iron skillet, heat the oil over medium-high heat until hot. Add the tofu and cook. Don't try to move or stir the tofu until the bottom is starting to brown. Fussing with it will only cause it to fall apart. When the tofu can be easily moved with a spatula or by shaking the pan, it's okay to turn the pieces over to brown the other sides. Just before the tofu is finished, sprinkle on the tamari. Shake the pan and continue to cook, allowing the liquid to reduce and thicken a bit. This only takes 5 to 8 minutes. Remove from the heat when the tofu is nicely glazed but before it sticks to the pan. Season with a bit of salt.

Crispy Seared Tofu

TO MAKE crispier seared tofu, sprinkle ¼-inch-thick slices with a little salt and dredge in cornstarch before searing in a the hot oil. I particularly like using crispy seared tofu in a sandwich—it has a lovely chewy texture—on whole wheat bread accompanied by a thick slice of tomato and a crunchy piece of lettuce.

Draining and Pressing Tofu

TOFU IS usually sold packed in water. Draining the excess moisture and pressing it to compact is very easy: to begin, remove the tofu cake from its container and set the tofu horizontally in a medium-sized colander in the sink (the tofu should lie flat). Set a bowl or small pot with water (weighing roughly a pound or two) on top of the tofu; the pressure of the weight will gently and uniformly compress the tofu and expel the excess water, which will drain out the bottom of the colander. Press the tofu for at least 30 minutes or up to several hours. The longer you press it, the flatter the cake and the denser the texture.

Tofu Sour Cream

TOFU SOUR CREAM *is the perfect nondairy substitute for regular sour cream. It's great as a base for spreads and dips, or simply scooped onto baked potatoes. On desserts, a dollop is the just the right replacement for crème fraîche.*

1. Place the tofu, oil, juice, vinegar, and salt in a food processor fitted with a metal blade. Process until smooth and creamy. Store in an airtight container up to 1 week.

One 14-ounce package firm tofu

⅓ cup extra virgin olive

¼ cup lemon juice

1½ tablespoons cider vinegar

2 teaspoons kosher salt

Baked Tofu Meatballs

MAKES 16 MEATBALLS, SERVING 4

3 tablespoons extra virgin olive oil

One 14-ounce package firm tofu, drained, pressed, and mashed

2 tablespoons walnuts, toasted (see page 86) and finely ground

½ cup wheat germ

¼ cup chopped parsley

2 tablespoons light soy sauce

2 tablespoons nutritional yeast (optional)

1 tablespoon onion powder

½ teaspoon garlic powder

¼ teaspoon oregano

THESE SAVORY BITES *are easy to prepare, high in protein, very low in fat, and satisfy any meat cravings that even those who have been eating vegetarian fare for a long time may occasionally experience. I sometimes serve them tumbled in Simple Tomato Sauce (page 186) for a classic spaghetti and meatball dinner. Or, hollow out a crusty roll, slather with spicy mustard, and add a few for a meatball hero. They're also good cold, plain, and eaten out of hand for a quick burst of protein energy. Many vegetarian recipes call for textured vegetable protein (a.k.a. TVP) as a meat replacement, but tofu is nutritionally superior so I opt for it whenever possible. The recipe easily can be doubled.*

1. Oil an 8 × 8-inch square or round baking dish with 1½ teaspoons olive oil. Preheat the oven to 350°F.

2. Mix the mashed tofu together with the walnuts, wheat germ, parsley, soy sauce, yeast (if using), onion powder, garlic powder, and oregano. Shape into sixteen 1½-inch balls and arrange in the prepared pan without touching each other. Drizzle with the remaining 1½ teaspoons olive oil. Bake, turning the meatballs every 10 minutes, for 30 to 35 minutes, until they're evenly brown and crispy. Be careful when turning these—especially during the first few minutes—because they're quite soft and will crumble if roughly handled.

Onion and Garlic Powder

MADE FROM crushed dehydrated onions and garlic, onion and garlic powder are available in supermarkets in the spice department. Look for organic varieties that have no additives. Alternatively, make your own powder in an instant by crushing dehydrated onion flakes or granulated garlic.

Tofu with Parsley Sauce

MY MOTHER MADE *a German family favorite, chicken with parsley sauce. I always liked the parsley sauce best, so it was one of the first dishes from my childhood that I converted to vegetarian. It has become a new family favorite. I accompany it with steamed potatoes or spoon it over wide, flat noodles.*

1. Heat the oil in a large skillet over medium heat. Add the tofu and a sprinkle of salt and cook, turning, until the tofu is browned and crispy. Drain on paper towels.

2. Without rinsing the skillet, add the butter and heat until it turns light brown. Add the flour, 3 tablespoons at a time, stirring continuously. When all the flour is blended in, whisk in the stock, a couple of cups at a time to keep the sauce from becoming lumpy. Once the sauce is smooth, add the tofu and simmer for about 5 minutes. Sprinkle in the parsley and stir well to combine. Season with salt and pepper before serving.

3 tablespoons canola or other vegetable oil

One 14-ounce package extra-firm tofu, drained, pressed, and cubed

Kosher salt

8 tablespoons (1 stick) unsalted butter or soy margarine

8 to 10 tablespoons all-purpose flour

5 cups Vegetable Stock (page 106)

1 cup chopped parsley

Freshly ground black pepper, to taste

Tofu Kebobs with Tamari-Ginger Sauce

Tamari-Ginger Sauce

½ cup tamari

½ cup pure maple syrup

1-inch piece ginger, grated or chopped finely

Kebobs

2 large sweet potatoes, peeled and cut into 1-inch cubes

12 Swiss chard leaves

One 14-ounce package extra-firm tofu, drained, pressed, and cut into 1-inch cubes

24 cremini or white mushrooms

YOU WON'T BELIEVE *how many ways you can use these kebobs: eat them right from the grill, place whole skewers over seasoned rice, or nestle the tofu and vegetables in pita bread and dress with Lime-Ginger Dressing (page 102). I eat leftovers for breakfast if I'm lucky enough to have any.*

Don't worry if the chard is raggedy after blanching. Once the "envelopes" are tightly folded and sealed, they hold up just fine. Use the leftover chard stems in soups or stir-fries. A bit of advice about skewering: threading kebobs on two skewers held ½ inch apart makes for a significantly more stable kebob that's much easier to handle as you grill. For this number of servings, you'll need 16 to 20 skewers, soaked in water for at least 30 minutes if made from bamboo or wood.

1. **TO MAKE THE SAUCE:** Combine the tamari, maple syrup, and ginger in a small bowl and refrigerate for at least an hour or up to several days, for the flavors to blend.

2. **TO MAKE THE KEBOBS:** In a medium saucepan, gently steam the sweet potato in a steamer basket just until barely fork tender, about 10 minutes. Immediately transfer to a bowl and let sit until cool enough to handle.

3. Bring a pot of salted water to the boil. Cut the chard leaves from their tough center ribs. Add the chard leaves to the boiling water and blanch for 1 minute. Drain in a colander, taking care not to tear the limp leaves. When cool enough to handle, drape each leaf over the side of the colander to drain for a few minutes longer. Pat the leaves dry with a paper towel.

4. Place one leaf with the tip facing you on a cutting board and tuck in the side edges until you have a strip 1½ to 2 inches wide. Fold the leaf lengthwise to make a neat little squareish package, then press between your palms to seal. The moisture in the leaf will help it to stay together. Repeat until all the leaves are used.

5. Preheat a grill to medium. Thread the sweet potatoes, chard packets, tofu, and mushrooms on skewers, alternating and arranging them by colors and textures and starting and ending each with a mushroom to use as a "brake." Leave about ⅛ inch between the pieces to facilitate cooking.

6. Brush the kebobs with the sauce. Grill the kebobs, basting frequently with the sauce to keep them from drying out and turning occasionally, until the kebobs show grill marks all over. Brush with additional sauce and serve.

RECIPE COURTESY OF CATHI DICOCCO

Tofu Pot Pie

MAKES FOUR 6-INCH PIES

Dough

2 cups whole wheat pastry flour, sifted

1 teaspoon fine sea salt

¾ cup (1½ sticks) cold unsalted butter or soy margarine, diced

Filling

6 tablespoons canola or other vegetable oil

One 14-ounce package extra-firm tofu, drained, pressed, and cubed

1 large onion, diced

2 medium carrots, diced

2 celery stalks, diced

1 medium baking potato, peeled and diced

½ cup all-purpose flour

4 to 5 cups Vegetable Stock (page 106), at room temperature

1 cup petit peas

½ cup chopped parsley

1 tablespoon chopped dill

2 tablespoons capers, rinsed and drained

Salt and freshly ground black pepper, to taste

THANKSGIVING DINNER CAN be lonely for vegetarians. While others are tucking into turkey, those who don't eat meat are often left with a bunch of side dishes that are heavy, sweet, and often bathed in butter and cream. Once you start serving tofu pot pie for your holiday dinner, everyone will flock to this dish. My children love it so much that I now make them individual pot pies all year-round. Substitute tempeh or vegetarian chicken-style strips for the tofu if you like. You can forgo the crust and spoon the filling over Vegan Corn Bread (page 131) or biscuits. Unbaked pot pies can be frozen: When ready to bake, cover with aluminum foil and place in a cold oven. Turn the oven to 325°F and bake for 25 minutes. Remove the aluminum foil after the first 10 minutes to brown the crust.

1. **TO MAKE THE DOUGH:** Combine the flour and salt in a large bowl. Add the butter and with a fork or pastry blender mix to pea-sized pieces. Add ice water, a tablespoon or two at a time and use your fingers to lightly knead just until a dough forms. Place the dough on a floured surface and shape into a ball. Divide into quarters, then shape each quarter into a disc. Wrap the discs individually in wax paper and chill for at least 30 minutes.

2. Preheat the oven to 350°F. Lightly grease four 6-inch ramekins or individual foil pot pie pans.

3. **TO MAKE THE FILLING:** Heat 4 tablespoons of the olive oil over medium heat in a heavy skillet. Add the tofu cubes and cook, turning, until browned and crisp, about 10 minutes. Transfer with a slotted spoon to paper towels to drain.

4. Heat the remaining 2 tablespoons oil in the pan. Add the onion, carrots, celery, and potato and sauté until crisp-tender, 6 to 8 minutes. Add the flour, stirring and tossing to coat the vegetables evenly. Continue stirring and cooking for an additional 2 to 3 minutes. Slowly add the stock, 1 cup at a time, stirring constantly, until a thick gravy develops. You may not need all 5 cups of the stock, so start with 4 cups and add more if needed. The sauce may appear a bit thin at first, but it will thicken considerably while baking. Add the tofu, peas, parsley, dill, and capers and stir to combine. Season with salt and pepper.

5. On a floured surface, roll each disk of dough into an ⅛-inch-thick circle, just slightly larger than a ramekin. Divide the tofu mixture among the ramekins, lay the dough on top, and press along the edges of the dishes to seal tight. Pierce the top of each pie with a fork to vent the steam. Bake for 20 to 25 minutes, until the crust turns a nice golden brown. Remove the pot pies from the oven, let cool for a few minutes, and then dig in.

TEMPEH AND SEITAN

REQUIRING LITTLE OR no pre-preparation, texture-rich tempeh is ready to use at a moment's notice. Made from fermented soybeans, tempeh is a wonderful source of protein, iron, calcium, and vitamin B_{12}. It's also low in fat, easily digestible, cholesterol-free, and—fried, sautéed, grilled, or baked— works beautifully with any cuisine.

Made from wheat gluten, seitan's firm and chewy texture is the ideal substitute for meat in many traditional recipes. It's also a low-fat source of protein, niacin, and calcium. My made-from-scratch recipe is hearty and dense as well as easy and economical.

Best Braised Tempeh

One 8-ounce package tempeh, any variety

3 tablespoons canola or other vegetable oil

Sweet and Spicy Marinade (next page)

SOUR, SALTY, AND *sweet—this tempeh brings all of these flavors together in one dish—with a succulent texture. Yes, store-bought versions of marinated tempeh can be had, but they're pretty pricey and the flavor doesn't come close to what you can achieve here, easily and inexpensively. I often serve the tempeh plain, with a crunchy cabbage salad dressed with Tofu-Lime Dressing (page 102) and a thick slice of tomato; it also complements stir-fried vegetables and makes a good sandwich filling. Because this is so irresistibly good, it never lasts, so I tend to make two packages' worth at one time.*

1. Cut the tempeh into quarters. Turn each quarter on its side and slice through the middle to make 8 thinner slices. Heat a deep skillet over medium-high heat until hot. Add the oil to the pan and heat. Lay the tempeh pieces in the skillet and cook, turning once, until nicely browned. Reduce the heat to medium and pour the sauce over the tempeh. It will bubble up quickly, so add ¼ cup warm water and then shake the pan to incorporate the water somewhat into the sauce. Allow the tempeh to cook vigorously for a few minutes, then reduce the heat to medium-low. Cover and simmer for 25 minutes. Check the tempeh from time to time to make sure there is still enough liquid in the pan. If not, add a tablespoon or so more water.

2. Reduce the heat to very low and uncover. Continue to cook until most of the liquid has reduced to a syrupy sauce. Transfer the tempeh to a dish and spoon any remaining sauce on top. Let the tempeh sit for a few minutes before serving or store in the fridge for up to 10 days.

Sweet and Spicy Marinade

■ **MAKES 1 CUP**

IF YOU ONLY *have one marinade recipe in your repertoire, this should be it. Whether for marinating, braising, baking, or as a basic brush-on barbeque sauce, it lends itself to many variations: Substitute 1 tablespoon Dijon mustard for the ginger. Use the same amount of honey or maple syrup instead of sugar. Add 2 tablespoons chopped parsley, cilantro, tarragon, or chives. Try lime zest instead of lemon, or use lemon or lime juice instead of vinegar. Substitute plum or balsamic vinegar for the cider vinegar. Replace shoyu with regular soy sauce or tamari. It's easy to create a sauce that suits your fancy.*

½ cup shoyu soy sauce
⅓ cup canola or other vegetable oil
¼ cup vegetarian Worcestershire sauce
2 tablespoons cider vinegar
2 tablespoons brown sugar
4 garlic cloves, crushed
1 tablespoon grated ginger
1 tablespoon grated lemon zest
1 tablespoon freshly ground black pepper

1. Whisk all the ingredients together in a bowl. Use immediately or store in a jar or covered container in the fridge for up to 2 weeks.

Tamari Tempeh

SERVES 2 TO 4

One 8-ounce package tempeh, any variety

¼ cup canola or other vegetable oil

2 tablespoons tamari soy sauce

SALTY TAMARI AND *nutty mild tempeh complement each other perfectly; I'll prepare tempeh this way to have it on hand for sandwiches, but it can add protein and chew to pasta or rice dishes. I eat it out of hand for a quick protein blast, cube it and add it to salads in place of bread croutons, or cut into thin strips to replace pork bacon in a classic vegetarian BLT.*

1. Cut the tempeh into quarters. Turn each quarter on its side and slice through the middle to make 8 thinner slices. Or slice into long thinner slices like strips of bacon, or into cubes. Heat the oil in a nonstick skillet over medium heat and cook each slice until golden brown. Turn the pieces and cook until crisped. Transfer to a plate and blot with a paper towel to remove any excess oil. Brush each side of the tempeh with tamari while still hot.

Barbequed Tempeh

SERVES 4 TO 6

I LOVE TEMPEH'S *nutty, chewy texture and how it readily accepts different flavorings. This recipe lends tempeh a classic sweet and sour barbeque zing with deep accents. I'll brush the cooked tempeh with a little vegetable oil, skewer with sweet red peppers, Vidalia onions, and mushroom caps, and grill as kebobs. Or, you can cut it into square burger shapes by cutting the tempeh in half, then cutting the halves in half through the middle to make 4 thinner slices, and then grill like burgers.*

1. Preheat the oven to 350°F. Cut each tempeh cake into quarters. Turn each quarter on its side and slice through the middle to make 16 thinner slices. Arrange the tempeh in a single layer in a 13 × 9 × 2-inch baking dish. Nestle the pieces right up against each other; it will be a tight fit.

2. In a medium bowl, whisk together the soy sauce, vinegar, maple syrup, vegetable oil, olive oil, and cumin until well blended. Pour over the tempeh and cover the pan tightly with foil. Bake for 30 minutes. Check the tempeh to see if most of the sauce has been absorbed. If it's still fairly soupy, re-cover and bake 15 minutes or so, until the tempeh is swollen with the sauce. Uncover the pan and bake another 10 to 15 minutes, until the tempeh has absorbed the sauce but isn't too dry. Serve hot, cold, or at room temperature.

Two 8-ounce packages tempeh, any variety

½ cup shoyu soy sauce

½ cup cider vinegar

⅓ cup maple sugar or syrup

¼ cup canola or other vegetable oil

2 tablespoons olive oil

2 teaspoons ground cumin

Jamaican Jerk Tempeh

SERVES 4 TO 6

Two 8-ounce packages
tempeh, any variety

½ cup shoyu soy sauce

½ cup cider vinegar

⅓ cup maple syrup

1 to 2 teaspoons Jamaican
jerk sauce

2 teaspoons ground cumin

1 teaspoon chipotle powder

¼ cup extra virgin olive oil

¼ cup canola or other
vegetable oil

WHEN I VACATIONED *in the Cayman Islands, I noticed small stands and snack shops all over, selling jerk style chicken and pork. Eager to try a vegetarian rendition of this Caribbean classic, I brought home some jerk spice and set out to concoct a meat-free version. One day I'll have the time to make jerk seasoning from scratch; in the meantime, Walkerswood Traditional Jerk Seasoning is my personal favorite; add it in small increments to control the kick. I like my tempeh sliced thin, but if you're using the tempeh as a burger on a bun, leave the tempeh in thicker quarters. Serve hot or cold (it keeps in the refrigerator for up to a week). I often serve with Vermicelli and Rice (page 226) and Caribbean Cabbage and Carrot Salad (page 78).*

1. Preheat the oven to 350°F. Cut each tempeh cake into quarters. Turn each quarter on its side and slice through the middle to make 16 thinner slices. Lay the tempeh in a single layer in a 13 × 9 × 2-inch shallow baking dish.

2. In a bowl, whisk together the soy sauce, vinegar, maple syrup, jerk sauce, cumin, and chipotle powder. Continue whisking as you slowly add the olive oil and vegetable oil to emulsify the sauce.

3. Pour the sauce over the tempeh, moving it around to make sure each piece is covered. Cover the entire pan tightly with foil and bake 25 to 30 minutes. Remove the foil and continue baking another 15 to 20 minutes, until the sauce is almost completely absorbed, being careful not to let it dry out completely.

Malaysian Curried Tempeh

MY FRIEND SANDRA *from South Africa—whom I also have to thank for the recipe for the Breakfast Rusks (page 241)—introduced me to this tart and spicy curry dish. She makes it with fish, but I substitute tempeh. Pile on slices of chewy, whole grain German bread and accompany with sliced apples and a bowl of Roasted Red Pepper and Leek Soup (page 116). Some toasted nuts will add crunch. Or layer fresh, ripe tomato slices on top. Although you can eat it right away, Malaysian curries are best when left to rest a day or two in the refrigerator to develop the flavors.*

One 8-ounce package tempeh, any variety

4 tablespoons canola or other vegetable oil

3 large yellow onions, thinly sliced into half moons

2 tablespoons organic cane sugar

1 tablespoon Madras curry powder

1½ teaspoons turmeric

1½ teaspoons chile powder

½ cup cider vinegar

3 bay leaves

1. Cut the tempeh into quarters, then cut the quarters in half through the middle, giving you 8 thinner slices. Heat 2 tablespoons of the oil in a wide sauté pan over medium heat. Add the tempeh pieces and cook, turning, until nicely browned on both sides. Transfer to a serving dish.

2. Heat the remaining 2 tablespoons oil in the same pan over medium heat. Add the onions and toss to separate the rings and coat with oil. Add the sugar, curry powder, turmeric, and chile powder and combine with the onions until well mixed. Add the vinegar and bay leaves and cook until the onions are soft, 8 to 10 minutes, being careful not to let them brown. Discard the bay leaves. Pile the spicy onion mixture over the tempeh. Serve immediately, or cool and refrigerate for up to 48 hours before serving. Serve at room temperature.

Greek Stuffed Cabbage

MAKES ABOUT 12 ROLLS

½ cup brown rice

3 tablespoons walnuts

4 ounces tempeh, any variety

3 tablespoons extra
virgin olive oil

1 bunch scallions, chopped

1 tablespoon currants

2 tablespoons minced parsley

2 tablespoons pine nuts,
toasted (see page 86)

2 tablespoons grated
Parmesan (optional)

2 large organic eggs, beaten
(optional)

1 head savoy cabbage

1 cup lemon juice

Lemon Cream Sauce (below)

THIS FESTIVE DISH *is vibrant and substantial enough to serve as the main dish for a spring holiday meal, yet easy enough for any day of the week. A filling of lemon, rice, nuts, and savory herbs will dispel your bad memories of tired stuffed cabbage forever. I use the crinkly leaved savoy cabbage because I prefer its chewier texture and visual appeal. For this amount of filling, you need 12 to 14 cabbage leaves, but because savoy cabbage leaves range so widely in size be prepared to use more or less. The rolls and sauce can be cooked ahead of time and stored in an ovenproof casserole dish to be reheated later. When ready, preheat the oven to 350°F and bake, covered, for about 30 minutes, until bubbly and heated through. If the sauce thickens too much, simply thin with water or milk, added a little at a time, until you reach the desired consistency.*

1. Bring 1½ cups water to a boil in a medium saucepan. Add the rice, cover, and cook for 10 to 15 minutes, over medium-low heat, then immediately drain and place in a large mixing bowl. Since the rice will be cooked further as part of the filling, it is deliberately undercooked at this point.

2. Place the walnuts in a food processor and pulse to roughly chop. Break the tempeh into chunks, add to the processor, and pulse until the mixture resembles coarse meal. Heat a small skillet over medium heat. Add 2 tablespoons of the olive oil and sauté the walnut-tempeh mixture until golden brown and fragrant, about 5 minutes.

3. Add the tempeh mixture, scallions, currants, parsley, pine nuts, Parmesan and eggs (if using) to the rice and combine with the remaining 1 tablespoon olive oil.

4. Bring 3 cups water to a boil in a deep, wide pan. Remove from heat. Pull off 12 to 14 cabbage leaves, discarding any outer leaves that are too ragged. Submerge the cabbage leaves under the hot water, cover, and let sit for 3 minutes. Transfer the leaves to a colander and quickly rinse under cold water. Blot the leaves dry. The leaves have to be pliable enough to fill and roll, but not limp.

5. Place a heaping tablespoon of the filling into the center of a leaf. It may look as if it's a stingy amount, but the rice will plump up as it cooks. Roll the leaf up like a burrito, folding the bottom of the leaf up about halfway over the filling and then folding in the sides. Roll from the bottom up to the top and set the roll, seam side down, in a 6-quart Dutch oven. Repeat to make the remaining rolls. Start with a single

layer in the pot, but then stack them as necessary. Once all of the filling is used up, coarsely chop the remaining cabbage to make 2 cups.

6. Pour the lemon juice into the pan over the cabbage rolls. Add enough water just to cover the rolls. Sprinkle the chopped cabbage around the edge of the pan, tucking them under the water and among the rolls with a wooden spoon. Place a small heatproof dish, such as a sandwich plate, over the rolls right in the pan to keep them submerged. Cover the pan and bring to a boil. Reduce the heat and simmer for 30 minutes. The cabbage is done when you tip the pot and there's about a cup or so of lemon cooking water remaining. When the cabbage rolls are tender, using tongs, transfer to a serving platter, and then carefully pour the hot lemon water into a bowl to reserve for the lemon cream sauce. Put the rolls back into the pan to keep warm.

7. Pour the lemon cream sauce over the rolls and gently shake the pot to insure the sauce collects at the bottom. Turn the heat up, cover the pot, and let everything heat through for 2 to 5 minutes. Serve immediately.

Lemon Cream Sauce

■ MAKES ABOUT 3 CUPS

THE TRADITIONAL SAUCE, *like so many Greek recipes, is usually made with two or three egg yolks, but in this version, the egg yolks are eliminated without any compromise in flavor. Use dairy or soy milk—both work equally well.*

4 tablespoons (½ stick) unsalted butter or soy margarine
¼ cup whole wheat or unbleached all-purpose flour
1½ to 2 cups dairy or soy milk
About 1 cup reserved lemon water from the cabbage
2 tablespoons lemon juice
1 to 2 tablespoon grated Parmesan (optional)
Salt and freshly ground black pepper, to taste

1. Melt the butter in a small saucepan over medium heat. Add the flour and stir or whisk constantly until well blended. This roux burns quickly, so watch the heat. Stir in 1 cup of the milk—the sauce will rapidly thicken—then begin adding the lemon water a tablespoon at a time, blending well with a whisk. Add more milk as necessary to obtain a creamy consistency that's not too thick, but keep in mind that the sauce will thicken in the final heating. Taste the sauce and season with lemon juice, salt and pepper, and optional cheese.

Tempeh and Cabbage

SERVES 4

2 to 3 tablespoons extra
virgin olive oil

2 yellow onions, thinly sliced

½ teaspoon caraway seed

1 red bell pepper, seeded and
cut into 1-inch dice

One 8-ounce package tempeh,
any variety, cut into
2-inch pieces

1 pound cabbage,
coarsely chopped

2 tablespoons mirin
(rice wine)

¼ cup light soy sauce

½ cup almonds, toasted
(see page 86)

GROWING UP IN *Germany, I ate a lot of cabbage. Germans use cabbage, red and green, in salads, with meats, pickled, stuffed—everything but dessert. Most often, cabbage is served alongside pork or fowl and accented with apples, caraway, and vinegar. Serve this vegetarian version of pork and cabbage over steamed sweet potatoes. For an added sweet and spicy kick, drizzle with some Sweet Chili Dipping Sauce (page 49). You can also thicken the sauce with 1 tablespoon cornstarch dissolved in 2 tablespoons water. Add slowly at the end until the sauce is the desired consistency.*

1. Heat a large skillet over medium heat and cover the bottom with a thin coating of olive oil. Add the onions and sauté until golden, then add the caraway seeds and toss to combine. Raise the heat and add the red pepper and tempeh pieces. Cook for 15 minutes, until the tempeh and onion are caramelized. Add the cabbage and sauté for 5 to 10 minutes longer.

2. Mix the mirin, soy sauce, and 1 cup water in a small bowl. Make a well in the center of the tempeh and cabbage and add the mirin mixture. Simmer for 10 minutes, until the cabbage is crisp yet tender. The mixture should be lightly glazed. Top with the toasted almonds and serve hot.

Moroccan Stew

FRAGRANT, SPICY, AND *loaded with vegetables and tempeh, this North African–inspired stew is a favorite on a cold winter day with some creamy polenta, couscous, or basmati rice. Baking the eggplant first makes it nice and chewy. This is another dish that is best made a day ahead to allow the mélange of spices to blend.*

1. Preheat the oven to 350°F. Arrange the eggplant in a single layer on a foil-lined baking sheet. Bake for 20 minutes, until the cubes become a light, golden color.

2. Meanwhile, heat a 5½-quart Dutch oven over medium-high heat and pour in the olive oil. Add the onion and sauté until soft, golden, and translucent. Add the crushed garlic and sauté for another 3 minutes. Add the diced tempeh and turn and cook until lightly golden. Add the cashews, currants, cumin, turmeric, chili sauce, coriander, cinnamon, and paprika, combining everything well. Sauté for another 5 minutes or so, until the spices release their fragrance. Add the eggplant, tomatoes, and 2 cups water. Simmer for 20 minutes, until the water and tomatoes create a thick, rich sauce. Top with lime zest and serve hot.

1 medium eggplant, unpeeled, cut into 1-inch cubes

3 tablespoons extra virgin olive oil

1 large onion, diced

6 garlic cloves, crushed

One 8-ounce package tempeh, diced

½ to 1 cup whole raw cashews

⅓ cup currants

1 teaspoon ground cumin

1 teaspoon turmeric

1 teaspoon chili sauce

1 teaspoon coriander

½ teaspoon ground cinnamon

½ teaspoon paprika

2 cups canned tomatoes, chopped

Zest of 1 lime

Tempeh Cacciatore

SERVES 4

One 8-ounce package tempeh,
any variety

3 tablespoons extra
virgin olive oil

1 medium red onion,
finely diced

1 medium carrot, diced

2 celery stalks, diced

3 garlic cloves, finely chopped

1½ teaspoons coarsely
chopped rosemary

Fine sea salt and freshly
ground black pepper

¾ cup dry white or red wine

1 cup drained canned
San Marzano tomatoes,
coarsely chopped

1 cup Vegetable Stock
(page 106) or water

THERE ARE AS *many versions of cacciatore as there are cooks in Italy. Some prepare it with a much a more pronounced tomato flavor, others add vegetables like mushrooms and peppers, while others add a variety of herbs. One thing everyone agrees on is that cacciatore tastes best when prepared one or two days before eating. This allows the elements to become infused with the subtle richness of wine and tomatoes, which simply can't be achieved without the extra time. When I don't have tempeh on hand, I substitute sautéed mushrooms or chicken-style TVP. Partner this with Crispy Roasted Potatoes (page 220) or spoon over polenta. A sprig of rosemary makes for a fragrant garnish.*

1. Cut the tempeh into quarters. Turn each quarter on its side and slice through the middle to make 8 thinner slices. Heat a heavy skillet over medium-high heat. Add the oil and when it begins to loosen and swirl, add the tempeh. Brown the tempeh on both sides; if the oil smokes, lower the heat. Remove the tempeh from the pan.

2. Into the same skillet, still hot and with any brown bits left on the bottom, add the onion, carrot, celery, garlic, rosemary, and a pinch of salt. Lower the heat so the vegetables don't brown and cook gently until the onion is translucent and soft, about 8 minutes. Add the wine and bring to a boil. Simmer about 5 minutes, until the wine is almost fully evaporated and fragrant. It should just cover the vegetables.

3. Stir in the tomatoes, stock, 1 teaspoon salt, and ½ teaspoon pepper and cook for 5 minutes. Add the tempeh, cover, and simmer on low until the carrot and celery are cooked through, 20 minutes or less. If the tomato broth is still too thin for your liking, uncover and cook on low for another few minutes. The flavor of this dish improves overnight. Season with salt and pepper to taste and serve.

Tempeh Fajitas

SERVES 4

WHENEVER I TRAVELED to Mexico, I visited the local markets to pick up a variety of dried and powdered chiles and spices. The secret to authentic Mexican food is in the spices, and these spices are now available everywhere. Chunks of spice-doused tempeh replace chicken, beef, or pork, and blend beautifully with the medley of grilled sweet bell peppers, hot jalapeños, and caramelized onions. Tucked into warmed tortillas and served with both Green Salsa Picada (page 70) and Chunky Avocado Salsa (page 71), these fajitas are almost as good as a trip to Mexico.

One 8-ounce package tempeh, any variety

6 to 7 tablespoons canola or other vegetable oil

2 to 3 tablespoons fajita seasoning

6 medium bell peppers, a combination of colors, seeded and coarsely chopped

2 medium yellow onions, coarsely chopped

1 to 3 jalapeño peppers, seeded and chopped, to taste

6 to 8 fajita wraps

1. Cut the tempeh block in half lengthwise, then slice into ¼- to ½-inch-wide strips. Place the tempeh strips in a plastic container with a lid, add 2 tablespoons of the oil and 2 tablespoons of the fajita seasoning. Cover and turn it to coat the tempeh. Let marinate at room temperature or in the fridge at least 30 minutes, but the flavor improves if marinated 6 to 8 hours.

2. Heat 4 tablespoons of the oil in a large skillet. Add the tempeh and sauté until golden brown. Add the peppers, onions, and jalapeños. Turn up the heat and stir-fry for 5 to 7 minutes, until the peppers start to blacken. If necessary, add the remaining tablespoon of oil while cooking. Season to taste with some or all of the remaining 1 tablespoon fajita spice.

3. Divide the tempeh mixture among the fajita wraps, roll up, and serve hot.

Tempeh Marsala

SERVES 4

One 8-ounce package tempeh, any variety

3 tablespoons extra virgin olive oil

2 medium yellow onions, coarsely chopped

1 pound cremini mushrooms, quartered

2 tablespoons chopped garlic

½ to ¾ cup dry Marsala wine

2 tablespoons chopped oregano

¼ to ½ teaspoon crushed red pepper, or less to taste

Salt and freshly ground black pepper, to taste

THIS RECIPE WAS *introduced on my show by chef and caterer Heidi Valenzuela, and while the flavors are complex and sophisticated, it couldn't be simpler to prepare. Crispy sautéed tempeh is combined with caramelized onions and cremini mushrooms. The whole dish is finished with a rich sauce highlighted by a measure of dry Marsala wine. Spoon over basmati rice and serve Sesame-Garlic Kale (page 209) on the side.*

1. Cut the block of tempeh in half horizontally, then each half in half again, making 4 pieces. Slice the tempeh quarters on the diagonal into 1-inch-wide strips.

2. Heat the olive oil into a wide skillet and over medium heat. Add the onions and sauté until golden brown and lightly caramelized, 15 to 20 minutes. Add the mushrooms and cook until fork tender. Transfer the onions and mushrooms to a bowl.

3. Add the tempeh and garlic to the pan and sauté over medium-high heat until crispy brown, 8 to 10 minutes. Add ½ cup of the Marsala and simmer to reduce the liquid by half. (If it becomes too dry, add an additional ¼ cup wine.) Add the oregano, crushed red pepper, and salt and pepper and stir to combine. Return the cooked mushrooms and onions to the pan and simmer for another 5 to 10 minutes. Serve immediately.

Homemade Seitan

MAKES ABOUT 1 POUND

DERIVED FROM PROTEIN-RICH *wheat gluten that is naturally fat- and starch-free, seitan is tasty and nutritious with a chewy, meaty texture. But pound for pound, prepackaged seitan is incredibly expensive, especially considering what it's made from. This (oh so) easy recipe produces a far superior product for far less money. The trick is to use bulk vital wheat gluten, which is gluten that is already separated from the starch. Vital wheat gluten is readily available in local food co-ops and natural food stores. Homemade seitan is ready to cook immediately, or you can submerge the chunks in the cooking broth and refrigerate for up to 10 days or freeze for later use. Seitan is delicious roasted or used in place of tofu or tempeh. I add a few sprigs of fresh herbs like rosemary and sage when refrigerating or freezing to infuse those deep flavors into the seitan and its broth. Bragg Liquid Aminos is a liquid protein concentrate derived from soybeans, then mixed with purified water. Containing both essential and nonessential amino acids, Bragg is an excellent low-sodium replacement for tamari or soy sauce.*

1. **TO MAKE THE DOUGH:** Combine the gluten, granulated garlic, and ginger in a large bowl and mix thoroughly. Combine the stock and liquid aminos in a separate bowl, then quickly add to the dry mixture. Mix with a fork until a dough forms. The gluten will almost immediately seize up into a semisolid state. With your hands, knead the dough a couple of dozen times; the consistency should be squishy but firm. Let the dough rest for 5 minutes. Knead another dozen times and let rest 10 minutes. Cut the dough into about 8 pieces and pull into 4- to 6-inch strips.

2. **TO MAKE THE BROTH:** Combine the stock, liquid aminos, ginger, garlic, and herb bundle in a large stockpot. Bring to a boil and add the gluten dough strips. Cover and reduce to a simmer. Cook for 1 hour. Check occasionally and add more water or stock if needed. Use at once or store in a container.

Gluten Dough

One 10-ounce box vital wheat gluten

1 teaspoon granulated garlic

½ teaspoon ground ginger

2 cups Vegetable Stock (page 106) or water

2 tablespoons Bragg Liquid Aminos, or reduced-sodium tamari or shoyu soy sauce

Broth

4½ cups Vegetable Stock (page 106) or water

¼ cup Bragg Liquid Aminos, or reduced-sodium tamari or shoyu soy sauce

2 teaspoons ground ginger

1 teaspoon granulated garlic

2 sprigs rosemary, 6 sage leaves, 10 peppercorns, and 3 sprigs thyme, wrapped in cheesecloth or placed in an herb infuser

Granulated Garlic

GRANULATED GARLIC is made from pure fresh organic garlic that has been cleaned, sliced, and dehydrated, then milled to its desired size. Intensely flavorful and easy to store, granulated garlic is inexpensive and superior in flavor to commercial garlic salt or artificially enhanced powders. Note: a small quantity goes a long way, so if you're substituting it for fresh garlic, ¼ teaspoon is equal to two average-size cloves.

PASTA

CONSIDERED BY MANY to be the ultimate in comfort food, pasta is economical, filling, a terrific source of energy, and a perfect base for any topping. Pasta comes in many shapes and sizes. You'd be hard-pressed to find a kid who doesn't like some form of pasta so by all means use that to your advantage.

Always cook your pasta in a roomy pot with plenty of salted water; it needs room to tumble. Despite what you may think, using less water will not make pasta cook faster. If you're tossing your pasta with a thick sauce or a pesto, be sure to reserve a cup or two of the cooking water to help thin out the sauce if necessary—it's an excellent habit to get into. Don't add oil to your water and don't rinse your pasta: the residual starch will help grab your sauce. Stir often and use the cooking times on the box as a guideline. There are many variables when cooking pasta, so taste along the way and cook just until al dente.

And finally, you must resist doing two things: 1) Eating enough for two; and 2) over-saucing. A well-balanced pasta dish can be put together in minutes by utilizing pantry ingredients that are on hand. Does it get any better than that?

Spaghetti Aglio e Olio

SERVES 4 TO 6

1 pound spaghetti

¼ cup extra virgin olive oil

3 to 4 garlic cloves,
finely minced

3 dried red pepper pods or ¼
teaspoon crushed red pepper
flakes, more or less to taste

Salt, to taste

SIMPLICITY ON A *plate. Spaghetti with garlic (aglio) and olive oil (olio) is made everywhere in Italy, from the north to the south. In Tuscany it's served with a sprinkle of fresh parsley or dried oregano; in Rome and Naples a small plate of dried hot peppers accompanies the spaghetti—but sometimes the peppers are tossed into the oil and garlic during the last minute of cooking. I enjoy the way the peppers complement the clean uncluttered flavor of the olive oil and garlic. Be aware that the success of this dish depends upon the garlic being cooked just until it's golden; it will be ruined if over-browned and bitter.*

1. Bring a large pot of generously salted water to a boil. Add the spaghetti and cook until al dente.

2. Meanwhile, heat the olive oil in a small saucepan over low heat. Drop in a small bit of the garlic. When it begins to sizzle, add the rest and give it a quick stir. Keep the heat moderately low, stirring often and making sure the garlic is sizzling. Cooking the garlic on too low a heat will cause it to absorb the oil; alternatively, too high a heat will burn the garlic. When the garlic is just golden, remove the pan from the heat.

3. Quickly drain the pasta, reserving some of the cooking water, and immediately transfer to a serving bowl. Pour the garlic and oil over the spaghetti and add the pepper flakes if using (if using red pepper pods, reserve in a small bowl for individual seasoning). Toss the spaghetti well, coating it evenly with the olive oil and garlic bits. If the spaghetti seems a little dry, add some of the reserved water a little at a time and toss well. Season with salt and serve immediately.

Spaghetti with Fennel Sauce

SERVES 6

THE SAUCE FOR *this Sicilian classic can be strained and silky, but I'm partial to a chunkier, more rustic texture. If you prefer a smoother consistency, just before adding the pasta, quickly blend the fennel and tomato with an immersion blender. This dish is especially good when fresh fragrant fennel is in season. The outer bulb layers can be tough, so pull those away; save the feathery fronds to garnish the finished dish. Chopped fresh parsley, sautéed cremini mushrooms, and torn arugula all make tasty additions.*

1. Heat the olive oil in a large skillet over medium-high heat. Add the fennel and sauté for 5 to 7 minutes. When the fennel begins to turn golden and caramelize, add the red pepper flakes and oregano. Sauté for a minute or so, then add the tomatoes and ½ tomato can of warm water. Reduce the heat to medium-low and simmer for 15 to 20 minutes, until slightly reduced. Season with salt and pepper.

2. Meanwhile, bring a large pot of salted water to a boil. Add the pasta and cook until al dente. Drain, reserving some of the cooking water. Add the pasta to the sauce and blend well. If the sauce is too thick, add some cooking water, a little at a time. Transfer to a large serving bowl and serve hot.

5 tablespoons extra virgin olive oil

2 medium fennel bulbs, trimmed and chopped into 1-inch dice

½ teaspoon crushed red pepper flakes

½ teaspoon dried oregano

One 28-ounce can crushed tomatoes

Salt and freshly ground black pepper, to taste

1 pound spaghetti rigati

Pasta with Peas

½ pound spaghetti

¼ cup extra virgin olive oil, plus additional for serving if desired

1 medium sweet onion, finely diced

2 garlic cloves, quartered

3½ cups fresh peas or defrosted frozen petit peas

Salt and freshly ground black pepper

½ cup minced mint or parsley

Freshly grated Parmesan or vegan cheese (optional)

FRESH, GREEN SWEET *peas are visually breathtaking against pale pasta. Make it during the brief season when peas appear in the market or garden. If the fresh pea season has come and gone, frozen petit peas work well. In lieu of cheese, try this with a sprinkle of crushed, preferably homemade, croutons. Or, add 2 cups shredded butter lettuce to the pan for a minute or two before the peas finish cooking.*

1. Bring a large pot of salted water to a boil. Add the pasta and cook until al dente.

2. Meanwhile, heat the oil in a saucepan over medium-low heat. Add the onion and cook until translucent but not brown, 3 to 4 minutes. Add the garlic and gently stir to coat with the hot oil but don't let it brown. Add the peas and gently toss, making sure everything is coated well. Add a few tablespoons of water and cover the saucepan, keeping the heat low and steaming the peas until they are crisp tender. This should take about 5 minutes.

3. Drain the pasta and place in a warmed serving bowl. Toss the peas into the pasta and season well with salt. Add the mint, cheese, and black pepper. Drizzle with a little additional olive oil, if desired and serve hot.

Penne with Onions and Vegetarian Bacon

SERVES 4

MY MOM ALWAYS *made a bacon-macaroni-onion dish as a way to use up left-over pasta. I can see why: lightly fried pasta is delicious with just about anything. Pasta that's a day or two old has a dense firm texture that works best with this recipe. This can certainly be prepared with freshly boiled pasta, but it won't get the same crispy exterior and chewy firm bite.*

1. In a large shallow skillet heat the oil over medium-high heat. Add the bacon and fry until crisp. Remove the bacon from the pan with a slotted spoon and drain on paper towels.

2. Sauté the onion and garlic in the remaining oil in the skillet until soft, about 3 minutes. Add the edamame and red pepper and sauté for another minute or two. Add the cooked pasta and toss well to combine and heat through. Add the bacon, radicchio, basil, salt, and lots of black pepper and toss again. Serve, if desired, with shaved Parmesan.

3 tablespoons extra virgin olive oil

4 ounces vegetarian bacon, coarsely chopped

1 red onion, finely chopped

2 garlic cloves, minced

2 cups edamame beans, cooked

1 teaspoon crushed red pepper flakes

1 pound penne or ziti, cooked (preferably a day ago)

1½ cups thinly sliced radicchio

Small handful of torn basil

Salt and freshly ground black pepper, to taste

Shaved Parmesan (optional)

Spaghetti Tofunese

SERVES 4

1 medium red onion

1 medium carrot

1 large celery stalk

4 tablespoons (½ stick) unsalted butter or soy margarine

2 tablespoons fruity extra virgin olive oil, plus more for drizzling

12 ounces vegetarian "beef" crumbles, tofu, or minced tempeh

3 to 4 slices vegetarian bacon, chopped (optional)

½ to ¾ cup good-quality dry white wine, to taste

One 15½-ounce can tomatoes, chopped

1 teaspoon fresh grated nutmeg

1 cup Porcini Stock (page 107) or Vegetable Stock (page 106)

Salt and freshly ground black pepper, to taste

½ to ¾ cup milk, cream, light cream, or unsweetened soy milk, to taste

1 pound spaghetti

Freshly grated Parmesan

BOLOGNESE IS A *rich and creamy tomato-based sauce typically made with a variety of meats, heavy cream, wine, and beef stock. I didn't think it would be easy to translate this dish to a lighter meatless version until I discovered that, as with many recipes that contain meat, it's actually the supporting "cast members"—the dry white wine, nutmeg, carrots, celery, and red onion—that give such dishes their distinctive flavor.*

1. Finely chop the onion, carrot, and celery in a food processor. Heat the butter and oil in a large shallow heavy pan. When they begin to bubble, add the chopped vegetables and sauté for 5 minutes. Add the crumbles and bacon and sauté for 10 minutes, stirring every so often just until they begin to lightly brown.

2. Add the wine and cook for 5 minutes, then add the tomatoes. Simmer for 15 minutes, stirring occasionally. Add the nutmeg and stock. Continue cooking for about another 20 minutes. Taste the sauce and season with salt and pepper as necessary. Lower the heat, stir in the milk, and simmer for another 10 to 15 minutes, stirring occasionally. Low heat is essential so the sauce doesn't burn.

3. While the sauce is simmering, bring a large pot of salted water to the boil. Add the pasta to the boiling water and cook until al dente. Drain the pasta quickly and add to the sauce. Combine well and heat gently over very low heat for 2 minutes. Divide the pasta among four pasta bowls and drizzle a little fruity olive oil and sprinkle freshly grated Parmesan over each serving. Serve immediately.

Fettuccine Walnut Alfredo

THE CREAMY EMULSION *of this sauce gets its smooth fluffy texture by rapidly blending hot water into nuts and garlic. This recipe is a perfect stand-in for the heavy butter- and dairy-based Alfredo sauce. Rich in monounsaturated fats, walnuts and pine nuts are also a good source of omega-3 fatty acids. If desired, sprinkle on some Parmesan or fresh herbs before serving. Don't add too much garlic as it will overpower the delicate mild flavor. The sauce can also be spooned over vegetables, such as green beans or asparagus.*

½ pound dried or fresh fettuccine

¾ cup walnuts or walnut pieces

1 garlic clove

¼ cup pine nuts

Few sprigs parsley

2 to 3 tablespoons extra virgin olive oil

Pinch of fine sea salt

Freshly grated black pepper

Freshly grated Parmesan (optional)

1. Bring a large pot of salted water to a boil. Add the pasta and cook until al dente.

2. Pulse half of the walnuts with the garlic in a food processor. Stop and scrape down the sides of the bowl with a spatula. With the processor running, add the remaining walnuts, the pine nuts, and parsley and then drizzle in the oil. When the sauce has a pesto-like texture, stop the processor and scrape down the sides of the bowl. The nuts should be very finely ground. Turn the machine on and slowly add ¼ to ⅓ cup very hot water, checking the consistency to make sure the sauce doesn't become too thin. The sauce should begin turning white with a fluffy creamy texture. Stir in the salt.

3. Have a large deep pasta bowl handy. Quickly drain the pasta and drop into the bowl. Toss with about 5 tablespoons of the sauce, more or less to taste. Serve immediately with a few grinds of black pepper and Parmesan, if desired.

Penne with Tomato and Chickpea Sauce

SERVES 4

3 tablespoons extra virgin olive oil, plus additional for serving

3 garlic cloves, crushed

One 28-ounce can San Marzano tomatoes, crushed

Small handful of coarsely chopped basil

One 15-ounce can chickpeas, drained and rinsed; or ¾ cup cooked dried chickpeas

1 teaspoon crushed red pepper flakes (optional)

1 pound penne, rigatoni, or other tube pasta of choice

Salt and freshly ground black pepper, to taste

Freshly grated Pecorino Romano (optional)

NORTH AFRICAN CULTURE *has had a tremendous influence on the regional cuisine of southern Italy and Sicily; because of this, it's very common to prepare this chickpea dish with a sprinkle of cinnamon and even raisins. Cinnamon adds a unique dimension, certainly worth the experiment. You can also throw in a few handfuls of fresh spinach and some chopped Kalamata olives and serve the thick sauce on Garlic Toasts (page 53) as a bruschetta.*

1. Bring a large pot of salted water to a boil.

2. Heat the olive oil and garlic in a large skillet over medium-high heat and cook until the garlic begins to sizzle but doesn't brown. Add the tomatoes, ½ tomato can water, and half the basil. Bring to a low simmer. Add the chickpeas and continue simmering until the chickpeas are tender and break easily when pressed, 10 to 15 minutes. Add the red pepper, if using. If the sauce feels dry, add a little pasta water (about ¼ cup) to loosen it up. When the chickpeas are thoroughly cooked, use a fork to mash them, leaving some whole. Continue simmering the sauce on very low.

3. Add the penne to the boiling water and cook until al dente. Drain the pasta, reserving a few cups of the hot cooking water. Add the hot pasta to the sauce and fold to combine. Ladle in some of the reserved cooking liquid a little at a time until the sauce is fluid but not runny. Add the remaining basil and season with salt and black pepper to taste. Serve hot with an additional drizzle of olive oil and a sprinkling of Pecorino, if desired.

Ziti with Summer Tomato Sauce and Arugula

IN THE SUMMER *when juicy tomatoes, vibrant greens, and fragrant herbs are in abundance at the farmers' markets, nothing beats this light, fresh, uncooked sauce for pasta. Dressed with just a hint of balsamic vinegar, sweet red onion, and spicy arugula, ziti becomes a colorful dish perfect for entertaining or just a casual simple supper on a warm night. Fontina is a mild, buttery, semi-soft cheese from northern Italy. Lightly grated onto hot pasta it melts smoothly and quickly.*

½ small red onion, chopped

1½ tablespoons balsamic vinegar

1 pound ziti

4 vine-ripened tomatoes, cut into a 1-inch dice

1 cup basil leaves

1½ cups baby arugula, roughly torn

½ cup pinenuts, toasted (see page 86)

¼ cup extra virgin olive oil

Salt and freshly ground black pepper, to taste

Italian Fontina (optional)

1. Bring a large pot of salted water to a boil. Combine the red onion and vinegar in a shallow serving bowl or casserole dish. Stir well and let stand for about 10 minutes.

2. Add the pasta to the boiling water and cook until al dente. Meanwhile, add the tomatoes, basil, arugula, pinenuts and oil to the onion. Toss to combine, then sprinkle in about a teaspoon salt and gently mix as you would a salad to coat all the vegetables with the dressing.

3. Drain the pasta and immediately add to the tomato mixture in the serving bowl. Gently fold in the pasta, bringing the vegetables up from the bottom to the top, until well combined. While the ziti is still warm, add a few gratings of Fontina if desired. Taste and season with more salt if necessary and plenty of black pepper. Serve at room temperature.

Penne with Roasted Eggplant Sauce

SERVES 6

1 medium to large eggplant

Scant ¼ cup extra virgin olive oil

3 garlic cloves, halved

Salt and freshly ground black pepper, to taste

Nice handful of chopped basil or parsley, or both

One 28-ounce can San Marzano tomatoes, crushed

1 pound penne

ECONOMICAL AND INCREDIBLY *versatile, eggplant is one of my favorite vegetables. Roasting transforms its mildly bitter undertones into sweet flavors. This robust sauce is wonderful tossed with penne, but you can also use it as a base for a stew or a rich dense vegetable soup, or as a pizza topping (for example, Roasted Eggplant Pizza with Olives, Capers, and Arugula, page 142). It's also perfect with Eggplant Meatballs (page 214), or spooned over creamy polenta and coarsely sautéed greens with a spinach salad on the side. For a bruschetta topping, omit the water, add 1 cup chopped pitted black olives and/or 1 cup sautéed mushrooms and pile on Garlic Toasts (page 53). The sauce will keep, covered in the fridge, for up to 5 days.*

1. Preheat the oven to 425°F. Wash the eggplant and prick a few times with a fork. Set on a foil-lined baking sheet and roast until the top feels dry and the eggplant is about ready to collapse, 45 minutes to 1 hour. Let cool for 10 minutes. Cut in half and scoop out the pulp. Chop the eggplant until the pulp is very fine. Discard the skin.

2. Heat the olive oil in a large skillet over medium heat. Add the garlic and sauté until golden. Add the eggplant pulp and about ½ teaspoon salt and cook until heated through. Add half the herbs and cook for 5 to 8 minutes. The eggplant will begin to take on a creamy consistency. Add the tomatoes and ½ tomato can of water. Bring to a simmer, then reduce the heat and simmer on low for about 15 minutes. Season with salt and pepper.

3. Bring a large pot of salted water to a boil. Cook the pasta in the boiling water until al dente. Drain well, reserving some of the cooking water. Add the pasta to the skillet with the sauce and toss to combine, adding some of the cooking water if it seems dry.

Tofu Ravioli with Butter and Sage

MAKES 16 LARGE RAVIOLI, SERVING 4

WHEN I LIVED *near Florence, my mom and I would frequent a small family-run trattoria tucked behind one of the city's lesser known piazzas and small churches. They made the most delicious ravioli with butter and sage sauce I've ever eaten, and I've had many versions. The pasta was homemade (of course), the ricotta filling was light and almost fluffy with a just a hint of nutmeg, and the ravioli were served with the perfect amount of butter and toasted sage. Tofu's neutral flavor makes it an ideal substitute for ricotta. Vegans, you can omit the cheese and substitute ¼ cup extra virgin olive oil or soy margarine for the butter.*

1. **TO MAKE THE RAVIOLI:** Using your hands, gently squeeze any remaining water out of the tofu block. Crumble the tofu into a bowl and mash well with a fork. Add the parsley, salt, nutmeg, pepper, and Pecorino, if using, and mix very well, almost beating the filling like you were scrambling eggs.

2. Prepare the dough by carefully stretching a sheet with your hands then laying it flat on a floured board. Dip a pastry brush in warm water and brush down the middle and along all 4 edges. With the wet brush, mark out 8 squares.

3. Place a heaping tablespoon of the filling into the middle of each marked square. Take a second dough sheet and lay over the filled side. Press gently along the outlines of the filling, almost creating the shapes of fried egg yolks. Press along the moistened lines to lightly seal, trying also to press out most of the air. Seal the edges securely. Using a ravioli cutter or a knife, cut away the outside edges, and then cut along the sealed lines into 8 square ravioli. A rough appearance only adds to their rustic homemade appeal, so don't worry about perfection here. The most important thing is that the outer edges be sealed so filling doesn't leak out when the ravioli are placed in boiling water. Place the cut ravioli onto a well-floured metal jelly-roll pan or cookie sheet to dry. Repeat to make 8 more ravioli. You can cover the ravioli with plastic wrap and refrigerate for up to 2 days. You can also freeze the ravioli: so they don't stick together in one big lump, arrange them individually on a cookie sheet and freeze. When frozen, place in a plastic freezer bag. Properly frozen, they will keep for up to 3 months.

Ravioli

One 12-ounce package firm or extra-firm tofu, drained

⅔ cup finely chopped parsley

1 tablespoon kosher salt

Few gratings of nutmeg, to taste

Freshly ground black pepper

½ cup grated Pecorino Romano (optional)

1 pound fresh pasta dough sheets

Butter and Sage Sauce

6 tablespoons (¾ stick) unsalted butter

6-10 sage leaves, washed and dried

Salt and freshly ground black pepper, to taste

Shaved Parmesan, to taste

4. **TO COOK THE RAVIOLI:** Bring a large pot of salted water to a boil. Add the ravioli and cook for about 3 minutes, until al dente.

5. **TO MAKE THE SAUCE:** While the ravioli are cooking, melt the butter in a large skillet over medium heat, being careful not to let it brown. Reduce the heat and allow the butter to foam for a minute or two. Add the sage and stir gently, making sure the butter doesn't burn. When the leaves are nicely crisped, the sauce is done. Season to taste with salt and pepper.

6. Drain the ravioli and place in a large serving bowl. Spoon the sauce over the ravioli and sprinkle on a little shaved Parmesan. Serve immediately.

Pasta Sheets

PREPARED FRESH pasta sheets are available in the refrigerator section of most supermarkets, health food stores, and specialty shops. Fresh pasta should always be chilled and rolled or cut on a cool floured surface. Wrap any unused pasta tightly in plastic and it will keep for up to 2 days in the refrigerator.

Cannelloni with Eggplant

SERVES 4 TO 6

THIS RECIPE IS *enormously popular with my television viewers. The traditional dish is made with pork and beef; my vegetarian version utilizes parboiled no-boil pasta sheets, roasted eggplant, and textured soy—without sacrificing any of the deep hearty flavor or texture of meat. If you wish, the vegetarian crumbles and béchamel may be replaced with an additional large roasted eggplant and Simple Tomato Sauce (page 186).*

1. Preheat the oven to 400°F. Place the eggplant on a foil-lined baking sheet and prick with a fork a few times. Roast until the eggplant begins to brown and collapses slightly, about 35 minutes. I lightly press the eggplant with my finger and if it leaves a dent, it's finished roasting. Reduce the oven temperature to 350°F. Let the eggplant rest until cool enough to handle, about 10 minutes. Slice the eggplant in half, scoop out the soft pulp, and coarsely chop. Discard the skin.

2. Heat the oil in a deep skillet over medium heat. Add the onion and cook for a few minutes, until soft and slightly translucent. Add the garlic, oregano, and pepper flakes (if using). Stir a minute or two to release the aromas and flavor. Add the crumbles, if using. Add the eggplant and cook until the filling is slightly browned, 5 to 7 minutes. If the mixture becomes dry, add a tablespoon of olive oil. Add the tomatoes and garlic salt, stir to combine, and cook an additional 3 minutes. Remove from the heat and stir in ¼ cup of the chopped basil and the cheese. Season with salt and pepper and add additional oregano and/or basil to taste.

3. Spread 1 cup béchamel in a large shallow casserole. Bring a large, preferably shallow, pot of salted water to a boil. Add the 2 or 3 lasagna sheets and move them around a bit. Boil until they become flexible and slightly softened, 2 to 3 minutes. You want these a little underdone since they will be further cooked in the oven. Using tongs, carefully remove the pasta and line them up on your work surface. Add another 2 or 3 sheets pasta to the boiling water. Meanwhile, place about 3 heaping tablespoons filling near the bottom of each sheet of parboiled pasta, leaving a 1-inch border. Roll the pasta around the filling into a tube. Place the cannelloni, seam side down, next to each other in the baking dish. Continue this method of boiling and filling. Depending on the shape and size of your dish, this may be done in a single layer—but if not, it's fine to stack a few.

1 large or 3 small eggplant, washed

3 tablespoons extra virgin olive oil, plus more if needed

1 medium onion, chopped

3 garlic cloves, chopped

2 tablespoons oregano, plus more if needed

¼ teaspoon crushed red pepper flakes (optional)

One 12-ounce package vegetarian "beef" crumbles, or one 8-ounce package tempeh, minced (optional)

½ cup canned fire-roasted tomatoes, chopped

1 teaspoon garlic salt

Coarsely chopped basil

¼ to ½ cup Pecorino Toscano or vegan Parmesan

Salt and freshly ground black pepper, to taste

Béchamel (see next page)

1 pound no-boil lasagna noodles

4. Ladle some additional béchamel over the cannelloni. Add a drizzle of olive oil and a little more fresh basil. Pour ¼ cup water around the edge of the dish, cover with foil, and bake for 20 minutes. Uncover and bake an additional 10 minutes, or until the top is just becoming golden.

Béchamel

■ MAKES ABOUT 3 CUPS

3 cups 2% dairy or unsweetened soy milk
6 tablespoons (¾ stick) unsalted butter, soy margarine, or extra virgin olive oil
6 tablespoons unbleached all-purpose flour
Salt and freshly ground black pepper, to taste
Good pinch of freshly grated nutmeg

1. Heat the milk until hot but not boiling. (Milk at room temperature will work, but using hot or warmed milk, in my experience, makes a smoother sauce.) Meanwhile, in a medium saucepan over medium heat, heat the butter, taking care not to let it become too brown or burn. Add the flour and stir or whisk until the flour has a light golden color, 5 to 7 minutes. Whisk in the milk, about a cup at a time, until you have a smooth consistency. Continue whisking while bringing the sauce up to a gentle boil. Cook, whisking, until the béchamel is nicely thickened, 8 to 10 minutes. Remove from the heat, season with salt, pepper, and nutmeg, and cover. The béchamel may continue to thicken as it sits. If this happens, whisk in hot water a few tablespoons at a time until you reach a looser creamy consistency.

Tofu Lasagna

MY LASAGNA IS *a glorious layering of pasta, light and tasty tofu "cheese," savory "beef" sauce, and a creamy béchamel that can be prepared with or without dairy products. When preparing a dairy-free version, I add 3 tablespoons of nutritional yeast flakes as a tasty substitute for the grated Pecorino. Oftentimes I'll skip the cream sauce altogether and dress the lasagna with a little extra fresh basil and Simple Tomato Sauce (page 186).*

The lasagna keeps well and is even more delicious the next day. I usually make two 8 × 8-inch pans and then freeze one for those days when I'm too busy to cook but want a quick, hearty, and nutritious supper.

1. **TO MAKE THE TOFU FILLING:** Crumble the drained tofu into a bowl and work it around with your fingers until smooth; the texture should be similar to ricotta. If you prefer you may blend the tofu for 2 minutes in a food processor. Add the cheese, parsley, spinach, nutmeg, and salt and mix together with a fork until well blended. Taste and adjust seasoning with the pepper and additional salt and/or nutmeg.

2. **TO MAKE THE "BEEF" SAUCE:** Heat 3 tablespoons olive oil over medium heat in a heavy sauté pan. Add the garlic and onion and sauté until translucent, about 5 minutes. Add the oregano and sauté for a few minutes, until the oregano becomes nicely aromatic. Add the crumbles and continue to sauté until everything is nicely browned and heated through. Add the 2 tablespoons tomatoes along with a sprinkling of olive oil and cook for an additional 3 minutes. Season to taste.

3. **TO ASSEMBLE THE LASAGNA:** Preheat the oven to 350°F. Coat the bottom of an 8 × 8-inch baking sheet with a drizzle of olive oil. Place all the lasagna ingredients within reach of the prepared baking dish. Reserve 1 cup of the béchamel and ¼ cup of the basil.

4. In the baking dish, place 2 lasagna sheets. Spoon some of the "beef" sauce onto the noodles, then a ladle of béchamel, and toss on some basil. Add another layer of the noodles, then some tofu filling, and more béchamel. Continue layering the ingredients however you wish, ending with the ½ cup tomatoes and then a layer of noodles. Spoon the reserved 1 cup béchamel over the top, making sure to cover the entire surface of the uncooked noodles. Pour ¼ cup water around the edges of the lasagna. The water will bring up the moisture content of

Tofu Filling

One 12-ounce package extra-firm tofu, drained well

½ cup freshly grated Pecorino Romano or vegan cheese (optional)

½ cup chopped parsley

2 cups chopped baby spinach

1½ teaspoons grated nutmeg, plus more to taste

1 tablespoon fine sea salt, plus more to taste

Freshly ground black pepper, to taste

"Beef" Sauce

Extra virgin olive oil

2 garlic cloves, mashed

1 medium yellow onion, chopped into ¼-inch dice

3 tablespoons dried oregano

One 12-ounce package vegetarian "beef" crumbles

2 tablespoons chopped San Marzano tomatoes or Simple Tomato Sauce (below)

Salt and freshly ground black pepper, to taste

Lasagna

Béchamel (page 184)

About ¾ cup coarsely chopped basil leaves

1 pound no-boil lasagna noodles

½ cup chopped San Marzano tomatoes or Simple Tomato Sauce (below)

Extra virgin olive oil for drizzling

the lasagna and help to cook the no-boil noodles. Drizzle a little additional olive oil over the top.

5. Cover the lasagna with foil and bake for about 35 minutes. Remove the foil and bake for about 15 minutes, until the lasagna is bubbling and the noodles are cooked through. Let the lasagna rest for 10 minutes. Sprinkle with the reserved ¼ cup chopped basil, additional olive oil if desired, and serve.

Simple Tomato Sauce

■ MAKES 4 CUPS

TRAVELERS TO ITALY *are usually impressed with the simplicity and fresh flavors of pasta dishes, particularly those made with tomato sauce. Italian tomato sauces tend to be cooked quickly and subsequently retain a clean, light, and naturally sweet flavor. The longer tomatoes are cooked, the more heavily concentrated and acidic they become. This classic tomato sauce, which I've been making for decades, is one that should be a part of every cook's repertoire. It is versatile enough for tossing with any pasta, spooning over warm polenta, using as a sauce for pizza, or simply scooping up with hot garlic bread. The addition of a little butter just before serving is a trick I learned in Naples; it softens and gently rounds out the flavor of the tomatoes. Fresh basil is a must and if you're able to find imported San Marzano tomatoes the flavor of the sauce improves tenfold.*

3 tablespoons extra virgin olive oil, plus additional for serving
2 garlic cloves, minced
One 28-ounce can San Marzano tomatoes
Few pinches of fine sea salt
Handful of basil
2 to 3 tablespoons unsalted butter (optional)
Freshly grated Parmesan, (optional)

1. Heat the olive oil in a medium saucepan over medium heat. Add the garlic and sauté for a minute. Add the tomatoes and salt and cook for 15 to 20 minutes. Add the basil and butter. After saucing and before serving your pasta of choice, drizzle with a little additional olive oil, sprinkle with Parmesan, and garnish with a fresh basil leaf.

Vegetable Lasagna

TOO OFTEN VEGETABLE *lasagna is soggy and limp. But by properly cooking sweet parsnips and carrots and bright zucchini and yellow squash to perfection, you can make a lasagna with vegetables that retain their flavor and shape. This lasagna freezes well, so pick up extra vegetables at the farmers' market and make two. On a busy day, it's a blessing to have a satisfying meal on the table in no time.*

1. **TO MAKE THE TOFU FILLING:** In a medium bowl, combine the tofu, Pecorino (if using), parsley, nutmeg, and salt and mix together with a fork, until you reach a ricotta consistency. If using nutritional yeast, stir it in now.

2. **TO MAKE THE VEGETABLE FILLING:** Heat the olive oil in a deep skillet over medium-low heat. Add the parsnips and carrots and sauté for 5 to 8 minutes, until crisp-tender. Add the zucchini and squash and heat through, about 3 minutes. Remove the pan from the heat and let sit while assembling the lasagna.

3. **TO ASSEMBLE THE LASAGNA:** Preheat the oven to 375°F. Coat the bottom of an 8 × 8-inch baking dish with olive oil. Spread about ½ cup of the tomatoes over the bottom of the dish and top with 2 sheets of lasagna. Add a layer of about half of the vegetable filling and a few spoonfuls of the tomatoes, then spread about ½ cup of the béchamel on top. Add a second layer of pasta, alternating the direction of the noodles. Top with the tofu filling, then the spinach, a drizzle of olive oil, a pinch of salt, and a third layer of noodles. Add the remaining vegetable filling, a few dollops of tomato, a little more of the béchamel, and cover with 2 more lasagna noodles. Top the lasagna off with a nice cover of béchamel, a sprinkling of salt and pepper, a drizzle of olive oil, and the basil. Finally, spoon a little more of the tomatoes and 3 tablespoons of water around the edges of the lasagna.

4. Cover with foil and bake for about 40 minutes. Remove the foil and bake another 15 minutes, until the top is bubbly and the lasagna is tender. If desired, top with any remaining tomatoes. Serve hot.

Tofu Filling

One 12-ounce package extra-firm tofu, drained and crumbled

½ cup freshly grated Pecorino Romano or 3 tablespoons nutritional yeast

½ cup chopped parsley

1½ teaspoons grated nutmeg

2 teaspoons fine sea salt

Vegetable Filling

2 tablespoons extra virgin olive oil

2 cups julienned parsnips

1 cup julienned carrots

2 to 3 small zucchini, thinly sliced lengthwise

1 to 2 small yellow summer squash, thinly sliced lengthwise

Lasagna

Extra virgin olive oil

6 tomatoes, skinned and seeded, or 1 cup canned chopped tomatoes

1 pound no-boil lasagna noodles

Béchamel (page 184)

3 cups baby spinach, coarsely chopped

Salt and freshly ground black pepper, to taste

½ cup coarsely chopped basil

BURGERS AND SANDWICHES

THE BEST THING about sandwiches and burgers is that everybody can personalize them by adding their favorite toppings: mustard, mayonnaise, ketchup, hot sauce, slices of onion, tomato, or cucumber These vegetarian burgers are scrumptious and satisfying served on a bun or plopped on a fresh, tart cabbage slaw.

The following recipes are among those most requested by viewers of my show. I think this is because they're easy to prepare, and they're fresher and tastier than store-bought. Like so many of my recipes, the ingredients are culled from familiar components—whole grains, nuts, and savory, cooked vegetables. I often accompany the burgers and sandwiches with a bowl of hearty soup or stew or a vegetable side dish.

Beet Burgers

MAKES 8

2 tablespoons canola or other vegetable oil

3 small beets, quartered

1 medium yellow onion, coarsely chopped

1 medium carrot, cut into chunks

Salt and freshly ground black pepper, to taste

1 cup millet

½ cup walnut pieces

2 garlic cloves, peeled and minced

½ cup toasted wheat germ

2 slices whole wheat bread, lightly toasted and torn into pieces

Handful of unblemished beet green leaves, torn

I DID SAY beet, *and not* beef. *These savory-sweet burgers are best cooked over steady, low heat, because the beet sugars burn quite easily. For a chewier burger, I throw in ¼ cup toasted pumpkin seeds. I partner the burgers with Caribbean Cabbage and Carrot Salad (page 78) or Cabbage Slaw with Tomatoes and Ginger (page 79) and a puddle of hot sauce. Refrigerate any leftover mixture or freeze individually wrapped uncooked patties you don't use.*

1. Preheat the oven to 375°F. Drizzle 1 tablespoon of the oil on a baking sheet. Arrange the beets, onion, and carrot on the sheet in a single layer and lightly season with salt and pepper. Bake until the beets are fork tender, 25 to 30 minutes. Let the vegetables cool for at least 10 minutes.

2. Bring 2½ cups of water to a boil and stir in ½ teaspoon of salt and 1 cup millet. Cover, reduce the heat to a simmer, and cook for 20 to 25 minutes, just until the water is absorbed. Do not overcook the millet, as it will become gummy. Fluff the grains with a fork, spoon into a large bowl and allow it to cool for a few minutes.

3. Combine the walnuts, garlic, wheat germ, and bread pieces in a food processor and process to fine crumbs. Add to the millet. Combine the vegetables and beet greens in the processor and pulse until everything is finely chopped. Add to the millet mixture. With a large spoon, mix everything well and season liberally with salt and pepper. Refrigerate for 1 hour.

4. Take a handful of the mixture and pat it firmly between your hands into a patty. Repeat to make 8 patties. Heat the remaining 1 tablespoon oil in a sauté pan over medium-low heat. Add the burgers a few at a time, being careful to leave enough room between them so you can flip them easily. Don't move them once they're in the pan because they're somewhat delicate and this might cause them to fall apart. Cook the burgers undisturbed for 5 to 10 minutes, then carefully flip, and cook for 5 to 10 minutes longer. The burgers will develop a nice caramelized crust on both sides. Repeat with the remaining burgers.

RECIPE COURTESY OF DIDI EMMONS

Kasha Krunch Burgers

MAKES 8 TO 10

THIS BURGER IS *my hands-down favorite. The key to its success is to pan-fry the burgers until a thick, crunchy crust forms; use a heavy-bottomed, well-seasoned skillet such as cast iron. I use cremini mushrooms, but you can substitute white button or portobellos. Also, I tend to prefer cashews, but walnuts or hazelnuts work just as well. Substitute fresh tarragon for the parsley when it's available to lend the burger a slight anise flavor. Try it bunless with a squirt of Thai sriracha (hot sauce) on a bed of Cabbage Slaw with Tomatoes and Ginger (page 79) or as a satisfying brunch dish with a poached egg on top*

1. Heat the olive oil in a saucepan over medium heat and add the onion and carrot. Cook, stirring occasionally, until soft, 5 minutes. Add the garlic and cook 2 minutes. Add the brown rice, mushrooms, salt, and 5 cups water and bring to a boil. Reduce the heat, cover, and simmer 25 minutes. Stir in the kasha, cover, and cook until both the rice and kasha are tender and the liquid is completely absorbed, about 20 minutes. Remove from the heat and blend in the cashews and parsley. Let cool.

2. In 3 batches, pulse the kasha mixture in a food processor until finely chopped. If you want a chunkier texture, don't process to a fine chop. Transfer to a bowl and cover with plastic wrap.

3. To form the burgers, dust your hands with flour, and form the mixture into 8 to 10 patties. Lightly dredge in the flour (to create the crust). Heat about ¼ inch vegetable oil in a large cast-iron skillet over medium heat. Add the burgers and cook until the undersides are dark golden brown, about 5 minutes, lifting and checking frequently to prevent them from blackening. Carefully flip the burgers, and brown the other side for 5 minutes.

2 tablespoons extra virgin olive oil

1 small yellow onion, chopped

1 carrot, chopped

2 garlic cloves, minced

2 cups long-grain brown rice

8 ounces (1½ cups) cremini mushrooms, coarsely chopped

2 tablespoons kosher salt, to taste

1 cup kasha (toasted buckwheat groats)

1 cup cashews, toasted (see page 86) and chopped

¼ cup chopped parsley

¼ cup (or less) unbleached all-purpose flour

About ⅓ cup canola or other vegetable oil

RECIPE COURTESY OF DIDI EMMONS

Freezing Burgers

FORM THESE burgers into patties, separate by waxed or parchment paper, and store in an airtight container in the refrigerator for up to 2 days, or freeze for up to 2 months. Always wrap the burgers individually before freezing. Frozen burgers need to be defrosted completely before cooking. Defrost in a microwave in their wrappers for 2 minutes on the defrost setting. The added bonus is that if the burger is already warm inside, it cooks and browns much faster. Microwaving also gives you the flexibility to cook up a burger at a moment's notice.

Black-Eyed Burgers

MAKES 4

One 15½-ounce can black-eyed peas, drained and rinsed

1 medium shallot, finely minced

1 scallion, white and green part, chopped

3 tablespoons chopped parsley

¼ teaspoon chili sauce

2 tablespoons extra virgin olive oil

6 ounces cremini mushrooms, coarsely chopped

½ cup chopped walnuts, toasted (see page 86)

2 garlic cloves, minced

Salt and freshly ground black pepper, to taste

½ cup all-purpose flour

1 to 2 tablespoons canola or other vegetable oil

4 soft whole grain sandwich buns

THIS HEALTHY BURGER *is long on onion flavors and chewy bean texture. Black-eyed peas, also known as cowpeas, are traditionally served Down South on New Year's Day to bring luck and prosperity. They hold their texture well when cooked and are loaded with nutrients, particularly vitamin A and calcium. Try a burger on a soft bun thickly spread with spicy brown mustard or horseradish-spiked ketchup, accompanied by Red Bliss Potato Salad (page 96) or Malibu Spicy Vegetables and Rice (page 211)*

1. Mash the peas in a large bowl and add the shallot, scallion, parsley, and chili sauce. Heat a skillet over medium-high heat. Add the olive oil and heat for a count of 10. Add the mushrooms and sauté until nicely browned, 5 minutes. Add the walnuts and garlic and sauté for 1 or 2 minutes longer, until the mushrooms are cooked through, but not watery.

2. Add the mushroom mixture to the pea mixture and season with salt and pepper. Blend well with your hands or a fork. The mixture should be a bit crumbly but easily shaped into patties. I like a big burger, so I form mine into 4 patties up to 4 inches across and ¾-inch thick, but you can make them smaller and thinner if you prefer, simply adjust your cooking time.

3. Heat a cast-iron skillet with a good coating of vegetable oil, up to 2 tablespoons, over medium-high heat. Pour the flour into a dish. Dredge each burger in the flour, then place in the hot skillet. Cook until the burgers develop a crispy brown coating, 5 to 7 minutes. Check by gently lifting a burger with a spatula. When they are done on one side, turn them over, being careful not to break them into crumbles, and cook the other sides the same way. Serve the hot burgers in the buns.

Eggplant Wraps
with Green Yogurt Sauce

MAKES 4

THESE WRAPS PACK *very well for school or office take-along lunches: roll in waxed or parchment paper, slice in half through the paper, then wrap tightly with foil.*

1. **TO MAKE THE SAUCE:** In a small bowl, mix the yogurt, mayonnaise, parsley, and mint. Season to taste with salt and pepper.

2. Heat the oil in a wide cast-iron skillet over medium heat. Add the eggplant slices and cook, turning once, until lightly golden, about 5 minutes. Drain on paper towels.

3. To assemble a wrap, arrange a few slices of eggplant in a sandwich wrap and cover generously with yogurt sauce. Layer on tomato, cucumber, jalapeño, lettuce, and finish with a sprinkle of cilantro. Fold in the sides of the tortilla, roll up burrito-style, and slice the wrap in half. Repeat to make 3 more wraps.

Green Yogurt Sauce

8 ounces plain dairy or vegan yogurt

3 tablespoons regular or vegan mayonnaise

1/4 cup chopped parsley

1/4 cup chopped mint

Salt and freshly ground black pepper, to taste

3 tablespoons extra virgin olive oil

1 medium eggplant, thinly sliced

4 sandwich wraps or tortillas, any flavor

1 firm ripe red tomato, thinly sliced

1 small cucumber, thinly sliced

1 jalapeño pepper, seeded and thinly sliced

4 to 5 leaves romaine lettuce, roughly chopped

Small handful of chopped cilantro

No-Egg Salad Sandwiches

MAKES 2 TO 4

One 14-ounce package firm tofu, drained

½ cup regular or vegan mayonnaise

2 tablespoons Dijon mustard

½ to 1 teaspoon cayenne pepper

½ teaspoon turmeric

2 tablespoons chopped parsley

1 tablespoon chopped dill

½ cup minced scallions

Salt and freshly ground black pepper, to taste

4 to 8 slices whole grain bread

THE FLAVOR AND *texture of the healthy tofu mix mimics traditional egg salad. I pile a generous scoop on top of a mixed green or fresh fruit salad, or serve it as a spread with crackers. Control the heat of the cayenne pepper by adding ⅛ of a teaspoon at a time and, of course, if you prefer a milder flavor, don't use it at all. If using vegan mayonnaise, add 1 teaspoon lemon juice or cider vinegar to bump up the flavor.*

1. With a fork, mash the tofu in a bowl, leaving some chunky texture to the mixture. Fold in the mayonnaise, mustard, cayenne, turmeric, parsley, dill, and scallions and mix until well combined. The color should be an even consistent golden color. Season with salt and pepper. Cover with plastic wrap and refrigerate for at least 30 minutes before serving to allow the flavors to mingle. Spread the salad between 2 slices of bread and enjoy. Leftover salad keeps for up to 10 days in the refrigerator, but it never lasts that long in my house.

Mock Fish Salad Sandwiches

MAKES 2 TO 4

IN ADDITION TO *making hearty sandwiches, this faux fish salad can be tossed with hot pasta or used as a filling for Mock Crab–Stuffed Mushrooms (page 52) or Marvelous Meaty Wontons (page 51). Blend it to a smoother spread and serve on crackers or melba toasts. If you're unable to find tempeh with sea vegetables, add 2 sheets of chopped nori or try some kombu dashi powder, a dried seaweed powder. If you go with the powder, add it slowly, bit by bit, until you have the "fish" taste you want.*

2 tablespoons extra virgin olive oil

1 small to medium onion, cut into $\frac{1}{4}$-inch dice

One 8-ounce package tempeh with sea vegetables, diced

1 sheet nori, cut into $\frac{1}{4}$-inch pieces

1 tablespoon regular or vegan mayonnaise

Salt and freshly ground black pepper, to taste

4 to 8 slices crusty Italian bread

4 to 8 leaves crunchy lettuce, washed and dried

1. Heat a heavy skillet over medium heat until hot. Add the olive oil and onion and sauté until the onion is translucent, 3 to 5 minutes. Add the tempeh and sauté until browned. Remove the pan from the heat and stir in the nori. Let cool for 15 to 30 minutes. Add the mayonnaise, mix everything very well, and season with salt and pepper to taste.

2. Spread the salad on half of the bread slices and top with the lettuce. Cover with the remaining bread and serve.

Mock Maryland Crab Cakes

MAKES 10

3 teaspoons canola or other vegetable oil

½ cup minced celery

½ cup minced yellow onion

⅓ cup minced carrot

½ small green or red bell pepper, minced

¼ cup chopped parsley

One 14-ounce package firm tofu, drained and pressed dry

5 slices whole wheat bread, toasted and processed into fine crumbs

1 cup panko (Japanese bread crumbs)

½ cup regular or vegan mayonnaise

1 sheet nori seaweed, chopped into flakes

1 tablespoon Old Bay seasoning

2 teaspoon dry mustard

1 teaspoon fine sea salt

Wedges of fresh lemon, for squeezing

Wasabi Mayonnaise (below)

AFTER A VISIT *to Baltimore, where I was unsuccessful in tracking down a vegetarian alternative to those famous Maryland crab cakes, I developed this version. They replicate the flavors and textures of traditional seafood-based croquettes quite well. Serve with a side of oven fries.*

1. Preheat the oven to 350°F. Heat 1 teaspoon of the oil in a skillet over medium heat. Add the celery, onion, carrot, pepper, and parsley and sauté until softened but still firm. Process the tofu in a food processor until the consistency of cottage cheese; do not purée. In a large bowl, combine the sautéed vegetables, tofu, half of the bread crumbs, the mayonnaise, seaweed, Old Bay, mustard, and salt and mix very well. Add the remaining crumbs a little at a time, until the mixture is easy to shape into patties.

2. Using a ⅓-cup measure, shape the mixture into ten ½-inch-thick cakes. Spread the panko on a plate. Carefully dredge the cakes in the panko to coat. These patties are delicate and must be handled gently to avoid having them crumble.

3. Heat the remaining 2 teaspoons oil in a nonstick skillet over medium heat. In batches, gently place the cakes in the hot oil and cook on one side, without fussing with them, until they're golden brown and move easily when you shake the pan, 5 to 8 minutes. With a spatula, gently flip the cakes and cook until golden brown on the other side. Serve hot with wedges of fresh lemon and the Wasabi Mayonnaise.

Wasabi Mayonnaise

■ **MAKES ABOUT ½ CUP**

4 ounces regular or vegan mayonnaise
1 to 2 teaspoons wasabi powder, adjusted to your desire for heat
1 tablespoon dairy or soy milk

1. Blend all the ingredients together with a wire whisk in a bowl.

Tempeh Club Sandwiches

THE COFFEE SHOP *club sandwich is usually prepared with mayonnaise, layers of chicken or turkey, bacon, iceberg lettuce, and tomato slices. In this grilled version, tempeh takes the place of turkey and bacon, romaine lettuce for iceberg, and Russian dressing for mayo. Plus, there's an abundance of healthy vegetables. If you don't want to use store-bought Russian dressing, make your own simple sandwich version by whisking together ¼ cup mayonnaise with 3 tablespoons ketchup and ½ teaspoon minced pickle or relish.*

1. Heat a stovetop grill pan or skillet. Prepare a slice of bread with a slather of Russian dressing, and then a layer of the cheese (if using), a slice or two of tempeh, a tomato slice, red onion pieces, pepper strips, and lettuce. Top with the another slice of bread and brush the top with butter. Flip the whole sandwich and place the buttered side down onto the hot grill or skillet. Brush the top with butter. Cook until the bottom is browned and crispy and carefully flip it over, using a spatula. Grill the other side. Repeat to make the remaining sandwiches.

8 to 12 slices hearty sandwich bread

5 tablespoons Russian dressing

4 slices Swiss cheese (optional)

Jamaican Jerk Tempeh (page 160) or Tamari Tempeh (page 158)

1 large fresh ripe tomato, thinly sliced

1 small red onion, thinly sliced

3 fresh or water-packed roasted red peppers, cut into wide strips

4 to 6 romaine lettuce leaves

Melted unsalted butter or vegetable oil, for brushing

Cornhusker's Reubens

2 slices Swiss cheese

4 slices New York rye bread

4 slices Tamari Tempeh
(page 158)

¾ cup sauerkraut, drained

2 tablespoons
Russian dressing

Soft unsalted butter
or vegetable oil

THE REUBEN SANDWICH *is usually made with corned beef or pastrami, sauerkraut, and cheese on rye bread, and then grilled or broiled until the cheese melts. Though the origins of the Reuben sandwich are disputed, this vegetarian version is named after the Nebraska hotel restaurant that boasts the oldest known menu reference to the American classic. Be sure to drain the sauerkraut very well, so the sandwiches don't become soggy. If you don't like sauerkraut, substitute with coleslaw which will make a sandwich called a Rachel. I serve the sandwiches with a lightly dressed pasta salad like Orzo, Basil, and Sun-Dried Tomato Salad (page 91).*

1. Heat a cast-iron skillet over medium heat. Build a sandwich by laying the Swiss cheese across a slice of bread. Top with 2 slices of tempeh laid side to side at an angle, then spread with Russian dressing, a generous spoonful of sauerkraut, and finish with another slice of bread. Butter or oil the top. Repeat to make a second sandwich.

2. Slide a spatula underneath an assembled sandwich and, holding the top piece of bread with your fingers to keep it from falling apart, flip the whole thing over and lay onto the hot pan. Butter or oil the top. Repeat with the other sandwich. Grill the sandwiches until golden brown. Flip them over to grill the other sides the same way, until everything is hot and the cheese is melted. Remove the sandwiches from the pan, cut on the diagonal, and serve.

New York Hot Dogs and Onions

WHEN I WAS *young, going into New York City always included a stop at my dad's favorite street vendor for a kosher hot dog slathered with mustard, piled with spicy cooked onions, and washed down with an Italian lemon ice. This meat-free version evokes those warm childhood memories. The key is in caramelizing the onions.*

I prefer Yves Meatless Hot Dogs, but everybody has a favorite and most natural food stores offer a dozen or more "dog" options. If you're not a hot dog person, the onions are just as good piled onto Kasha Krunch Burgers (page 191) or in a submarine sandwich made with Eggplant Meatballs (page 214).

Spicy Onions

¼ cup canola or other vegetable oil

2 to 3 pounds yellow onions, thinly sliced into half moons

3 generous pinches kosher salt

1 tablespoon (or less) tomato paste, to taste

1 to 2 teaspoons sriracha, or 1 teaspoon red pepper flakes, or to taste

Dogs

Mustard

6 to 8 whole grain hot dog buns

6 to 8 vegetarian hot dogs, any variety, steamed or boiled

1. **TO MAKE THE ONIONS:** Heat a large Dutch oven over medium-low heat. Add the oil and heat for a count of 10. Add the onions and stir to coat evenly with the hot oil. Sprinkle with the salt so they sweat and release their sugars. Toss the onions again and cook, keeping an eye on the heat and turning it down if needed and stirring occasionally, until they become soft and buttery, 30 to 40 minutes. Don't let the onions brown. When the onions are tender and most of any liquid has evaporated, remove them from the heat. Add the tomato paste, a teaspoon at a time, using a wooden spoon to blend them well. The onions will take on a nice, pink color. Add 1 teaspoon of the sriracha. Blend well and taste, adding more sriracha if you like. I like my onions pretty spicy, so I go with the full measure. (When adjusting the heat level of spices, always add a little at a time.) Makes 4 cups onions. Refrigerate unused onions in a lidded jar for up to 2 weeks.

2. **TO MAKE THE DOGS:** Slather mustard on the buns, put the cooked hot dogs into the buns, and pile on the onions.

Cooking Hot Dogs

VEGETABLE-BASED dogs contain little or no fat, therefore they cook quickly and have a tendency to become dry and chewy. I've discovered the best way to keep them firm and moist is to steam or boil them—in the microwave or on the stovetop—for 3 to 5 minutes. If you're grilling them, brush them first with a little bit of vegetable oil and cook until just heated through, about 5 minutes.

Soysage-Pepper Sandwiches

MAKES 4

2 to 3 tablespoons extra virgin olive oil

4 to 6 Italian-style vegetarian sausage links

2 large yellow onions, thinly sliced into half moons

Salt and freshly ground black pepper, to taste

3 to 4 orange, yellow, or red bell peppers, seeded and thinly sliced

2 to 3 garlic cloves, finely chopped

½ cup tomato sauce

2 to 3 tablespoons chiffonade basil (see page 57)

Red pepper flakes, to taste

4 crusty Italian-style rolls or 8 slices crusty bread

4 slices provolone (optional)

I SERVE THE *sausage and peppers tucked into crusty Italian bread rolls and garnished with shreds of fresh basil. A sprinkle of dried oregano and thyme on the softened peppers adds fragrance and even more Italian flavor. If you're a cheesehead, definitely go with the melted provolone on top. The hearty sausage mixture also perks up brunch when accompanied by scrambled eggs or as a topping for Creamy Polenta (page 229). If using breakfast-style vegetable links, add ¼ teaspoon fennel seed and ¼ teaspoon red pepper flakes when browning the sausage.*

1. Place a large skillet over medium heat and add 1 tablespoon of the olive oil. Wait for a count of 10, then add the sausage links. Cook until browned evenly on all sides. Transfer to a plate.

2. Into the same pan, pour another tablespoon (or two) of olive oil, add the onions, and sprinkle with a bit of salt. Sauté the onions until they begin to soften and start to turn golden, 7 to 10 minutes. Add the peppers and cook, stirring occasionally, until softened and browned, 10 to 15 minutes. If the peppers stick, just add a splash more olive oil. Add the garlic and cook for 1 or 2 minutes. Add the tomato sauce and half of the basil and season with red pepper flakes, salt, and pepper. Cook until the mixture is hot and neither too saucy nor too dry, 5 to 7 minutes. Return the sausages to the pan and heat through. Remove the pan from the heat and let it rest for 5 minutes.

3. Spoon the sausage mixture into the rolls or place between slices of bread and sprinkle with the remaining basil. If you like, top each sandwich with a slice of provolone, then quickly broil until the cheese melts.

VEGETABLES

THEY MAY BE called side dishes, but recipes like this often function—at least for me—as the foundation for a meal; therefore you want them to be delicious, nutritious, and inspiring, yet simple to prepare. In my experience, dishes that start with fundamental ingredients don't need to be intricate in order to taste fabulous.

When you're working with vegetables, a simple squeeze of fresh lemon, a drizzle of fruity olive oil, and a little garlic intensify the flavors of most without the clutter of heavy sauces or cheese. By following my easy preparation techniques, vegetables you didn't even know you liked may soon become your new favorites. Partnered with an entrée, or shining on their own, these dishes encourage you to use your imagination and inspire you to explore new flavor possibilities.

Marinated Portobello Mushrooms

6 large portobello mushrooms, stems removed and saved for stock

vegetable oil spray

2 tablespoons canola or other vegetable oil

2 tablespoons dark soy sauce

2 tablespoons vegetarian Worcestershire sauce

Freshly ground black pepper, to taste

GRILLING MARINATED RAW *mushrooms has never quite worked for me for two reasons: One, the raw mushrooms don't sufficiently absorb the marinade's great flavors. And two, they can make a real mess of a grill. But because I adore grilled mushrooms, I grill or roast mushrooms first, and then marinate them in a favorite dressing. Like the sponges they are, the mushrooms absorb the marinade without any mess. Sometimes, instead of marinating them in strips, I leave them whole or halved and serve on a toasted whole grain bun spread with mustard and mayonnaise and topped by a crunchy leaf of romaine. For a Sunday night family dinner, serve with Porcini Gravy (page 107) and Mashed Potatoes, Two Ways (pg 218).*

1. Preheat a large, well-seasoned cast-iron or grill pan for 15 minutes or so over medium-low to medium heat; you want it hot but not burning. While the pan preheats, use a spoon and gently scrape the dark gills out of each mushroom cap. Removing the gills removes a lot of the water, which allows the meaty texture of mushroom to be enhanced by cooking and much more receptive to the marinade.

2. Rinse the caps quickly under cold water and blot dry with paper towels. Remove the hot pan from the heat and lightly coat with vegetable oil spray. Return to the heat and place the mushrooms on the hot surface, hollow side down. Cook the mushrooms slowly over medium heat, pressing them with a spatula against the surface of the pan every so often. When the undersides begin to turn a dark, uniform color, turn and cook the other side in the same manner, pressing down every so often with the flat of a spatula. When the mushrooms are nicely colored, flattened, and cooked through—about 10 minutes—transfer to a plate and let cool slightly. You may have to do this in batches if your grill pan isn't large enough to hold all of the mushrooms.

3. In a medium bowl, combine the oil, soy sauce, Worcestershire, and black pepper, and whisk into an emulsion. When the mushrooms are cool enough to handle, cut into ¼-inch-thick slices and add to the marinade. Toss well to make sure the mushrooms are evenly coated. Add several grindings of black pepper and allow them to absorb the flavors for at least 10 minutes.

Grilled Asparagus with Lime

ASPARAGUS IS THE *culinary harbinger of spring. When it's plentiful, I buy it whenever I see it. I add asparagus tips to scrambled eggs or tofu for breakfast; for lunch, they are lightly steamed and laid across a sandwich in place of lettuce; and for dinner, I grill them, as in this recipe. Everybody knows lemon and asparagus go well together, but once I tried lime, I never went back; the key is to slightly undercook the asparagus because the lime helps tenderize it. Look for thick asparagus stalks with tight tips; they're easier to grill than the skinny ones. Don't cut off the tough ends; instead, snap off the bottom end of each spear just above where the woody stalk meets the tender spear. You can grill these outside over gas or hot coals or inside on a grill pan. Any leftover stalks are tasty eaten cold right out of the refrigerator. As they sit, they will become more tender.*

Good-size bunch of fresh asparagus, about 14 stalks, tough ends snapped off

1 tablespoon extra virgin olive oil

Kosher salt and freshly ground black pepper, to taste

1 lime, halved

A few shavings of Pecorino cheese (optional)

1. Preheat a grill, grill pan, or charcoal grill until hot. Blanch the asparagus spears in salted, boiling water for 1 to 2 minutes, only until bright green. Immediately transfer to a colander and rinse under cold water to stop the cooking. Place the spears in a wide bowl where they'll fit in the bottom and lightly brush with the olive oil.

2. Place the spears sideways on the hot grill, being careful that they don't fall through. If you prefer, use a flat-bottomed grill basket designed to hold smaller vegetables. Using long-handled tongs, turn the asparagus until all sides begin to turn golden and the spears are slightly tender, 5 to 10 minutes, depending upon the level of heat. When the asparagus is cooked but still retaining some crunch, pull off the grill and arrange on a serving platter. Season with salt and pepper, Pecorino cheese, and then give them a good squeeze of fresh lime. I usually use at least half, if not more, of the lime.

Sesame-Ginger Green Beans

SERVES 4

1 pound fresh green beans, trimmed and diagonally cut into 2-inch pieces

2 tablespoons hoisin sauce

2 tablespoons mirin (rice wine)

1 teaspoon sesame oil

1 tablespoon canola or other vegetable oil

1 tablespoon sesame seeds

1½ to 2 tablespoons minced ginger

1 garlic clove, minced

Salt and freshly ground black pepper, to taste

THIS EASY ASIAN-INSPIRED *sauce works with just about any vegetable. Crisp green beans, which I use here, are my favorite but fresh asparagus comes in a close second. I serve with Best Braised Tempeh (page 156) and Millet (page 233). You could also pile the beans onto brown or white rice for a quick hot lunch.*

1. Bring a large pot of salted water to a boil. Add the green beans and cook for 5 to 7 minutes, until tender. Drain in a colander and rinse under cold water to stop the cooking.

2. Combine the hoisin, mirin, and sesame oil in a small bowl and whisk until smooth. Heat a large nonstick skillet over medium heat and add the canola oil. Add the sesame seeds to the center of the pan—they will pop and move toward the outside of the pan on their own. Shake the pan until the seeds begin to brown, 3 to 4 minutes. Add the ginger and garlic, shake the pan again, and cook for 1 minute. Using a wooden spoon, add the hoisin mixture, turn the heat up just a bit, and add the green beans with a sprinkle of salt. Cook, stirring frequently and coating the green beans with the sauce, just until they're heated through and tender, 3 to 5 minutes. The sauce should be a shiny glaze on the green beans. Season with salt and pepper and serve.

Hoisin Sauce

HOISIN IS a thick, dark brown, sweet and spicy sauce made from a blend of soybeans, chile peppers, garlic, sugar, and spices. Available in supermarkets and Asian markets, hoisin can be used as a table condiment, a seasoning, or a barbeque sauce. Stored in a tightly sealed glass or plastic container in the refrigerator, hoisin will keep for up to 2 years.

Lemony Broccolini

SERVES 2

THE COMBINATION OF *fresh lemon, garlic, and olive oil goes with so many things, but it is especially good with the delicate, asparagus-like flavor of broccolini—a hybrid of broccoli and Chinese chard that is loaded with vitamin C, potassium, and other vitamins and minerals. Use this basic recipe to prepare broccoli and broccoli rabe as well. Greens that lean toward the bitter side benefit first from parboiling or steaming for few minutes. If you're out of lemon, substitute 1 to 2 tablespoons of a good balsamic vinegar to add a tart-sweet flavor.*

1 bunch broccolini, rinsed well

1 tablespoon (or less) extra virgin olive oil

2 garlic cloves, minced

Grated zest and juice of ½ lemon

¼ cup toasted (see page 86) pine nuts (optional)

Salt and freshly ground black pepper, to taste

Crushed red pepper flakes

1. Using a steamer insert in a medium saucepan, steam the broccolini until bright green and tender enough to be pierced with a knife, 5 minutes or less. Transfer to a colander and rinse under very cold water, then drain well.

2. Heat a large skillet over medium heat. Add the oil and as soon as it appears to be moving, add the garlic and working quickly, stir to prevent browning. With the garlic sizzling, add the broccolini and toss everything to coat with the oil and garlic. Continue cooking for 5 to 10 minutes, just until the broccolini is very tender. Transfer to a serving plate and dress with the lemon juice, zest, and pine nuts, if using. Season with salt and pepper, sprinkle with the red pepper, and serve.

Boiling Broccolini

IF YOU don't have a steamer basket, bring 1 cup water to a boil in a 4-quart saucepan. Drop in the broccolini, cover, and cook for 5 to 10 minutes (or less), until the broccolini is very tender. Boiling imparts more water than steaming, so be sure to drain well.

Properly Cooking Vegetables

UNDERCOOKED VEGETABLES—especially those in the broccoli and cabbage family—can be difficult for many people to digest, causing discomfort, gas, and bloating. In Italy undercooked vegetables are rarely served; in fact, you are more likely to see vegetables well boiled or steamed. We're often told that overcooking vegetables removes valuable nutrients. But in some cases, as with broccoli, cooking can actually increase the variety of nutrients that are released inside our digestive tracts, and most nutrition experts agree that there is no significant loss of nutrients in well-cooked vegetables. Since it's much easier to digest well-cooked vegetables, I've become an advocate of doing just that. Even if you're a fan of crunchy, undercooked vegetables, try my method to test the difference in digestion.

Oven-Dried Tomatoes

MAKES 12 TO 14

3 pounds Roma tomatoes

¼ teaspoon kosher salt

Few pinches of freshly
ground black pepper

OVEN DRYING ENHANCES *the sweetness of tomatoes while preserving summer's favorite crop at the same time. When tomatoes are in season, affordable, and abundant, buy extra to dry in this manner. Slow cooking in the oven dehydrates the tomatoes and prepares them for preserving; you'll want them to be dry, a bit leathery, yet flexible. To preserve the tomatoes in oil, they must be very dry because any water will cause the tomatoes to become rancid. Cover your oven-dried tomatoes with olive oil in a lidded jar to preserve in the refrigerator and add to any recipe for a rich, sweet, tomato flavor. You can follow the same technique for cherry tomatoes, but don't scoop out the insides, and cut them in half at the equator, not from stem to tip.*

1. Preheat the oven to 200°F. Line a baking sheet with parchment or foil. Cut off the stem ends of the tomatoes, then cut each tomato in half lengthwise. With a teaspoon, gently scoop out the juicy insides and compost them. Place the tomatoes, cut sides up, on the prepared baking sheet and sprinkle with the salt and pepper.

2. Bake for 2 to 3 hours. Resist the urge to turn the heat up and hurry this process along, or the tomatoes will burn. Since Roma tomatoes vary in size, at the end of the cooking time some may be nice and dry while others remain a little moist. Return the moist ones to the oven to dry further.

Wine-Braised Fennel

I CREATED THIS *recipe after enjoying fennel lightly braised with fresh tomatoes in white wine in Sorrento. When braised or roasted, fennel becomes lighter and sweeter and its anise flavor mellows. I serve the wine-scented fennel spooned over brown rice, piled onto rye toast, or over Tuscan bread for bruschetta.*

4 fennel bulbs

4 tablespoons (½ stick) unsalted butter or extra virgin olive oil

⅓ cup dry white wine

Kosher salt and freshly ground black pepper, to taste

2 tablespoons grated dairy or vegan Parmesan

1. Remove any discolored, woody outer layers of the fennel bulbs and slice the bulbs crosswise into ½-inch-thick slices. Heat a heavy sauté pan large enough to hold the fennel in a single layer over medium heat. Add the butter and heat until the foam subsides. If using olive oil, heat slowly just until warmed through but not smoking. Add the fennel in a single layer, pour the wine over, and season with salt and pepper. Cover and simmer for 10 to 15 minutes, until the fennel is fairly tender when poked with a knife. The fennel should appear caramelized, turning a light golden brown underneath, and most of the liquid should be absorbed. Turn the fennel pieces, cover, and continue cooking until the other side colors, another 5 minutes or so. Sprinkle with cheese, if using, and serve hot.

Sicilian Fennel

SERVES 4

6 fennel bulbs

6 ripe plum tomatoes

2 tablespoons extra virgin olive oil

1 small yellow or white onion, chopped

¼ cup raisins

1 tablespoon pan-roasted cumin seeds, crushed

Salt and freshly ground black pepper, to taste

Fruity Sicilian extra virgin olive oil

THE BEST FENNEL *in Italy is grown under the hot sun of Sicily, which is also the inspiration for this recipe. Known as* finocchio *(fee-NO-kee-o) in Italy, the tender white bulb can be eaten raw, alone or in salads, or cooked in a variety of ways.*

1. Trim the leafy tops of the fennel, slice off the tough root ends, and peel off any tough outer leaves. Quarter the bulbs.

2. To skin the tomatoes, drop them one by one into a small saucepan of boiling water. After just a few seconds, the skins will pucker and loosen. Immediately remove the tomatoes from the water with a slotted spoon and run under cold water. When cool enough to handle, slide the tomato meat out of the skin and coarsely chop the pulp.

3. Heat the oil in a deep skillet over medium heat. Add the onion and sauté until softened. Add the fennel and sauté for 5 minutes or so. Add the tomatoes, raisins, and cumin. Stir everything well, cover, and simmer for 25 to 30 minutes, until the fennel quarters are easily pierced with a knife. Season with salt and freshly ground pepper to taste, dress with Sicilian olive oil, and serve.

Sesame-Garlic Kale

BESIDES CARRYING LOADS *of vitamins and minerals, kale offers a delightful sharp flavor that's enhanced when combined with garlic and toasted sesame seeds. I steam-cook my kale before sautéing; it saves time and preserves vitamins. Look for bright green, crispy kale with no yellow leaves. Tear the leaves away from the tough center ribs; be sure to rinse the kale thoroughly to wash away any sand hiding among the curly leaves. This recipe works with any variety of kale, such as purple Russian or lacinata (dinosaur) kale.*

1. Fill a large pot about one-fourth full with water. Add the kale leaves; it isn't necessary to submerge the strips—the goal is to steam them. Cover the pot, return the water to a boil, and steam-cook for 2 minutes. Transfer the greens to a colander and rinse under cold water. Drain thoroughly to remove most of the water. When cool enough to handle, squeeze out any additional liquid with your hands.

2. Heat a large deep skillet over medium heat. Add the olive oil and garlic and sauté for 3 to 5 minutes. Add the toasted sesame seeds, and turn up the heat to medium-high. Add the cooked greens and toss and sear for 5 minutes, until the kale is crisp-tender. Remove the pan from the heat, season with the salt and pepper, toss again to combine, and serve.

2 generous bunches kale, washed, ribs removed, leaves chopped into strips

2 tablespoons extra virgin olive oil

2 to 3 tablespoons chopped garlic

2 tablespoons sesame seeds, toasted

Salt and freshly ground black pepper, to taste

RECIPE COURTESY OF HEIDI VALENZUELA

Peas and Pecans

1 pound frozen organic petit peas

1½ tablespoons unsalted butter or extra virgin olive oil

1½ tablespoons honey or maple syrup

¼ cup chopped pecans

VEGETABLES CAN BE *a tough sell to children. On the other hand, sugar and sweetened foods seem to go over without a hitch. This recipe takes naturally sweet peas and makes them even sweeter so kids tend to gobble them up. Make sure you don't overcook them—texture plays an important role in how kids accept food and most like things chewy, not mushy. Pecans add even more chewy texture, as well as sweet, nutty flavor and a boost of nutrition. If the kids go for these peas, try preparing green beans, lima beans, or carrots the same way. My son loves the peas in a bowl mixed with crispy Golden Tofu Bites (page 50), but they're also fantastic cascading over steamed or roasted sweet potatoes, accompanying Kasha Krunch Burgers (page 191).*

1. Cook the peas according to the package directions and drain well. Heat the butter in a saucepan over medium heat and add the honey and pecans. Cook, stirring, for 2 to 3 minutes, just until the pecans are evenly coated and bubbly. Add the cooked peas, stir everything to combine, and serve immediately.

Malibu Spicy Vegetables and Rice

INSPIRED BY A *chopped salad I once had in California, this rice dish is studded with sautéed fresh corn and sweet red peppers, red cabbage, and fresh scallions. I created it in late summer, when fresh corn was available, but if you're making it in midwinter, substitute frozen corn. I use brown basmati rice cooked in stock, but you can substitute long-grain brown rice cooked in water if you prefer a more neutral flavor. No matter the ingredients, the key is to make sure to dice your vegetables small to create the right "chop" texture. I often have this for lunch or dinner with Tempeh Fajitas (page 167). Bump up the heat with a generous sprinkle of cayenne pepper. The dish tastes even better after a day or two in the refrigerator; I've been known to scoop it onto my plate next to scrambled eggs for breakfast.*

1 cup brown basmati rice

2½ cups Vegetable Stock (page 106)

2 tablespoons extra virgin olive oil

4 ears corn, kernels sliced off the cob

1 large red bell pepper, seeded and finely diced

1 small head red cabbage, cored and finely diced

1 bunch scallions, white and green parts, finely chopped

1 tablespoon pan-roasted cumin, crushed

2 tablespoons red wine vinegar

¼ teaspoon sriracha

Salt and freshly ground black pepper, to taste

1. Gently dry-roast the rice in a heavy saucepan over medium heat until toasty-smelling, about 2 minutes. Add the stock and bring to a boil. Reduce the heat to low, cover, and cook for 50 minutes, until the rice is tender but firm. Uncover and let cool for 10 to 15 minutes.

2. Meanwhile, heat a wide skillet over medium heat, pour in the olive oil, and wait half a minute. Add the corn and red pepper and sauté for 5 to 10 minutes, just until the vegetables are tender but retain some bite. Transfer the vegetables to a large serving bowl, add the cabbage and scallions, and turn to combine.

3. Combine the crushed cumin with the red wine vinegar and sriracha and blend with a fork. Add the rice to the vegetable mixture, pour the spicy vinegar over everything, and toss to coat the rice and combine all the ingredients. Season with salt and pepper. Serve warm or at room temperature.

Rosemary-Roasted Winter Vegetables

SERVES 4

1 good-size head cauliflower, pulled apart or cut into small florets

1 medium butternut squash, peeled and cut into 2-inch pieces

6 to 10 garlic cloves, unpeeled

1 shallot, coarsely chopped

¼ cup extra virgin olive oil

Kosher salt and freshly ground black pepper, to taste

3 to 4 whole sprigs rosemary

¼ cup pine nuts, toasted (see page 86)

¼ cup freshly grated Parmesan (optional)

WITH ITS BRILLIANT *orange flesh, sweet butternut squash is a perfect partner for cauliflower. Roasted together with fragrant rosemary, garlic cloves, and buttery pine nuts, this is delicious as a side dish accompanied by warm, crusty bread to sop up the savory juices or tucked into Chickpea Crepes (page 132). Sometimes I toss in currants or raisins and pecans for sweetness and crunch. While I usually melt a bit of Parmesan over the hot roasted vegetables, vegans can either omit the cheese or substitute vegan Parmesan.*

1. Preheat the oven to 425°F. Combine the cauliflower, squash, garlic, and shallot in a roomy work bowl. Drizzle the olive oil over the vegetables, season with 1 teaspoon salt and a few grinds of pepper, and toss to coat. Pile the vegetables into a roasting pan or terra cotta baking dish. The vegetables shouldn't be in a single layer—they'll stay moist and steam each other when piled into the dish. Arrange the rosemary sprigs all around. Sprinkle with the pine nuts.

2. Roast the vegetables for 20 minutes. If they become a bit dry, drizzle with additional oil and add a few tablespoons of water—not a lot, just enough to bump up the moisture. After 20 minutes or so, the vegetables will be browning on top, so turn them with a spoon and continue roasting another 15 minutes, or until the squash is fork tender and caramelized on the bottom of the dish. Remove the baking dish from the oven. Adjust the seasonings and sprinkle with Parmesan if using. Cover the baking dish lightly with foil to allow vegetables to sweat and rest. After 5 minutes, the rosemary should be soft and fragrant. Any leaves remaining on the twigs can easily be pulled off and mixed with the juices.

Roasting Vegetables

THE DIFFERENCE between baking and roasting is the temperature. Roasting is accomplished at a higher heat, usually 400°F or more, in an open casserole or pan that cooks vegetables from the outside in. Almost any vegetable can be roasted. By searing and caramelizing, their succulent rendered juices become more concentrated, creating tremendous depth of flavor. Flavor, nutrients, and fiber lie in the skin so, with the exception of winter squash, I usually scrub my vegetables well and roast them with skins intact. Don't hesitate to add garlic or your favorite fresh herbs to a roasted vegetable mélange.

Roasted Balsamic Golden Beets

FRESH-FROM-THE-FARMERS'-*market-beets are perfect for roasting. Be sure to save the sweet tender greens for salads, soups, or stir-fries—they're full of vitamins and minerals. Golden beets have a sweeter, milder flavor than red; I prefer roasting the golden variety with a good-quality balsamic vinegar. Roasting beets allows their natural sugars to become caramelized. The skin is edible and will easily slide off the beet after cooking so it's a matter of personal preference whether or not you remove it; either way, scrub the beets well. If I have any leftovers, I slice them for salads or a sandwich garnish. Sometimes I dress the roasted beets with tart Creamy Curry Dressing (page 103) instead of balsamic vinegar.*

6 large golden beets, scrubbed clean, trimmed of any rootlets, and halved

1 tablespoon extra virgin olive oil, plus more for drizzling

Kosher salt

Good-quality balsamic vinegar

1. Preheat the oven to 375°F. Rub the beets with the olive oil and arrange cut side down on a foil-lined lined baking sheet. Roast until the beets are tender and caramelized 40 to 45 minutes. Let cool for 30 minutes, until you can handle them.

2. Cut the beets into smaller, bite-size chunks and place in a serving bowl. Drizzle with olive oil, add a sprinkle of salt, and then a light drizzle of balsamic vinegar.

Eggplant Meatballs

2 to 3 tablespoons extra virgin olive oil, or more if needed

1 medium onion, diced

1 medium eggplant, unpeeled, cut into ¼- to ½-inch dice

1½ cups walnuts, toasted (see page 86) and coarsely chopped (optional)

Fine sea salt and freshly ground black pepper, to taste

2 cups dried bread crumbs

2 large organic eggs, beaten; or ½ cup firm tofu, processed until smooth

½ cup dairy or vegan Parmesan, grated

½ cup grated Pecorino, or vegan cheese

3 garlic cloves, crushed

Zest of 1 lemon

¼ cup chopped fresh parsley or 1 tablespoon dried

1 tablespoon dried oregano

½ cup coarsely chopped basil

vegetable oil spray

STORE-BOUGHT VEGETARIAN *meatballs are expensive—and a bit too bland for my taste. This recipe is the perfect alternative: easy, affordable, and delicious. (It's also one of the few recipes in which I substitute dried parsley if I don't have fresh, so do make these even if that's the one ingredient you're without.) I drizzle the meatballs with a little basil-oil slurry and serve with a side salad of tomatoes and onions. You can shape them into burgers and serve with Lemony Garlic-Smashed Potatoes (page 221). Use leftover meatballs in lasagna or as a taco filling. To give these a Middle Eastern flavor, replace the basil with a generous handful of chopped mint and serve with garlicky Tzatziki (page 65).*

1. Preheat the oven to 375°F. Lightly oil a baking sheet.

2. Heat a large skillet and sprinkle in 2 tablespoons olive oil. When the skillet is hot, add the onion and sauté on medium-low until translucent, about 5 minutes. Add the eggplant and a sprinkle of salt and sauté until the vegetables are soft and fragrant, 8 to 10 minutes. If the eggplant dries out too quickly and begins to stick, add a bit more olive oil. Transfer to a large mixing bowl.

3. Add the walnuts, if using, to the eggplant and mix thoroughly. Transfer a generous cup of the eggplant mixture to the food processor. Process until pureed and return to the bowl. Add the bread crumbs, eggs, Parmesan, Pecorino, garlic, zest, parsley, oregano, basil, 1 teaspoon salt, and black pepper and mix well. If the mixture seems too dry, add the remaining tablespoon or more olive oil. Rub a little olive oil on your palms and shape the meatballs with your hands, using 2 heaping tablespoons of the mixture at a time. Each meatball should be about the size of a golf ball.

4. Place the eggplant balls on the prepared baking sheet and spray with vegetable oil spray. Bake 25 to 30 minutes, until a deep golden brown with a nice crust. Don't let them overbake or they will get too dry. Remove the pan from the oven, cover with foil to slightly steam the balls, and allow them to rest for a few minutes.

Stuffed Sugar Pumpkins

SERVES 4

DRIED CURRANTS, PECANS, *cooked spelt, and tempeh are transformed into a chewy pilaf and spooned into roasted sugar pumpkin halves for an impressive Thanksgiving or autumnal entrée. I suggest you try this recipe using spelt, but barley or farro (which it resembles) are both good substitutes. Because spelt is often confused with farro, when you purchase farro, make sure it's labeled Triticum dicoccum (farro's Latin name). Like spelt, it requires overnight soaking, but it takes longer to cook, about 2 hours.*

To lighten your holiday workload, make the stuffing up to 24 hours ahead and store in the refrigerator. To prepare for stuffing the pumpkins, add up to ½ cup water to the stuffing to rehydrate it a bit and then reheat the mixture in the microwave or on the stove over very low heat. The pumpkins can be baked and kept warm for up to 3 hours before stuffing and serving. I use any leftover filling as a lunch accompaniment to a vegetable burger or sandwich. If you can't find sugar pumpkins, this recipe works very well using acorn squash.

1. In a large, heavy-bottomed pot, combine the spelt and 4 cups water and bring to a boil. Reduce the heat and simmer 45 minutes, until the spelt is firm tender. It should be chewy but not stick in or to your teeth.

2. Preheat the oven to 375°F. Lightly oil a baking sheet. Using a large, very sharp chef's knife, halve both the pumpkins horizontally, around the equator. Cut very thin slices off the stem and bottom ends of each pumpkin so the halves will sit flat in the pan without wobbling. Scoop out the strings and seeds and throw to the squirrels. Place the pumpkin halves, flat side down, on the prepared baking sheet and roast until the flesh is soft, 45 minutes to 1 hour.

3. Meanwhile, in a large deep skillet, heat the oil over medium heat. Add the onion and cook until soft and translucent, 8 to 10 minutes. Add the nutmeg and half the garlic and cook another minute or so. Add the currants, tempeh, and 1 teaspoon salt and stir and cook for 5 minutes or so. Add the spinach, chopped cilantro, and remaining garlic and season with salt and pepper. Cook another 3 minutes, stirring often to make sure it doesn't burn. Stir in the cooked spelt and half of the pecans.

4. To assemble, place a pumpkin half on each plate. Fill the hollowed-out halves with the stuffing. Garnish with the remaining toasted pecans and the cilantro sprigs and serve.

1½ cups whole grain spelt, picked over, washed, and soaked overnight (8 hours) and drained

2 sugar pumpkins, about 4 pounds each, rinsed and wiped dry

3 tablespoons extra virgin olive oil

1 large onion, finely chopped

¼ teaspoon freshly grated nutmeg

4 garlic cloves, minced

½ cup currants

4 ounces tempeh, cut into ¼-inch pieces

Kosher salt and freshly ground black pepper, to taste

10 ounces baby spinach

½ cup chopped cilantro leaves and stems, plus 4 whole sprigs

¾ cup chopped toasted pecans (see page 86)

RECIPE COURTESY OF DIDI EMMONS

POTATOES, GRAINS, AND BEANS

WHETHER MAIN DISH, side dish, or appetizer, potatoes, grains, and beans add heartiness to any meal. Nutritious and filling, potatoes don't deserve their bad rap as starchy fillers—in fact, potatoes are a great source of fiber and vitamin C and can be prepared innumerable ways. Chewy nutty whole grains such as millet, quinoa, rice, and bulgur go from ho-hum to wow when properly prepared and seasoned. And beans are, without a doubt, one of my favorite protein and fiber sources, offering versatility with their smooth texture and mild flavor. The addition of beans, whole grains, and potatoes instantly transforms simple salads, pasta, or soups into satisfying main dishes.

Mashed Potatoes, Two Ways

MOST SUPERMARKETS OFFER *many varieties of potatoes these days and selecting the right potato for a particular dish is essential. For mashing, I prefer russet, white, or Yukon Gold, in that order. If I have a few of one and some of another, I mix them, but I don't go out of my way to do this. Once you decide how you like your potatoes, matching the potato to the desired texture is easy. Fluffy and smooth are best achieved with russets. Yukon Gold and white potatoes lend themselves better to a waxier rustic mash. Smooth, "whipped" potatoes require the addition of cream and butter. I prefer a more rustic "smash" with the potato skins left on and the natural texture of the potato intact. Any leftovers can be used in recipes like Potato-Cabbage Patties (page 224). Consider adding a spoonful or two of Garlic Confit (page 62) and chopped fresh parsley as well.*

Rustic Smashed Potatoes

SERVES 4

2 pounds Yukon Gold potatoes, peeled, if you like, and quartered

½ teaspoon fine sea salt

4 to 6 tablespoons extra virgin olive oil

Kosher salt and freshly ground black pepper, to taste

1. Place the potatoes in a large pot and cover with water by 3 inches. Add the sea salt and bring to a boil. After 5 minutes, reduce the heat and simmer gently until fork tender, another 5 to 10 minutes depending upon the size of the potatoes. Rapidly boiling the potatoes the entire time causes them to absorb water and fall apart, so after the first boil keep the water at a simmer. Drain in a colander, then return to the pot over very low heat and toss and turn the potatoes with a wooden spoon until they appear dry. Transfer to a serving bowl and add the olive oil and kosher salt and pepper. With a fork, smash the soft, hot potatoes, leaving some chunks for texture. Serve immediately.

Fluffy Mashed Potatoes

RUSSET POTATOES WORK *best for smooth whipped potatoes. Pressing the potatoes through a ricer gives the best results. If you don't want to use dairy or soy milk, almond or rice milk does the trick.*

3 pounds russet potatoes (4 to 5), peeled and quartered

2 tablespoons unsalted butter or extra virgin olive oil

1 cup 2% milk or unsweetened soy milk

Salt and freshly ground black pepper, to taste

1. Fill a large pot with enough water to cover the potato quarters. Since potatoes, especially floury russets, disintegrate quickly, bring the water to a boil first so there is less total cooking time. Put in the potatoes and cook at a gentle boil until they're tender but still a little firm, about 15 minutes.

2. Meanwhile, combine the milk and butter in a small saucepan and heat over low heat until just warm. When the potatoes are done, drain immediately and return to the pot. Heat over very low heat for 1 to 3 minutes, tossing and turning the potatoes until all traces of excess water have disappeared. Mash the potatoes with a masher or put through a ricer, then slowly add the milk and butter mixture, mashing as you go. The potatoes can now be whipped by hand or with an electric mixer, until as smooth as you like. Use care with the electric mixer—overbeating will cause the potatoes to become sticky. Season with salt and pepper to taste and serve hot.

Crispy Roasted Potatoes

SERVES 4

2 to 3 pounds Red Bliss
or Yukon Gold potatoes,
scrubbed and cut into
1-inch pieces

4 to 5 tablespoons extra
virgin olive oil

Few sprigs rosemary, leaves
only, coarsely chopped

Kosher salt and freshly
ground black pepper, to taste

4 small shallots, sliced

5 to 6 garlic cloves, unpeeled

A VERY HOT *oven is essential if you want potatoes with golden brown exterior and a soft interior. If you have a pizza stone, all the better: place the pan right on it. If you cut up your potatoes a few hours ahead of time, cover them with cold water so they don't turn black.*

While these are delicious right out of the oven, they can also be dressed simply with olive oil and fresh herbs, or try mixing Greek yogurt with fresh chives or scallions and toss with the potatoes for a Mediterranean-inspired potato salad. For another variation, omit the garlic, shallot, and rosemary and toss the plain roasted potatoes with Creamy Curry Dressing (page 103), Tarragon Vinaigrette (page 99), or Cilantro Mint Pesto (page 74).

A note to potato lovers: I always make extra of these to use the leftovers as home fries, mix into a green salad, or skewer on kebobs with tofu and vegetables for grilling. The leftovers also make a nice addition to omelets.

1. Heat the oven to 475°F. Coat a baking sheet large enough that the potatoes aren't piled on top of each other with a little olive oil. Place in the oven to preheat for 10 minutes.

2. Blot the potato pieces with paper or cloth towels to dry, then toss with the olive oil in a deep bowl. Add the rosemary and salt and pepper. Add the shallots and toss. Lightly tap each clove of garlic with the side of your knife just to break the skin. Toss into the potato-shallot mixture. (Leaving the garlic with skins intact will allow it to exude mellow flavor without burning it in the high heat needed to roast the potatoes.)

3. Slide the rack out of the oven and carefully pour the potatoes into the hot pan. Give the pan a shake to separate the potatoes into a single layer. Bake for 15 minutes. Check the potatoes and if they're crispy give them a rough turn. If the potatoes haven't quite crisped up yet, wait 5 minutes or so, then turn. Bake for another 15 minutes, until the potatoes are fragrant and tender but not mushy. Season with additional salt and pepper and serve.

Lemony Garlic-Smashed Potatoes

SERVES 4

THESE DELICIOUS POTATOES *have two garlic options: you can use raw crushed garlic, as I do below, for intensity with a bright lemony kick; or substitute roasted cloves (see Garlic Confit, page 62) for a deeper, more mellow garlic flavor. I use a mortar and pestle whenever I'm crushing garlic, but if you don't have one, a garlic press is fine. I love these potatoes accompanying any vegetarian burger meal or with Tempeh Marsala (page 168). When I serve the potatoes partnered with Greek Stuffed Cabbage (page 162), I either cut back on the lemon, adding just a tablespoon or two of juice, or eliminate it altogether. If you like a smoother texture, use peeled russets and whip the cooked potatoes with a mixer.*

3 pounds Red Bliss potatoes, peeled if you like

1 small head garlic, cloves separated and peeled

Kosher salt and freshly ground black pepper, to taste

½ cup extra virgin olive oil

Juice of 3 to 4 lemons

1 tablespoon chopped parsley

1. If the potatoes are small, leave them whole, if they're large, cut them into golf ball–size pieces. Boil the potatoes in salted water for 10 to 15 minutes, until tender but not mushy; drain well.

2. Crush the garlic in a mortar along with a sprinkle of salt. Put the crushed garlic in the bottom of a large bowl. Drop the cooked potatoes into the bowl and, with a fork, smash into a rustic texture, turning the smashed potatoes to blend well with the garlic. When you achieve the consistency you're looking for, alternately add the olive oil and lemon juice, mixing well and tasting after each addition. Both lemon and garlic impart a great deal of flavor, so hold back or use it all, according to your taste. Keep in mind that the garlic flavor will intensify as it rests. Top with the parsley and serve warm.

Hearty Home Fries

1 to 2 tablespoons extra
virgin olive oil

5 medium Yukon Gold
potatoes, cut into
1-inch cubes

2 to 3 shallots or
1 small onion, diced

1 small red or orange bell
pepper, seeded and diced

1 cup canned black beans,
drained and rinsed

1 to 2 plum tomatoes,
seeded and diced

Small handful of parsley,
coarsely chopped

Salt and freshly ground
black pepper, to taste

Pure maple syrup

SERVED WITH SCRAMBLED *eggs or tofu, these potatoes make a hearty, nutritious breakfast. I also serve them during the day with Beet Burgers (page 190) or Black-Eyed Burgers (page 192) to make a comforting diner meal that's far healthier and less fat-laden than the traditional burger and fries. You can cook them entirely on the stovetop, but roasting them in the oven creates a crustier potato, which I happen to like. And don't be afraid to double the recipe, because the leftovers are as delicious as the firsts.*

1. Preheat the oven to 450°F. Heat a large ovenproof skillet (such as cast iron) over medium-high heat for about 10 minutes. Add the olive oil and when it's hot but not smoking, add the potatoes. Don't move them around or fuss with them too much because you want to create a crust. When the bottoms are browned and crusty, gently turn the pieces over with a spatula. Spread the shallots and pepper over the top of the potatoes. Bake in the oven until the peppers are softened and the shallots are golden, about 10 minutes. Add the beans to the pan and continue baking for 5 minutes or so, until the beans are heated through. Carefully remove the pan from the oven, toss in the tomatoes and parsley, and season with salt and pepper to taste. Drizzle with a little maple syrup and serve.

Caribbean Spicy Sweet Potatoes

SWEET POTATOES ARE the most nutritious vegetable available; loaded with dietary fiber, which helps control cholesterol, they also contain naturally occurring sugars, complex carbohydrates, protein, vitamins A and C, iron, and calcium. Among root vegetables, sweet potatoes offer a low glycemic index rating because they are digested slowly and make you feel satisfied longer—important if you're trying to shed excess pounds. With so many people in fear of "bad carbs" these days, sweet potatoes belong on the good carb list. Which is something the folks in the Caribbean seem to know all about. I picked up this spicy recipe on a trip through the islands where sweet potatoes literally overflow from bins in local groceries. I leave the peels on, but if you prefer, peel the potatoes before roasting. I use honey for this recipe, but vegans can substitute ⅓ cup maple syrup and, of course, if you're allergic to nuts, omit the peanuts. Make an entire Caribbean meal by tucking these tasty potatoes along with a slice of spicy Jamaican Jerk Tempeh (page 160) into Chickpea Crepes (page 132). Wrap leftovers in a large whole wheat tortilla with avocado, more chopped scallions, lettuce, and tomato. These are also a delicious substitute for home fries for a hearty brunch or breakfast.

5 to 6 sweet potatoes, peeled, if you like, and cubed

½ cup honey

3 tablespoons grated ginger

3 tablespoons extra virgin olive oil

1 tablespoon ground cardamom

1½ teaspoons chipotle powder

Kosher salt and freshly ground black pepper, to taste

½ cup chopped roasted peanuts (optional)

1. Preheat the oven to 400°F. Combine the sweet potatoes, honey, ginger, olive oil, cardamom, chipotle powder, 1½ teaspoons salt, and ½ teaspoon pepper in a large bowl. Transfer to a large terra-cotta baking dish or cast-iron skillet. Bake uncovered for 20 minutes. Stir well. Bake for another 20 minutes, until the sweet potatoes are fork tender and caramelized on the bottom. Stir once again and adjust seasonings. Top with the chopped peanuts if using and serve.

Potato-Cabbage Patties

One ½-pound chunk of cabbage

3 cups Rustic Smashed Potatoes (page 218)

3 roasted garlic cloves (see page 98), mashed into a paste

1 large organic egg, beaten

½ cup shredded Fontina (optional)

3 tablespoons chopped parsley

¾ teaspoon freshly grated nutmeg

Salt and freshly ground black pepper, to taste

Canola or other vegetable oil, for frying

½ to 1 cup panko (Japanese bread crumbs)

GREAT FOR USING *up leftovers, this recipe transforms mashed potatoes into delicious patties with a bit of mellow, roasted garlic, some cabbage, and a well-oiled skillet. They make a tasty substitute for bread with a poached egg perched on top, but my favorite way of serving them is with Homemade Seitan (page 169) in a puddle of Porcini Gravy (page 107). Vegans may substitute ¼ cup unsweetened soy milk for the eggs, and nondairy cheese for the Fontina. I like the crunchiness of panko, but if you don't have it on hand, dredge the patties in all-purpose flour.*

1. Bring a pot of water with just enough water to cover the cabbage chunk to a boil. Add the cabbage and cook 8 to 10 minutes, until just tender. Drain and let cool. When cool enough to handle, shred thinly and place in a mixing bowl. Stir in the mashed potatoes, garlic, egg, Fontina (if using), parsley, and nutmeg and season with salt and pepper. Chill for at least 1 hour, preferably 2, to make it easier to form the patties.

2. Heat ½ inch olive oil in a large skillet over medium-high heat until hot. Using your hands, shape the potato mixture into 8 patties, 3 to 4 inches in diameter. Dredge 4 of the patties in the panko and carefully lay in the hot oil. Fry on each side for about 3 minutes, until golden brown and crisp. Transfer to paper towels for a minute or so to blot up excess oil. Season with a sprinkle of salt and pepper. Keep warm in low oven while you fry the 4 remaining patties. Serve hot.

Caribbean Red Beans and Rice

THIS CLASSIC ONE-POT *dish can be modified to suit your own personal taste—spicy or mild. It's satisfying tucked into warmed flour tortillas and packed for lunch on the go, or as a main dish meal served with a little Green Salsa Picada (page 70) on the side. For extra heat, spoon on some Orange, Jalapeño, and Cilantro Dressing (page 100).*

1. Heat a saucepan over medium heat and add the oil, then sprinkle in the cumin and chipotle powder. Stir well, add the rice and cook, stirring to coat the rice, for 2 minutes. Add 3 cups water and bring to a boil. Reduce the heat and simmer for 45 to 50 minutes, until the rice is tender but still chewy. Remove from the heat and stir in the beans with their liquid and the annatto. Squeeze in the juice of half a lime, or more if you like. Season with salt and pepper. Serve hot or at room temperature.

1 to 2 tablespoons canola or other vegetable oil

2 teaspoons ground cumin

2 teaspoons chipotle powder

1½ cups brown rice

One 15½-ounce can red beans with liquid

¼ teaspoon ground annatto

Juice of ½ lime

Salt and freshly ground black pepper, to taste

Annatto

ANNATTO SEED is also known as *achiote*. It grows on the annatto tree and is mostly used in Caribbean and Latino dishes. Annatto imparts a beautiful yellow or orange color and subtle peppery flavor to foods at a fraction of the cost of saffron, but it doesn't duplicate saffron's delicate flavor. I purchase ground annatto in a local Latino market and store it with my spices.

Vermicelli and Rice

SERVES 4 TO 6

3 tablespoons unsalted butter
or soy margarine

1½ cups vermicelli broken
into ½-inch pieces

1½ cups long-grain white rice

2 tablespoons vegetarian
bouillon powder

3 tablespoons minced parsley

WHEN I WAS *young, my mother rarely kept boxed food in the house, but Rice-A-Roni was an exception. I loved that San Francisco treat. I just had to come up with a vegetarian version—and this one is obviously less processed and easy to prepare. I use regular long-grain white rice, but basmati or short-grain rice works fine. Vermicelli is a thin spaghetti that lends this dish an authentic Rice-A-Roni look. Substitute orzo for the vermicelli to turn it into a Greek-style pilaf. Leftovers become fried rice with the simple addition of scallions, diced carrots, petit peas, and scrambled eggs or tofu.*

1. Melt the butter in a heavy skillet over medium heat. When the fat is bubbly, add the broken vermicelli and stir-fry until nicely browned. Add the rice, tossing and stirring until coated and toasted. Add the bouillon powder and mix well. Add 3 cups hot water and bring everything to a boil. Reduce the heat, cover, and simmer for 15 minutes, or just until the rice is tender but not mushy. Remove the pan from the heat and spoon the rice mixture into a bowl. Sprinkle with parsley and serve.

Chickpea Mash

THIS IS A *protein-packed side dish that can be served as an alternative to mashed potatoes or polenta. Spread on toasted pita or whole grain bread to accompany Moroccan Stew (page 165). I use red onion here because it has a bit more bite, but sweet Vidalia or yellow onion works just fine.*

1. Heat the olive oil in a small skillet over medium heat. Add the onion and sauté for 2 minutes. Add the garlic and continue sautéing until the onion is translucent, another 3 to 5 minutes.

2. Bring the beans and stock to a low boil in a small saucepan. Simmer for 10 minutes. Add the onion and garlic and simmer for 5 minutes. Remove from the heat and mash, or place in a food processor and pulse until coarsely mashed. You don't want a smooth puree like hummus. Transfer to a serving bowl. Fold the cilantro into the mashed beans and season with salt, pepper, and a drizzle of olive oil. Serve warm.

1 tablespoon extra virgin olive oil, plus a drizzle

1 small red onion, diced small

3 garlic cloves, chopped

One 15½-ounce can chickpeas, drained and rinsed

½ cup Vegetable Stock (page 106)

1 tablespoon chopped cilantro

Salt and freshly ground black pepper, to taste

Spinach Tortillas with Potatoes

SERVES 4 TO 6

3 tablespoons canola or other vegetable oil, or more if needed

½ large yellow onion, sliced into thin half moons

Salt and freshly ground black pepper, to taste

2 cups Homemade Seitan (page 169)

3 Yukon Gold potatoes, cut into 1-inch dice and parboiled until barely tender

1 tablespoon paprika

⅓ cup Vegetable Stock (page 106)

4 cups loosely packed baby spinach

10 to 12 fresh corn tortillas

WE THINK OF *tortillas as wraps for beans and beef, but here is a different spin from the kitchen of chef Heidi Valenzuela. Instead of seitan, the tortillas can be made with any TVP product of your choice, or tofu or tempeh. This recipe is somewhat neutral in flavor, making it a wonderful accompaniment to Green Salsa Picada (page 70), Chunky Avocado Salsa (page 71), and Caribbean Red Beans and Rice (page 225).*

1. Preheat a griddle or flat pan over medium heat for heating the tortillas.

2. Heat a large skillet over medium heat Add the oil, onion, and a little salt and sauté until the onion begins to soften, 3 to 4 minutes. Add the seitan and stir to combine. If the seitan seems too dry, sprinkle a teaspoon or so additional oil into the pan. Add the potatoes, paprika, and stock, stir well, and cook for a minute or two, until the stock reduces to a thin sauce. Add the spinach and stir to blend everything together. Continue cooking just until the spinach is wilted but retains a bit of texture, 2 to 3 minutes. Season with salt and pepper. Cover the pan and remove from the heat.

3. Place a tortilla on the hot griddle and cook until it begins to puff a little, develop brown spots, and release a toasty aroma. Using tongs, lift and place on a serving plate. Repeat with the remaining tortillas, covering them with foil to keep them warm and steamy. Place a hot tortilla on each plate, then spoon the seitan-spinach mixture onto half, and fold over.

Creamy Polenta

POLENTA IS A *staple food in many parts of northern Italy. Despite its fickle rep-* *utation, it's easy to prepare and can be served hot or cold, and baked or fried once* *cooked. I use polenta for every meal of the day, from breakfast to supper. If you* *want creamy polenta, serve it immediately once it's cooked because it sets quickly* *(see below). I prefer the clean corn flavor of polenta cooked in water, but you can* *also cook it dairy milk or soy milk.*

If you want to add cheese, do so when the butter or oil goes in. Grated Italian *cheeses like Parmesan, Pecorino, and Fontina work well. If frying polenta, wait to* *top with cheese until after frying. To fry, grill, or bake polenta, immediately spread* *the cooked polenta into an oiled 9 × 13-inch pan and allow it to cool for 20 to 30* *minutes. Cut the polenta it into any shape or size desired, and use accordingly.*

This recipe calls specifically for the quick-cooking variety of polenta. Look for *it in most supermarkets or your local Italian or natural foods grocery store. The* *recipe can easily be doubled and polenta keeps well, covered tightly with plastic,* *for up to 7 days in the refrigerator.*

1 teaspoon fine sea salt

1½ cups quick-cooking Italian polenta

5 tablespoons unsalted butter or 3 tablespoons extra virgin olive oil

1. In a heavy saucepan, bring 5½ cups water and the salt to a rolling boil. Reduce to a simmer and slowly begin whisking in the polenta in a steady stream. Whisk or stir with a wooden spoon continuously to prevent lumps, until the polenta comes back to a boil. It will sputter and spit a bit. Reduce the heat to low and continue whisking for 5 to 8 minutes, until the polenta thickens. When the polenta is thick and creamy, remove the pan from heat and stir in the butter. Serve immediately for soft polenta, or pour into a prepared pan and allow to set for 20 to 30 minutes before continuing.

Polenta con Fungi Porcini

SERVES 4 TO 6

Polenta

1 tablespoon fine sea salt

2½ cups quick-cooking Italian polenta

4 tablespoons (½ stick) unsalted butter or ¼ cup extra virgin olive oil

½ cup grated Fontina (optional)

Mushroom Topping

2 cups (about 4 ounces) dried porcini mushrooms

2 tablespoons extra virgin olive oil

3 garlic cloves, chopped

1 large onion, thinly sliced

3 cups mixed sliced cremini, button, and shiitake mushrooms (stems removed)

2 plum tomatoes, peeled; or 1 cup canned tomatoes, chopped

½ cup chopped mixed parsley, basil, thyme, and tarragon

¼ cup dry white wine

Salt and freshly ground black pepper, to taste

I BELIEVE MUSHROOMS *are truly a gift from nature, and with their earthy, robust flavors and meaty texture, they're precious to the vegetarian cook. Fresh wild mushrooms are sometimes difficult to find—fresh porcini nearly impossible. Some of you may be wary of dried mushrooms; I was too until I had this dish, made with dried porcinis, while visiting Montalcino in Tuscany, a beautiful hilltop town in the heart of wine country near Siena. There, the local shops were brimming with packages of dried porcini, so I took some home and gave them a try. From then on, I began cooking regularly with dried mushrooms. Look for high-quality dried porcini imported from Italy or France. The sliced caps should be dark brown and at least 2 inches in length. The polenta will keep in the fridge for about a week.*

1. **TO MAKE THE POLENTA:** In a heavy saucepan, bring 6 cups water and the salt to a rolling boil. Slowly sprinkle the polenta into the water, whisking constantly. Reduce the heat and continue to whisk and cook until the polenta thickens and pulls away from the sides of pan, about 5 minutes or less. Remove from the heat and add the butter and Fontina, if using.

2. Spray a 9 × 13-inch roasting pan with water and then pour in the hot polenta. Using a wooden spoon, work quickly to spread the polenta evenly to every corner. If the polenta mixture sticks to the spoon, spritz the polenta with a little bit of water. Let the polenta stand until set, 45 to 60 minutes. Wrap the pan tightly with plastic and refrigerate until you're ready to use.

3. **TO MAKE THE TOPPING:** Rinse the dried mushrooms under running water to clean them of any debris. Cover with about 1½ cups hot water and soak for 20 minutes.

4. Heat the olive oil in a wide sauté pan over medium heat. Add the garlic and onion and sauté until just beginning to soften. Turn up the heat a little and add the fresh mushroom mixture. Sauté until the mushrooms begin to soften, 5 to 7 minutes.

5. With your hands, pull the reconstituted dried mushrooms from their broth and squeeze to remove any excess water and reserve the liquid. Add the porcini whole to the sauté pan. Stir to combine with everything

else. Strain the mushroom broth through a paper towel–lined sieve. Add about 1 cup of the reserved soaking liquid to the mushroom mixture and bring to a simmer. Cook the sauce until thickened, about 10 minutes. Add the tomatoes and half the herbs. Simmer 10 to 15 minutes, until the sauce is thick and rich. Add the wine and remaining herbs. If the mixture seems too dry, add a bit more of the reserved soaking liquid, up to ¼ cup. Season with salt and freshly ground black pepper.

6. **TO ASSEMBLE THE DISH:** Preheat the oven to 475°F. Grease a baking sheet with olive oil. Slice the cooled polenta into ½-inch-wide planks and place on the baking sheet. Drizzle with additional olive oil and bake for about 10 minutes, until the tops of the polenta pieces are brown and bubbly. Sliding a spatula under each of the polenta pieces and place on serving dishes. Spoon mushroom topping over each and serve hot.

Quinoa with Fresh Herbs and Almonds

SERVES 4

2½ cups Vegetable Stock (page 106) or water

1½ cups quinoa, rinsed well

Salt and freshly ground black pepper

3 tablespoons mixed chopped parsley, thyme, and tarragon

1 tablespoon unsalted butter or olive oil

½ cup toasted sliced almonds, toasted pine nuts, or peanuts (optional)

QUINOA IS TREATED *as a grain in cooking but the plant is actually more closely related to leafy greens such as spinach, kale, and chard. The tiny power-packed quinoa grains have a wonderfully light and fluffy texture with the perfect touch of crunch. Mix quinoa with rice or millet or serve on its own as an accompaniment to stews or sautéed greens.*

1. Bring the stock to a boil in a medium saucepan. Add the quinoa and 1 teaspoon salt. Reduce the heat, cover, and cook for about 20 minutes, until firm-tender and all the liquid is absorbed. Remove from the heat and add the herbs and butter. Cover and let the quinoa rest for 5 minutes. Just prior to serving, fluff the quinoa with a fork, season with salt and pepper, and serve topped with nuts if you like.

Quinoa and Millet

MILLET AND quinoa are versatile, underused grains that can be combined with any number of ingredients: fresh herbs like cilantro, parsley, or thyme jazz them up; chopped dried fruits like cranberries or apricots add a subtle tart-sweet twist; and chopped shallots or scallions offer mild onion flavors. You can also blend quinoa or millet with brown or white rice and chopped walnuts or pecans for a delicious pilaf, mix them into homemade vegetable burgers, add to soups, or enjoy them simply as is, partnered with roasted vegetables. I serve leftover cooked grains for breakfast, reheated with a splash of soy milk, maple syrup, and raisins; or cold sweetened with brown sugar and topped with fresh cut fruit. The idea is to bring variety, fiber, and extra nutrition to your diet. In my experience, children readily dig into these basic grain dishes because the flavors are mild and the texture delicate yet chewy. Dry-toasting grains before cooking them teases out their delicate flavors.

Quinoa

■ **MAKES 3 CUPS**

1 tablespoon unsalted butter or extra virgin olive oil
¼ teaspoon fine sea salt
1½ cups quinoa, rinsed well

1. Combine 2½ cups water, the butter, and salt in a heavy saucepan. Bring to a boil, then reduce the heat and add the quinoa. Cover and simmer for about 20 minutes, until the quinoa is tender and cooked through.

Millet

■ **MAKES 3 CUPS**

1 cup millet
¼ teaspoon salt

1. Bring 2½ cups water to a boil in a heavy saucepan and add the millet and salt. Cover, reduce the heat to a simmer, and cook for 20 to 25 minutes, just until the water is absorbed. Do not overcook the millet, as it will become gummy. Fluff the grains with a fork or a single chopstick, and let it rest for a few minutes before serving.

Lentil Tabbouleh

SERVES 4 TO 6

¾ cup fine or medium grain bulgur wheat

1 cup green or brown lentils

1 bay leaf

Fine sea salt and freshly ground black pepper

6-8 scallions, white and green parts, thinly sliced

2 garlic cloves, minced

Zest of 2 lemons

¼ cup lemon juice

½ cup extra virgin olive oil

1 teaspoon paprika

2 cups finely chopped parsley

¼ cup chopped mint

A GLORIOUS BLEND *of many of my favorite ingredients—lentils, bulgur wheat, parsley, garlic, and lemony zest—this easy salad is packed full of protein. Serve warm or at room temperature to be scooped up with wedges of pita bread or spooned onto Fried Polenta Squares (page 59). Or tuck into radicchio or endive leaves for an appetizer. And it's better the next day once all the flavors have mingled.*

1. Place the bulgur in a bowl and pour in just enough boiling water to cover. Allow the bulgur to stand for 25 to 30 minutes, until the grains are swollen and tender and most, if not all, of the water is absorbed.

2. In a saucepan, cover the lentils with water. Add the bay leaf and ½ teaspoon salt and bring to a boil. Reduce the heat and simmer uncovered for 20 minutes, until tender but firm.

3. In a deep serving bowl, whisk together the scallions, garlic, lemon zest and juice, olive oil, paprika, and 1 teaspoon salt. Drain off any excess water from the tender-firm lentils, and fold them gently into the dressing. Pour off or press out any excess water from the bulgur and add to the lentil mixture, along with the parsley and mint. Toss all the ingredients gently. Discard the bay leaf. Season with salt and pepper and serve.

Parsley

ONCE USED only as a garnish to be discarded, parsley is an outstanding source of vitamins A and C, outperforming both carrots and oranges. Parsley is also high in iron and is a beneficial aid for digestive disorders. Add chopped parsley liberally to lend its piquant refreshing taste to any savory dish.

GOOD MORNINGS

BREAKFAST IS THE most important meal of the day, as we've all been told, and unfortunately the one where most people make the wrong food choices. Whole grains and fiber-rich foods are digested more slowly, leaving you with a satiated feeling for longer periods. Ultimately a breakfast that's high in sugar and low in fiber and protein will leave you hankering and reaching for snacks all morning. Here are some simple, fast breakfast options that can also work well as a light lunch or nutritious low-fat snack. There's something here for everyone, even for those days where you're craving something a little rich and sweet or creamy and comforting.

Homemade Cereal, Hot or Cold

SERVES 6 TO 8

4 cups whole organic oats

½ cup wheat germ

½ cup chopped dates

½ cup chopped dried apricots

1 cup sliced almonds, toasted (see page 86)

1 cup chopped walnuts, toasted (see page 86)

Small handful of unsweetened shredded coconut

Handful of dried cranberries

Handful of raisins

Small handful of vegan chocolate chips (optional)

THIS IS A *healthy and inexpensive take on Muesli, a Swiss invention that has become popular as a breakfast cereal staple. My recipe is composed of a base of rolled oats combined with nuts and dried fruits. Add more of whatever you especially like, as this is not an exact recipe. Two of my favorite ways to eat this are: 1) pour milk or soy milk over it and eat immediately, or 2) overnight, soak it in soy milk, cover, and refrigerate. The latter method gives it a chewy, moist texture that's similar to cooked oatmeal and is ready in the morning when you are. You could also sprinkle the mix with a little brown sugar and chopped fresh fruit like strawberries, raspberries, or kiwi. My favorite fruit to add is banana, which I then top with 3 to 4 tablespoons of Mediterranean-style yogurt. The combination of sweet and sour flavors with the crunch of nuts and oats, is sensational. I've served it this way as a light dessert. It's lovely in individual dishes garnished with mint leaves. The blend will keep for many weeks, but is best when consumed within 2 weeks.*

1. Combine all the ingredients together and store in an airtight container.

Mixed Pepper Frittata

SERVES 4

A FRITTATA IS *a savory open-faced version of an Italian omelet. Although not traditionally served in Italy as a morning meal, this comforting all-purpose dish moves effortlessly through breakfast, brunch, and right into a light supper. The recipe is so versatile, I'll also serve it at room temperature, cut into individual portions for parties or packed for a picnic. For a hearty breakfast, serve with warm Maine Berry Muffins (page 242) or a toasted bagel. And wedges, topped with a dash of fruity olive oil and chopped fresh herbs and accompanied by a simple green salad and Tuscan bread rubbed with garlic, make a satisfying Mediterranean-inspired dish any time of day.*

1. Preheat the broiler with the oven rack in the center position. Heat a 10-inch cast-iron or ovenproof skillet over medium heat. Pour in 2 tablespoons of the olive oil and add the potatoes. Cook, turning the potatoes every few minutes, until tender but not falling apart.

2. Add the remaining 1 tablespoon olive oil to the potatoes. Stir and add the onion, jalapeño pepper, and Cubanelle pepper. Sauté for about 5 minutes, until the peppers and onion are slightly softened. Stir in the dill. Pour the beaten eggs evenly over the vegetables and season with salt and pepper. Remove the pan from the heat and add the tomatoes, lightly pressing the pieces into the top of the frittata. Top with the grated cheese, if using.

3. Place the pan under the broiler and broil, keeping a close eye on it, until the top is set, 5 to 8 minutes. The top should not brown or the frittata will be dry. Look for a golden color once the eggs are set. Remove from the oven, let sit for a few minutes, and slice into wedges. Serve hot or cold.

3 tablespoons extra virgin olive oil

2 small Yukon Gold potatoes, scrubbed and cut into ¼- or ½-inch dice

½ small red onion, diced

1 jalapeño pepper, diced

1 cubanelle pepper, diced

½ teaspoon chopped dill

3 large organic eggs, beaten with 2 tablespoons water

Salt and freshly ground black pepper, to taste

1 medium tomato, cut into 1-inch dice

¼ cup grated Fontina or Asiago (optional)

Cubanelle Peppers

CUBANELLES ARE elongated sweet mild peppers ranging in color from yellow to green to red. Look for peppers that are firm, smooth, and glossy. They are usually available year-round, but if you're unable to find one, simply use sweet bell pepper. Unwashed peppers can be stored in a plastic bag in the refrigerator for up to 1 week. As with any variety, the redder the pepper the more mature it is; storage life diminishes significantly with age.

Cucumber and Radish Sandwiches

4 flatbreads or whole grain rye bread, toasted

1 tablespoon unsalted butter or soy margarine

12 to 16 slices cucumber

4 radishes, sliced

1 scallion, green parts only, minced

Salt and freshly ground black pepper, to taste

I GREW UP *eating these sandwiches as a child in Germany. My mother still makes them for us, especially in the summer when cucumbers and radishes are crispy fresh. European-style cucumbers have thin skins and tiny seeds, so they work best, but any cucumber will do. Simply peel and slice.*

1. Spread the toast with the butter, then scrape it off so that only the dimples in the toast have butter in them. Cover two of the toasts with the cucumber slices, overlapping the edges. Sprinkle with a bit of salt. Cover the remaining toasts with the radish slices, a sprinkling of scallions, and a bit of salt. That's it.

Pfannkuchen

IN BERLIN, WHERE *I spent the first six years of my life,* pfannkuchen *means "doughnut." In another part of Germany near the French border, where I lived when I was older,* pfannkuchen *means "pancake." In a sense both are true: this German sweet is a cross between a pound cake and a pancake. It's a fun recipe to play around with: try almond extract in place of vanilla, or omit both and add lemon juice and a grating of tangy rind. I've found I can use less sugar if I add fruit, like raspberries, strawberries, or those extra sweet, tiny, Maine blueberries when they're in season.*

As a breakfast treat, it's a great time-saver because you're not stuck over the griddle making pancakes one by one. Top your pfannkuchen *with warmed, pure maple syrup. Or do as we did in Germany and fill the cake with whole fruit jam and top it with a sprinkle of granulated or powdered sugar. To do this, cool the* pfannkuchen *completely, then turn it on its side and with a very sharp knife carefully slice it across the middle. Spread the jam, replace the top half of the cake, and sprinkle with some sugar. It looks very pretty and makes the perfect dessert.*

3 large organic eggs

1 cup 2% milk or soy milk

¼ to ½ cup organic cane sugar

1 teaspoon vanilla extract

½ teaspoon fine sea salt

1½ cups all-purpose flour

1 tablespoon baking powder

2 tablespoons unsalted butter or soy margarine

1. Preheat the oven to 400°F. In a large bowl, whisk together the eggs, milk, sugar, vanilla, and salt. In a separate bowl, using a fork, mix together the flour and baking powder until blended. Dump the dry ingredients into the wet and whisk into a smooth batter. Let stand for at least 10 minutes.

2. Put the butter into an 8- or 10-inch cast-iron skillet and place in the preheated oven. I usually use an 8-inch pan because it makes the *pfannkuchen* a bit higher, more like a cake. A 10-inch pan will give you a flatter cake. The recipe works either way. When the butter is melted and bubbly, carefully remove the pan from the oven and pour the batter into the hot pan. Return the pan to the oven and bake until the cake is a light golden color, puffed up, and a toothpick comes out clean when inserted in the center, about 15 minutes.

Rye Bread French Toast

1 cup soy milk

1 teaspoon vanilla

1 teaspoon organic cane sugar (optional)

¾ teaspoon ground cinnamon

Pinch of fine sea salt

2 tablespoons (or less) canola or other vegetable oil

8 slices deli-style rye bread

I ENCOURAGE FREQUENT *thinking outside of the bread box! When I first mentioned to friends that I use rye bread and no eggs when I make French toast, they were a little skeptical. But after their first taste of this marvelously sweet, custardy yet egg-free version of the classic, they were hooked—and didn't miss the eggs. I serve it with or without butter or margarine, but always with warmed, pure maple syrup poured over the top. The combination of maple flavor with the nutty rye is fabulous. You could also serve as a dessert accompanied by fresh, preserved, or roasted fruit and soy or regular ice cream.*

1. In a deep, wide dish, whisk together the milk, vanilla, sugar if using, ½ teaspoon of the cinnamon, and the salt.

2. Heat a nonstick or cast-iron skillet over medium heat and add enough vegetable oil to evenly coat the bottom of the pan. A nonstick pan requires only a light brush of oil. Dip a slice of bread into the milk mixture, making sure it absorbs some of the mixture. Depending upon the freshness of the bread it can soak up too much too quickly, so pay attention: you don't want mushy crumbles. Transfer the slice to the hot skillet to cook. Continue soaking and adding slices to the skillet—I can usually only fit about 4 slices in mine, so I do it in 2 batches. Sprinkle a bit of the reserved cinnamon over each slice. When the first side is nicely browned, flip, sprinkle with a bit more cinnamon, and cook until browned on the other side. Serve immediately.

Breakfast Rusks

MY DEAR FRIEND *Sandra, who hails from South Africa, came for coffee one afternoon with a tin of what I thought were biscotti. With their crunchy, dry, double-baked texture, rusks are similar to the Italian cookie, but with a buttermilk tang. In other words, completely addictive: I hid them from everyone and ate them for breakfast, lunch, and dinner for an entire week. Sandra gave me her recipe but I misplaced it, so one stormy, winter night when she was visiting again, we made a batch in the wee hours, happily dunking them in hot cups of coffee and tea the next morning. This time when Sandra left, I made sure to tuck away that recipe in a safe place. Note that the rusks have to dry out in a slow oven for at least eight hours. I suggest doing this overnight.*

1 pound (4 sticks) unsalted butter or soy margarine

1⅔ cups organic cane sugar

About 4½ cups self-rising flour

5 teaspoons baking powder

½ teaspoon fine sea salt

1 large organic egg

2 cups buttermilk

5 cups 100% bran flakes

2 cups sunflower seeds

1. Preheat the oven to 350°F. Lightly grease two 9 × 5-inch loaf pans. In a large saucepan, melt the butter. Remove from the heat and stir in the sugar until well blended. Add the flour, baking powder, and salt. Mix well. Whisk the egg and buttermilk in a small bowl and add to the flour mixture, stirring to combine. Fold in the bran flakes and seeds. Divide the batter between the prepared loaf pans. Bake for about 1 hour, until a cake tester inserted in the centers comes out clean.

2. Reduce the oven to 200°F. Let the pans cool completely. Carefully remove the loaves from pans and cut the bread into 1-inch-thick slices. Then cut each slice into two or three finger-size pieces. Arrange the pieces on a nonstick cookie sheet and bake until very dry, usually 8 or more hours. It's important that the rusks are very dry, otherwise they'll become moldy when stored. If they're still moist when you remove them from the oven, return them for an additional few hours. Baked this way, the cookies store well for up to 4 weeks.

Self-Rising Flour

IF YOU don't have self-rising flour on hand, you can make your own: for every 1 cup of regular all-purpose flour, add 1½ teaspoons baking powder and ½ teaspoon salt. Blend well—I use a whisk—and use according to the recipe directions.

Maine Berry Muffins

MAKES 12

2 cups all-purpose flour, plus 1 teaspoon to toss with the berries

½ cup organic cane sugar

1 tablespoon baking powder

½ teaspoon fine sea salt

1 teaspoon ground cinnamon

3 tablespoons canola oil, melted soy margarine, or melted unsalted butter

1 large organic egg

1 cup milk

½ teaspoon fresh lemon zest

1 cup fresh blueberries

MAINERS ARE KNOWN to brag that their blueberries are the best in the world. When I first moved here I was skeptical, but it turns out the natives are right: Maine's wild blueberries are without comparison. When berry-harvesting time comes in mid- to late August, Mainers swarm the farmers' markets in search of the first harvested berries or go out and pick their own. I even know people whose berry-picking caches are held sacred and the paths leading to these wild harvests kept secret and passed down through generations. If you can't get Maine blueberries, standard-issue blueberries are a totally acceptable alternative—or you can substitute fresh cranberries and add 2 teaspoons fresh orange zest and ¾ cup walnuts or pecans.

1. Preheat the oven to 400°F. Prepare a muffin tin by spraying with vegetable oil spray or using paper or silicone muffin liners.

2. In a large bowl, combine the 2 cups flour, the sugar, baking powder, salt, and cinnamon. In a small bowl or large measuring cup, mix the oil, egg, milk, and zest with a fork until combined. Quickly stir the wet ingredients into the dry, folding them in just until a moist batter begins to form.

3. Drop the berries into a third bowl, sprinkle with the remaining teaspoon flour and toss with a fork to coat. (Coating the berries with flour helps keep them from sinking to the bottom of the batter.) Gently fold the berries into the batter. Try not to overmix: the batter should be lumpy and rather thick, but evenly moistened.

4. Divide the batter among the muffin cups. Bake 25 minutes, or until a skewer inserted into the center of a muffin comes out clean. Let the muffins rest for a few minutes, then serve warm.

Berry Nice

🌿 FRESH BERRIES are always best—but frozen works quite well for year-round muffin pleasure.

Loaded Bagel

THIS IS A GREAT *morning meal, especially since you can eat it on the fly. Cutting out the dairy cream cheese and adding seeds and tomato make this fabulous, filling, and healthy. Feel free to add cucumber and/or radish with the tomato. Unlike cheese, when it comes to fresh vegetables, the more you eat, the better you feel. Needless to say, it takes little effort to double, triple, or quadruple this recipe— even up to a dozen or more bagels, if you're throwing a brunch party. Just be sure you've got plenty of tomatoes on hand, so everyone gets their two fair slices.*

1. Slice the bagel in half and lightly toast. Spread with the cream cheese and top with the sunflower seeds, tomato, and basil.

1 whole grain bagel, preferably with poppy, sesame, and sunflower seeds

1 tablespoon tofu cream cheese

1 tablespoon raw, hulled sunflower seeds

2 slices tomato

Few leaves basil

Salt and freshly ground black pepper, to taste

SWEET FINISHES

I USUALLY JUST pick something up at a local bakery when I'm in the mood for a sweet and dreamy indulgence. While heavy, complicated desserts are not my thing, I do love roasted fruit, like pears or apples, fresh fruit salad, or plain nuts after a nice meal. Remember that dessert is a treat, not an essential part of every meal, and moderation is key. Either that or plan on walking wherever you go, and always taking the stairs.

Maple-Baked Pears

4 to 6 Bosc pears

1 to 1¼ cups maple syrup

2 to 3 tablespoons
organic cane sugar

2 tablespoons calvados or
other apple brandy

2 teaspoons unsalted butter
or soy margarine,
broken into small bits

Juice of ½ lemon

I USE BOSC *pears here because they remain firm, but any pear will work; in fact, any firm fresh fruit may be substituted. Serve the pears alone or garnish with yogurt, whipped topping, or ice cream. For an extra treat, perch a few Breakfast Rusks (page 241) or Nutty Shortbread Cookies (page 249) on each plate. For breakfast, they're delicious with Pfannkuchen (page 239).*

Calvados is a dry apple brandy from Normandy, France. Often served as an aperitif or a digestive, its complex flavor complements and enhances the sweetness of fruity desserts beautifully.

1. Preheat the oven to 350°F. Trim a small piece off the bottom of each pear so they stand upright. Place the pears in a shallow 9 × 11-inch baking dish and pour the maple syrup over them to coat. Sprinkle with the sugar and add the calvados, butter, and lemon juice.

2. Bake the pears, uncovered, until the bottoms are tender when pierced with a knife, 25 to 30 minutes. Serve warm, with the juices from the pan as a sauce.

Sautéed Bananas

THERE ARE ENDLESS *ways to serve these: Top with a scoop of vanilla ice cream. Sprinkle with toasted coconut to add chewiness and tropical flavor. Serve with waffles for brunch. Use bananas that don't have any green, but don't do have any black either. If you see some brown mottling on the skin, they're ripe.*

2 ripe bananas

2 to 3 tablespoons unsalted butter or soy margarine

¼ cup unbleached all-purpose flour

2 tablespoons organic cane sugar

Maple syrup

1. Remove the peel from the bananas and slice in half at the middle and then again lengthwise. You'll have eight banana quarters. Put the flour on a plate and dredge each banana quarter in the flour, gently shaking off any excess.

2. Heat a large skillet over medium-high heat and add the butter. When it is hot and no longer foamy, add the banana quarters. Cook, turning, until the color deepens to golden, 8 to 10 minutes. Bananas have high sugar content and will brown quickly, so watch them to make sure they don't burn. Sprinkle with the sugar and cook for another minute. Remove from the heat and serve warm, drizzled with maple syrup.

Mango Fruit Salad

SERVES 2 TO 4

1 mango
1 cup blueberries
1 pomegranate
2 teaspoons lime juice

MAKE THIS FRUIT *salad your own by adding some unsweetened coconut, a handful of raisins, or broken pieces of Breakfast Rusks (page 241).*

1. Because of the shape of the mango stone (or seed), the fruit will have two thinner sides. With a thinner side pointing up, begin to cut away the fruit on one side as close to the seed as possible, then cut the other side. You will have 2 halves. With the skin side down in your hand, carefully score the fruit vertically and horizontally with a knife, creating a grid or a series of small ½-inch squares. Push up against the skin and gently pop the fruit upwards toward you. Slice the squares off the skin, as though you were shaving, into a bowl. Cut the remaining fruit from the stone in smaller pieces.

2. Toss the blueberries in with the mango. Halve the pomegranate and gently knock out the seeds with a wooden spoon into the mango-berry mixture. Dress with lime juice and serve.

Nutty Shortbread Cookies

MAKES 6

SOMETIMES YOU NEED *a little cookie to go with an espresso or a cup of scented tea, like jasmine or chamomile. In the summer, I use these instead of biscuits for strawberry shortcake—I pile fresh, local strawberries on them. For the holidays, I use them to make linzer torte by adding ½ to 1 teaspoon ground cinnamon, ¼ teaspoon allspice, an additional ½ teaspoon vanilla, and 1 teaspoon fresh lemon zest to the dough and spreading the finished cookies with raspberry preserves and a dusting of confectioners' sugar. This recipe doubles and triples well. Try it and let the good cheer begin.*

1. Preheat the oven to 350°F. In a food processor, pulse the nuts until finely chopped. Add the flour, sugar, cardamom, and salt. Pulse to combine, then process until everything is finely ground. Add the butter, vanilla, and zest and process until everything comes together into a ball.

2. Place the ball on a parchment-lined baking sheet and pat into a thick circle. With a rolling pin, roll into an 8-inch round about ⅛-inch thick. Prick the dough lightly all over with a fork to prevent it from puffing as it bakes. Using a knife, gently score the top of the dough into 6 wedges.

3. Bake for 10 to 15 minutes, until golden brown. Allow the shortbread to cool and then, using the knife or your hands, break into wedges.

¼ cup whole hazelnuts, almonds, or walnuts (or a blend of all three)

1 cup unbleached all-purpose or whole wheat flour

⅓ cup organic cane sugar

¼ teaspoon cardamom

Pinch of fine sea salt

8 tablespoons (1 stick) unsalted butter or soy margarine, cut into small pieces

1 teaspoon pure vanilla extract

½ teaspoon grated lemon zest

Tofu Cannoli

MAKES 6 TO 8

One 14-ounce package firm tofu, pressed to release most of the water

1 cup confectioners' sugar, sifted, 1 tablespoon reserved for garnish

2 to 3 drops orange oil (*not* orange extract)

¼ teaspoon ground cinnamon

½ cup semisweet chocolate bits, roughly chopped

6 to 8 prepared cannoli shells (available in supermarkets and specialty shops)

ONCE WHILE TRAVELING *through southern Italy, I waited in a local café for the ferry to Ischia, a beautiful island near Capri in the bay of Naples. On a whim, I bypassed my usual marmalade-filled brioche and decided instead on a creamy cannoli to accompany my morning cappuccino. It was smallish, not overstuffed, and fresh and crisp. And delicious.*

When I started experimenting with soy foods, I was impressed with how well tofu replicates ricotta. Sweetened whipped tofu paired with just a touch of orange and cinnamon and lightly garnished with chocolate bits, reminds me more of that cannoli I had in Naples than any other since. Replace the chocolate with chopped pistachios if you wish.

1. Process the tofu in a food processor until fairly smooth but textured, about 15 seconds. It should have the consistency of ricotta. Add the confectioners' sugar, pulse a couple of times to blend, then process for 10 to 15 seconds. Add the orange oil, cinnamon, and 3 tablespoons of the chopped chocolate. Pulse again for 10 seconds, just until all the ingredients are incorporated. Transfer the mixture to a bowl and chill for at least 1 hour or more. This resting time intensifies the flavor of the filling considerably and should not be skipped.

2. Just before serving, using a teaspoon, divide the filling among the cannoli shells. Dip each end of the filled cannoli into the remaining chopped chocolate. Dust the cannoli with the reserved confectioners' sugar and serve.

Tofu Coconut Cream Pie

SERVES 6 TO 8

REMOVING THE DAIRY *from the traditional recipe keeps the creamy texture and sweet coconut flavor, yet allows it to sit more gently on the palate. I make my own graham cracker crust since I find the ready-made crusts to be full of chemicals and often taste too sweet and flat. The pie keeps for up to a week in the refrigerator, but it rarely lasts that long in my house.*

1. Preheat the oven to 350°F. Process the graham crackers and sugar in the food processor until fine. Transfer to a bowl and drizzle in the margarine. Mix well with a fork or wooden spoon. Pat onto the bottom and up the sides of a 9-inch pie pan. Bake the crust for 15 minutes. Let cool.

2. Place the coconut on a baking sheet and toast in the oven until light brown, 10 to 15 minutes. Keep an eye on it, because coconut burns very quickly. Transfer the coconut to a bowl and fluff with a fork.

3. Process the tofu in a food processor until smooth. Add the sugar, milk, vanilla, and ½ cup of the coconut, and process for 10 seconds. Pour the filling into the prebaked crust and top with the remaining 2 tablespoons coconut. Chill for at least 2 hours before serving.

18 graham cracker squares

3 tablespoons organic cane sugar

6 tablespoons (¾ stick) soy margarine, melted

½ cup plus 2 tablespoons sweetened shredded coconut

One 14-ounce package firm tofu, drained and rinsed

¼ cup lightly packed light brown sugar

2 to 3 tablespoons coconut milk

⅛ teaspoon vanilla extract

Coconut Cream Squares

FOR COCONUT squares, press the graham cracker crust onto the bottom of a 9-inch square pan and bake as directed above. Add the filling, refrigerate for 4 hours, and cut into individual squares.

Basmati Rice Pudding

¾ cup white basmati rice

1½ teaspoons fine sea salt

4½ cups soy milk

½ cup organic cane sugar

1 slightly heaping tablespoon cornstarch

1½ tablespoons vanilla extract

¼ teaspoon ground cardamom

Pinch of fine sea salt

I MODIFIED THIS *recipe from one that called for 4½ cups half-and-half, 1 cup heavy cream, and 2 eggs: I felt stuffed just looking at it. This smooth, creamy rice pudding—without dairy or eggs—can be enjoyed for dessert or breakfast with fresh fruit and a sprinkling of crunchy raw granola. For a festive holiday brunch, I mix ¾ cup raisins and 2 tablespoons rum in a bowl, let stand for half an hour, and then add to the warm pudding just before serving.*

1. Combine 1½ cups water, the rice, and the salt in a saucepan and bring to a boil. Cover and simmer over very low heat 8 to 9 minutes, until most of the water is absorbed. Check frequently and stir to make sure it doesn't stick. Add 3½ cups of the soy milk and the sugar. Continue simmering on very low heat for an additional 20 to 25 minutes, until the rice is soft and most of the milk absorbed. You want a spongy texture, with no bite. Remove the rice from the heat.

2. Pour ¼ cup of the remaining soy milk into a bowl and whisk in the cornstarch to dissolve. Add the vanilla extract and cardamom. Pour the cornstarch-milk mixture along with the remaining ¾ cup soy milk into the hot pudding and stir to combine. At this point, I usually add a pinch of salt, which helps to draw out the subtle sweetness of the pudding. Serve warm or at room temperature.

Tarte Tatin

I'M SUCH A *go-with-the-flow cook that the inflexible formulas required for baking often intimidate me. This is not such an inflexible-formula recipe. You can substitute any fruit for the apples; I have a weakness for pears. If desired, dot the fruit with Gorgonzola just before covering with pastry.*

Half 17-ounce package (1 sheet) Pepperidge Farm frozen puff pastry dough

6 to 8 firm cooking apples such as Granny Smith or Golden Delicious, peeled, cored, and quartered

Juice of 1 lemon

8 tablespoons (1 stick) unsalted butter or soy margarine

½ cup organic cane sugar

Confectioners' sugar

1. Preheat the oven to 400°F. With a rolling pin, gently roll the puff pastry dough to slightly larger than a seasoned 10-inch, slope-sided, cast-iron skillet (about a ½ to 1 inch of overlap will do nicely). Place the dough on a cookie sheet, cover with a piece of waxed paper or plastic wrap, and refrigerate until ready to use.

2. In a medium bowl, toss the apple with the lemon juice to prevent the apples from turning brown. Meanwhile, preheat the cast-iron skillet over low heat for 10 minutes.

3. Raise the heat under the skillet to medium-low and add the butter. As soon as it melts, add the cane sugar and slowly stir until the sugar dissolves into a syrup. Be careful, this is very hot. Arrange the apples in the skillet in a snug circular pattern, pressing them slightly into the warm syrup in the skillet. Cook the apples over low to medium heat for 15 minutes, until they are slightly soft and the syrup begins to caramelize. Keep an eye on the heat so the caramel mixture doesn't burn.

4. Remove the skillet from the heat and place the pastry sheet over the apples. Using the back of a soupspoon, tuck the edges of the pastry down under the outer edge of apples. Work quickly, as you don't want the layers of pastry to fuse. Immediately place the skillet in the oven and bake for 12 to 15 minutes, until the pastry is puffed and golden brown. Allow the tart to rest for 5 minutes, then loosen the pastry edge with a knife and give the pan a little shake to release the apples. Place a serving platter over the pan and flip the entire thing upside down so that the crust is now on the bottom. Serve warm, sprinkled with confectioners' sugar.

Maine Blueberry-Nectarine Crostata

Dough

2 cups unbleached
all-purpose flour

2 to 3 tablespoons organic
cane sugar

¼ teaspoon fine sea salt

Grated zest of 1 lemon

¾ cup (1½ sticks) unsalted
butter or soy margarine,
cut into small pieces

1 large organic egg, separated

Filling

2 cups fresh Maine
blueberries, rinsed and
picked over for stems

3 to 4 unpeeled nectarines,
pitted and sliced

2 tablespoons organic
cane sugar

1½ to 2 tablespoons
unbleached all-purpose flour

Pinch of fine sea salt

Juice of ½ lemon

CROSTATA, AN ITALIAN tart, is traditionally made by folding the dough over the top of the filling; its rustic look adds to its appeal, and less fuss is always better when I'm making dessert. This pastry utilizes only 1 egg yolk (so it's not vegan), but it tastes as rich as something you'd find in an expensive pastry shop. I use Maine blueberries because they're so small and incredibly sweet, especially when paired with the sweet-tartness of nectarines. In the winter, when fresh fruit isn't available, fill the crostata with blueberry and nectarine preserves. Serve as you would American apple pie, with a scoop of vanilla soy or dairy ice cream.

1. **TO MAKE THE DOUGH:** Combine the flour, sugar, salt, and lemon zest in a bowl and blend with a whisk. Add the butter pieces. With a pastry blender or your hands, work the butter into the flour until it resembles coarse crumbs. Add the egg yolk and work into the flour mixture. Add 2 to 3 tablespoon ice water, a little at a time, working it in until the dough comes together but isn't sticky or wet. If the dough doesn't pull together, add more water a teaspoon at a time. Shape the dough into a flattened disk, wrap in plastic wrap, and chill for 30 minutes.

2. **TO MAKE THE FILLING:** Combine the blueberries and nectarine slices in a bowl and sprinkle with the sugar, flour, and salt. Gently toss to combine.

3. Preheat the oven to 375°F. Roll out the chilled dough on a floured surface to a ¼-inch-thick round, 12 to 14 inches in diameter; don't trim the edge, this adds to the rustic look. Transfer the dough to a cookie sheet. Arrange the fruit in the center of the dough, leaving a 2-inch border. Mix the egg white with a few teaspoons water. With a pastry brush, paint the edge of the crust with the egg white mixture. Fold the outer edge inward toward the center—creating a crimped 2- to 3-inch edge and leaving most of the fruit exposed in the center. Brush the top and edge of the crust with the remaining egg white mixture. Bake 20 to 30 minutes, until the crust is nicely browned and the fruit is bubbling. Remove the crostata from the oven and let it cool a bit. Serve warm.

Apple Cake

LIKE MOST OF *my recipes, this cake is basic and adaptable: Use pears or plums for the apples. Highlight different flavors by adding cinnamon or allspice. Or add texture, protein, and fiber by adding some pine nuts, pistachios, or walnuts. For another dessert idea, cut the cake into thick slices and place on a greased griddle, just as you would French toast, and grill until the undersides are brown. Sprinkle the tops with ground cinnamon, turn, and brown the other sides. Serve with a drizzle of pure maple syrup or sprinkling of fresh berries.*

1. Preheat the oven to 350°F. Grease an 8-inch square or round springform cake pan.

2. In a large bowl, toss the apples with 1 tablespoon of the lemon juice and the 2 tablespoons sugar. In a medium bowl, combine the ½ cup sugar, the flour, cardamom, and salt. Add the eggs and butter and mix, either by hand or with an electric mixer, until the batter is stiff. If the batter is too thick or dry, add the milk 1 tablespoon at a time, until you have a stiff but moist batter. Fold the apples into the batter, along with the remaining 3 tablespoons lemon juice. Make sure all the apples are coated equally with the batter. Pour into the prepared pan, smooth the top, and sprinkle with 2 to 3 tablespoons sugar. Bake for 45 minutes, until the top is a light, golden brown and a toothpick or cake tester inserted in the center comes out clean. Serve warm or at room temperature.

2 medium cooking apples such as Granny Smith or Golden Delicious, peeled, cored, and chopped

4 tablespoons lemon juice

2 tablespoons plus ½ cup organic cane sugar, plus more for sprinkling

1½ cups unbleached all-purpose flour

¼ teaspoon ground cardamom

⅛ teaspoon fine sea salt

2 large organic eggs

6 tablespoons (¾ stick) unsalted butter or soy margarine

2 to 3 tablespoons 2% milk, soy milk, or water, if needed

Banana–Chocolate Chip Cake

SERVES 6

vegetable oil spray

1¾ cups unbleached all-purpose flour or whole wheat pastry flour

1 cup organic cane sugar

2 teaspoons baking powder

¼ teaspoon fine sea salt

½ cup safflower oil or any light vegetable oil

¾ cup soy milk

1 teaspoon vanilla extract

2 bananas, mashed

¾ cup vegan chocolate chips

Confectioners' sugar

I MADE THIS *cake for the show's second season and it quickly became one of our most popular recipe downloads. Because there are no eggs or dairy products, the dessert is low in fat and cholesterol-free, with a great taste. To serve, I sprinkle with confectioners' sugar or spoon crushed pineapple or berries over individual slices.*

1. Preheat the oven to 350°F. Spray a 9-inch square or round baking dish with vegetable oil spray. Combine the flour, cane sugar, baking powder, and salt in a bowl and blend with a fork. Add the oil, soy milk, and vanilla and stir just until the mixture comes together into a batter, but be careful not to overmix. Fold the mashed bananas into the batter, and then fold in the chocolate chips. Pour the batter into the prepared pan. Bake on the center rack for 35 to 40 minutes, just until a toothpick or cake tester inserted in the center comes out clean. Place the cake on wire rack to cool. Sprinkle with confectioners' sugar and serve.

Walnut Cake with Lemon Icing

SERVES 6 TO 8

I HAD SO *many viewer requests for egg- and dairy-free desserts that I came up with this cake. If you don't have brown rice syrup, use pure maple syrup or ¾ cup organic cane sugar. I ice the cake with a light lemon icing, but feel free to use traditional vanilla frosting or a simple dusting of confectioners' sugar.*

1. **TO MAKE THE CAKE:** Preheat the oven to 350°F. Grease and flour a 9-inch round or square cake pan. In a large bowl, sift together the flour, nuts, baking powder, baking soda, and salt. In a small bowl, blend ⅔ cup water, the margarine, rice syrup, vanilla, and vinegar. Add the wet ingredients to the dry and blend just until moistened. Pour into the prepared pan. Bake for 20 to 25 minutes, until a toothpick or cake tester inserted in the center comes out clean. Set the pan on a wire rack to cool.

2. **TO MAKE THE ICING:** Combine the confectioners' sugar and lemon zest in a small bowl. Add the lemon juice and stir until well blended. Let the icing rest while the cake is baking.

3. While the cake is still warm, gently pierce the top all over with a fork (about a quarter of the way down). Spread on half the icing. Let the warm cake absorb the icing, about 30 minutes, then top with the remaining icing.

Cake

2 cups unbleached all-purpose flour

1 cup ground walnuts or almonds, or a combination

1 teaspoon baking powder

1 teaspoon baking soda

½ teaspoon fine sea salt

⅓ cup soy margarine, melted

1 cup organic brown rice syrup

4 teaspoons vanilla extract

2 teaspoons white vinegar

Lemon Icing

2 cups confectioners' sugar

Grated zest of 1 lemon

2 to 3 tablespoons lemon juice

If You Like... Then Try...

THIS CHART WILL help you find my vegetarian alternatives to a wide variety of dishes traditionally made with meat and poultry, fish, eggs, and dairy. I often hear from viewers who express surprise at how easy it is to eat more vegetarian food, more frequently—and even to make the switch to an entirely vegetarian diet. Even if meat, poultry, dairy, and/or eggs have been staples in your diet for many years, you'll likely be surprised to find how many dishes you can easily make that are every bit as delicious and filling—and often much more nutritious—than the traditional fare you have been eating. Additionally, I've included a guide to help you readily find my recipes for vegetarian versions of some favorites from diners, street fairs and festivals, and Tex-Mex fare.

MEAT DISHES

Hamburgers	➡ Beet Burgers (page 190) ➡ Kasha Crunch Burgers (page 191) ➡ Black-Eyed Burgers (page 192)
Meatballs	➡ Eggplant Meatballs (page 214) ➡ Baked Tofu Meatballs (page 148)
Beef	➡ Marinated Portobello Mushrooms (page 202) ➡ Tofu Lasagna (page 185) ➡ Cannelloni with Eggplant (page 183)
Jamaican jerk pork or chicken	➡ Jamaican Jerk Tempeh (page 160)
Pork wontons	➡ Marvelous Meaty Wontons (page 51)
Chicken fricasee	➡ Tofu with Parsley Sauce (page 149)
Chicken pot pie	➡ Tofu Pot Pie (page 152)
Chicken cacciatore	➡ Tempeh Cacciatore (page 166)
Chicken Marsala	➡ Tempeh Marsala (page 168)
Chicken or beef Rice-A-Roni	➡ Vermicelli and Rice (page 226)
Chopped liver	➡ Cashew Pâté (page 69)
Lamb stew	➡ Moroccan Stew (page 165)
Lamb-stuffed cabbage	➡ Greek Stuffed Cabbage (page 162)
Beef stock	➡ Porcini Stock (page 107)
Chicken stock	➡ Vegetable Stock (page 106)

FISH

Crab cakes	➡ Mock Maryland Crab Cakes (page 196)
Tuna salad	➡ Mock Fish Salad Sandwiches (page 195)

DAIRY- AND EGG-BASED DISHES

French toast	➡ Rye Bread French Toast (page 240)
Crepes	➡ Chickpea Crepes (page 132)
Cornbread	➡ Vegan Cornbread (page 131)
Gratin	➡ Rosemary-Roasted Winter Vegetables (page 212)
Mashed potatoes	➡ Lemony Garlic-Smashed Potatoes (page 221)

Cream soups
➡ Roasted Red Pepper and Leek Soup (page 116)
➡ Parsnip-Carrot Ginger Soup (page 113)
➡ Cream of Green Pea Soup with Mint (page 110)
➡ Watercress-Potato Soup (page 117)

Caesar salad
➡ Vegetarian Caesar Salad (page 76)

Creamy salad dressing
➡ Tahini Dressing (page 104)
➡ Tofu-Lime Dressing (page 102)
➡ Creamy Curry Dressing (page 103)

Sour cream
➡ Tofu Sour Cream (page 147)

Cake
➡ Banana–Chocolate Chip Cake (page 256)
➡ Walnut Cake with Lemon Icing (page 257)

Cole slaw
➡ Caribbean Cabbage and Carrot Salad (page 78)
➡ Cabbage Slaw with Tomatoes and Ginger (page 79)
➡ Fennel Cabbage Slaw (page 80)

BREAD, PIZZA, AND PASTA

Pepperoni or sausage pizza
➡ any of my pizza recipes (page 136–144)

Fettucine Alfredo
➡ Fettucine Walnut Alfredo (page 177)

Pasta Bolognese
➡ Spaghetti Tofunese (page 176)

Cheesy, creamy, pasta
➡ Tofu Ravioli with Butter and Sage (page 181)
➡ Cannelloni with Eggplant (page 183)
➡ Tofu Lasagna (page 185)
➡ Vegetable Lasagna (page 187)

DAIRY-BASED DESSERTS

Coconut cream pie
➡ Tofu Coconut Cream Pie (page 251)

Cannoli
➡ Tofu Cannoli (page 250)

Rice pudding
➡ Basmati Rice Pudding (page 252)

OTHER FAVORITES

Diner food
➡ No-Egg Salad Sandwiches (page 194)
➡ Mock Fish Salad Sandwiches (page 195)
➡ Tempeh Club Sandwiches (page 197)
➡ Cornhusker's Reubens (page 198)
➡ Hearty Homefries (page 222)

Street fair and festival food
➡ Soysage-Pepper Sandwiches (page 200)
➡ New York Hot Dogs and Onions (page 199)
➡ Fried Polenta Squares (page 59)
➡ Tofu Kebobs with Tamari-Ginger Sauce (page 150)
➡ Barbecued Tempeh (page 159)

Tex-Mex food
➡ Tempeh Fajitas (page 167)
➡ Mexican Sweet Potato–Black Bean Salad (page 90)
➡ Chunky Avocado Salsa (page 71)
➡ Tomato Salsa (page 70)
➡ Green Salsa Picada (page 70)
➡ Black Bean, Tomato, and Corn Salad (page 89)
➡ Chilled Avocado Soup (page 111)
➡ Orange, Jalapeño, and Cilantro Dressing (page 100)
➡ Black Bean and Fire Roasted Tomato Soup (page 120)

Acknowledgments

MY HEARTFELT THANKS to my mother and best friend for her love, wisdom, and strength; my daughter, Noelle, for her determination and love; my son, James, for motivating me to continue moving forward with my life; my father, my brother Jim and his wife Daniela, and my sister Tina for their culinary enthusiasm, passion, and patience.

In addition, many thanks to:

My dear friends Andy Alley, Peter Rice, Annemarie Dawson, Caryl Widdowson, Janet Polinsky, and Sandra Kotze, for always being within reach. Your humor, love, kindness, guidance, unconditional support, and belief in my abilities helped make my dreams become reality.

Kate Kaminski, for being a wonderful friend, writer, and co-creator of *Delicious TV*. Special thanks for your enthusiastic recipe testing. Your incredible talents have saved the day on more than one occasion.

Jane Ratcliffe, for kindly and patiently guiding me through the writing process; as well as for reading and re-reading this book until the very end. I couldn't have done this without you. Thank you.

Didi Emmons, Cathi DiCocco, and Heidi Valenzuela, for your fabulous vegetarian recipes, culinary insights, and for being delightful guest chefs on *Delicious TV*. Your energy, talent, and enthusiasm for great food continues to inspire me.

To all the talented technicians, artists, and donors who helped *Delicious TV* persevere: Ronda Wanser, Tom Pierce, Susannah SanFillipo,

Jeff Griffiths, Justin Maxwell, Nat Ives, Chris and Ronnie, Steve Allen, J.P., Bob Irish, Stephen Turcotte, the Maine Animal Coalition, and Yoshino Ishii.

Rob Draper, for your advice, optimism, and support.

My agent, Mary Ann Naples, for finding me, sharing my vision, and assisting me through this project. Thank you, thank you.

Matthew Lore, for your extraordinarily detailed and passionate queries, culinary expertise, sharp eye, confidence, and gentle prodding which inspired me to think harder and dig deeper.

Harriet Bell, for your guidance and exceptionally skillful editing.

My cat, Cadie, for eighteen years of love and faithful friendship. Thank you for being by my side through many chapters of my life and every chapter of this book.

And Betsy Carson, my dear friend, partner, producer, editor, and photographer extraordinaire. The journey has just begun.

Index

About the Author

TONI FIORE is the creator and host of *Delicious TV's Totally Vegetarian*. which airs on more than one hundred public television stations nationwide. A vegetarian for nearly twenty years, she is a self-taught chef who embraced Mediterranean culinary techniques and philosophy while growing up in Italy. She lives in Portland, Maine.